DEMOCRACY, DIALOGUE, AND COMMUNITY ACTION

Democracy, Dialogue, *and* Community Action

TRUTH AND RECONCILIATION IN GREENSBORO

SPOMA JOVANOVIC

The University of Arkansas Press
Fayetteville
2012

Copyright © 2012 by The University of Arkansas Press

All rights reserved
Manufactured in the United States of America

ISBN-10: 1-55728-991-3
ISBN-13: 978-1-55728-991-9

16 15 14 13 12   5 4 3 2 1

Designed by Liz Lester

⊖ The paper used in this publication meets the minimum requirements
of the American National Standard for Permanence of Paper for
Printed Library Materials Z39.48-1984.

LIBRARY OF CONGRESS CATALOGING-IN-PUBLICATION DATA

Jovanovic, Spoma, 1958–
    Democracy, dialogue, and community action : truth and reconciliation
in Greensboro / Spoma Jovanovic.
        p.   cm.
    Includes bibliographical references and index.
    ISBN 978-1-55728-991-9 (cloth : alk. paper) — ISBN 1-55728-991-3
    1. Greensboro (N.C.)—Race relations. 2. Truth commissions—North
Carolina—Greensboro. 3. Reconciliation—Social aspects—North Carolina—
Greensboro. 4. African Americans—North Carolina—Greensboro.
5. Massacres—North Carolina—Greensboro—History—20th century.
6. Ku Klux Klan (1915–)—North Carolina—Greensboro—History—
20th century. 7. Nazis—North Carolina—Greensboro—History—
20th century. I. Title.
    F264.G8J68   2012
    305.8009756'62—dc23
                                        2012031047

CONTENTS

ACKNOWLEDGMENTS

This book was written to document poignant, sometimes painful, and unquestionably significant community conversations. Those chances for meaningful dialogue begin with an open heart as well as the invitation to others to speak. Longtime activists I met over the course of researching and writing this book who enacted those practices of speaking and listening with courage and conviction include Z Holler, Carolyn Allen, Nelson Johnson, Signe Waller, Alan Brilliant, Joyce Johnson, Steve Sumerford, Mary K. Wakeman, Lewis A. Brandon III, Joya Wesley, Joe Frierson, Willena Cannon, and Jill Williams. Their work was complemented by the integrity of other community members who devoted large measures of time and talent to the quest for truth and reconciliation: Emily Harwell, Alex Goldstein, Lisa Magarrell, Lucy Lewis, Bob Foxworth, Margaret Arbuckle, Eric Ginsburg, and Wesley Morris.

My colleagues and students at the University of North Carolina at Greensboro, in the College of Arts and Sciences, and with the Department of Communication Studies offered unwavering support for my research activities, including the funding of two year-long Ashby Dialogues to engage critical questions surrounding truth and reconciliation, a Center for Critical Inquiry stipend, and a research leave to complete a large portion of the writing of this manuscript. Specifically, I extend my gratitude to the following people for entertaining my questions, curiosities, and attempts to "do right" through extended conversations, moral support, and intellectual inquiry: Chris Poulos, Tim Johnston, Marsha Paludan, Pete Kellett, Etsuko Kinefuchi, Roy Schwartzman, Cathy Hamilton, Cynthia Dew, Matt Barr, Glenn Hudack, Carol Steger, Donata Nelson, Sarah Symonds, Kristi Parker, Stephen Sills, Belinda Walzer, and Steve Flynn.

I depended as well on colleagues elsewhere, friends, and family as important sounding boards for this challenging work. So often, they said one small thing or suggested a direction I had not previously considered that helped me to more clearly define the focus for this project. Thank you, H.L. Goodall, Jr., Dan DeGooyer, Stephen Bloch-Schulman,

Sherry Giles, Ed Whitfield, Dan Malotky, Larry Morse, Claire Morse, Jay Mattson, Sander Mattson, Lena Mattson, Cliff Mattson, Roy Wood, Michael Hyde, Larry Frey, and Kevin Carragee. My appreciation goes out as well to UNCG's Office of Leadership and Service-Learning and Office of Undergraduate Research and to the University of Denver's Center for Civic Ethics for their financial support.

Many thanks to Jean Rodenbough and Alicia Sowisdral for the use of their creative and important poetic expressions in this book.

To Lawrence Malley, director and editor of the University of Arkansas Press, I offer my sincere appreciation for the enthusiasm, support, wisdom, kindness, and guidance provided throughout the development of this book. My thanks extend as well to the press production folks including Brian King, Deena Owens, and Melissa King and copyeditor Deborah Upton.

My father died before I finished writing this book, but his dogged pursuit of the truth continues to influence my deep sense of responsibility to engage the political dimensions of our social world so that we can uplift the human spirit. That commitment I happily share today with my husband, Lewis Pitts, whose prophetic vision for peace, justice, and the promise of democracy makes my life more meaningful, as it has for the survivors of November 3, 1979.

Time to Talk

America is an idea—a beautiful one. Democracy is an experiment, an ongoing one. Both ideals require telling the truth so that justice at home and abroad isn't blind. Both require reliable information disseminated widely, so that our passionate engagement and active, intelligent participation in the political process aren't rendered victims of power, privilege, and the silent protection of those who have abused their power and flaunted their privilege. Even then there are no guarantees.

—H. L. GOODALL JR.

IN 2004, THE first Truth and Reconciliation Commission in the United States was installed in Greensboro, North Carolina, to examine the impact of a tragedy twenty-five years earlier, one that sparked a worldwide cry for justice. Five people were murdered on November 3, 1979, when the Ku Klux Klan and the American Nazi Party fired into a crowd of protestors one Saturday morning. Television crews captured the shootings on video, from start to finish, yet none of the killers ever served time for the crime. That tragedy—known as the Greensboro Massacre—exposed what many believed to be the inadequacy of judicial, political, and economic systems in the United States. Before examining that disturbing day, it is important to recognize that the particulars of November 3 were not a staple of most people's day-to-day conversations when Greensboro's Truth and Reconciliation Commission was launched. In fact, many people had never heard of November 3, while others had long purged the violent episode from their memories. Why, then, would talking about an event that occurred twenty-five years earlier be desirable or even necessary? As is often the way, not talking about something does not mean it ceases to have impact. Indeed, the effect of November 3 was felt far and wide in the fabric of the southern city. Trust of the police and local government was perilously low, racial tensions persisted, and political protest had been effectively silenced.[1] Despite repeated attempts, the city was faltering in its efforts to envision a new identity following the collapse of its textile industry that had long formed the community's economic base.

Former Greensboro mayor Carolyn Allen and co-chair of the task force formed to initiate a truth and reconciliation process believed a thoughtful, sustained inquiry into the causes and consequences of November 3 could improve the city's affairs she had seen decline over the previous twenty years—relationships between blacks and the police, trust of city leaders by citizens of all races, and communication among residents (Cose, 2003). An alliance of blacks and whites mobilized to establish the Greensboro Truth and Community Reconciliation Project (GTCRP), a grassroots organization that would eventually lay the foundation for the United States' first Truth and Reconciliation Commission (TRC). The TRC was to be a process and a tool by which citizens could feel confident about the "truth" of the city's history in order to reconcile divergent understandings of past and current city priorities.

In looking at the experiences of Greensboro's citizens during this process, on-lookers from around the country and throughout the world asked if truth and reconciliation commissions could work for their communities as well. They wanted to know in what ways can and do people depend upon one another to assert the common good and transform a pain-filled past into a more hopeful, prosperous future?

Communities that have experienced racial and class injustice, pain, suffering, and lingering resentment often point to the less than full exoneration of past wrongs as contributing to a gripping, existential mistrust and even cynicism among the populace. To correct the painful condition, citizens and leaders alike seek guidance in how to constructively resurrect past issues in order to implement reflective responses for the benefit of all citizens. These matters point directly to the ethical posture and communicative processes that undergird democratic action. It is *people* who imagine, construct, and sustain their communities by interacting, dreaming, and struggling with one another over conceptions of how to best live together. TRC processes invest resources to encourage deliberation that confronts conflict, welcomes differing views, seeks deep understanding, and constructs a future path to restore the well-being of the community. In doing so, TRCs recognize that it is communication that awakens people's critical awareness, reflection, and action, not legal records, detailed reports, or judicial proceedings.

> With respect to communication, it is difficult to overstate its importance in a society that aspires to be democratic. The relative absence of communication is to that extent an approximation of fascism. If we think in terms of communication among individuals, groups and constituencies within a society, a democracy should be expected to promote an interest in and familiarity with one another. Any failure to do so is equivalent to promoting or at least tolerating a degree of isolation that breeds suspicion, distrust, even hatred . . . A democratic society simply can not tolerate such conditions, not if it seriously desires to advance and strengthen its democratic character. (Ryder, 2008, 3)

What came to light in the truth and reconciliation process was that the honest conversations needed following November 3, 1979, were diverted toward image management and misplaced blame, rather than a scrutiny of the underlying factors contributing to the tragedy, factors that persisted and plagued the city.

In 1979 and for many years after, the trauma led many to believe that the most reasonable course of action was to forget or suppress the details and features surrounding November 3. Fear, uncertainty, confusion, distress, and pressure from others to remain silent prevented a full accounting of the shootings.

It was not until the TRC was launched that many people in the community would or could finally share their stories. With time, more residents, law enforcement officials, and protest participants were willing to speak, but even twenty-five years after the fact, the Truth Commissioners admitted that some people were still scared to publicly share what they had always known.

In the unsettled times of the twenty-first century, or perhaps because of them, Greensboro's citizens of different political persuasions, ethnic identities, religious affiliations, and racial associations joined together to strengthen the quality of their interactions. In doing so, they confronted conflicting views and understandings of their community. Leaning on alternative discourse pathways, they formed new alliances with the express aim of affecting cultural shifts in the city.

My involvement with the TRC coincided with the public announcement of its formation in 2003. I attended community meetings, initially alongside a group of twelve graduate students at the University of North Carolina at Greensboro in the Department of Communication Studies, and later with hundreds of other students and fellow community members who learned of Greensboro's history with me over the next many years. We read past accounts of the Greensboro Massacre, researched other episodes of protest and violence in the South, reviewed and edited TRC planning documents, drafted outreach materials, organized volunteers, helped coordinate special events, conducted surveys, interviewed city leaders, sat with fearful community members, ushered guests into the TRC hearings, and transcribed testimonies. Though we were initially unfamiliar with Greensboro's activists and complete history, it was clear that our city had a unique opportunity to address a past wrong by talking about it in order to reconsider the facts that could lead to new understandings. Greensboro, like many of its sister cities in the South, has had a checkered record of atoning for racial violence and improving poor race relations, often denying the ramifications of systemic conditions that continue to keep blacks in a disadvantaged position economically, educationally, and politically.

This writing aims to contribute to the scholarly literature surrounding TRCs and add a distinct dimension few publications feature; here is documented the community's involvement, disorder, and celebration during the process. In other studies of TRCs, what is instead often the focus of research inquiry are the events, testimonies, and public documents, absent the community's voice (Verdoolaege, 2008). Immersing myself in this project brought forward insights I could not have anticipated at the start; it was an effort inspired by "stumbling into possibilities" (Poulos, 2009, 66). This research method permitted me to take a sustained view into the norms, practices, routines, and values embedded in the community. It reflects a research tradition initially used to study foreign cultures (Geertz, 1973) but is now the inspiration for new ethnographies studying people closer to home (Goodall, 1999; Poulos, 2009; Towns, 2007).

In the process of researching and writing this book, I learned a lot from more seasoned activists and their "radical" ideas.[2] Throughout, they held fast to their deepest convictions that the community benefits when there is more, not less deliberation, inclusion, and equality.

Overview of the Book

The purpose of this book is threefold. First, there is need to preserve the historical significance of a people's effort to seek truth and work for reconciliation. Greensboro's TRC, unlike any other Truth and Reconciliation Commission prior, convened and operated without government sanction. Despite the perseverance of Greensboro's citizens to solicit local government involvement, the resistance by elected bodies prevailed, leaving the grassroots project to fend for itself financially and in every other way. This situation started out as one that put the TRC supporters in a disadvantaged position to fully engage the community in its process. Once underway, however, the operation of the project sans government support was heralded as a point of pride. Alex Boraine, deputy chair under Archbishop Desmond Tutu on the South African Truth Commission, proclaimed his support for the Greensboro model as a new means by which to carry out future Truth Commissions, noting that the moral suasion of the people was stronger than any possible government mandate for truth and reconciliation (Covington, 2007).

The second purpose of this book is to show a variety of discourse models for other communities to use in seeking to redress past harms. In Greensboro, there continues to be a need for training to facilitate conversation that cuts across social class and racial lines, but training programs by themselves are not enough. Supporters of the truth and reconciliation process did not, for the most part, instigate large-scale programs to talk about race. Instead, they relied on many small group settings and creative forms of expression to prompt discussion. These informal, inexpensive avenues to dialogue yielded impressive results for the community organizers and are valuable tools to encourage deep conversation on difficult subjects.

Finally, this book attempts to demonstrate the power of community action to promote participatory democracy. As scholar James

Darsey (1997) asserts, our country is not lacking in opportunity for civil discourse, but rather people have refused radical engagement with the deeply important and meaningful issues of our times. As a result, our communication has faltered, tending toward the bland and safe that purposefully avoids conflict. As a nation and as individuals, the retreat from public discourse has proven dangerous. When diplomacy, for instance, is forsaken, conversation ceases to be a meaningful arbiter of peace and all too often, cultural or military or other kinds of conflict ensue. Absent trust, the willingness of citizens to actively engage the ideas of others evaporates. What follows is a democracy that ceases to exist as a vibrant pathway to equality and justice for all.

In Greensboro, the recognition that our future as a democratic society depends upon an engaged citizenry was the fuel that kept the GTCRP supporters connected to a process whose outcome was uncertain. The community members poured their faith into the belief that individual and collective actions could shape a new, more promising future. Thus, Greensboro's foray into truth and reconciliation serves to deepen our understanding of the role of communication in community organizing.

The understandings, interpretations, and conclusions in this volume emerged from more than six years of contact and study of Greensboro's Truth and Reconciliation process. Together, the experiential data collected from weekly meetings, home dinners, coffee shop chats, interviews, and sustained observations, along with the methodical study of archived legal records, media materials, and commissioned reports, form the basis of this book's argument that ordinary people can deepen democratic public life, independent of government cooperation.

This book and Greensboro's TRC reveal how some stories of our past have been submerged under veils of civility. Howard Zinn artfully showed in *A People's History of the United States* (1980) that the failure to document historical tragedies does not mean they did not happen. The quest to conceal the roots of citizen uprisings is real, but so too, is the dedication of social change agents to set the records straight. This book, then, should be read as a resource and case study of how citizens in one community used its TRC as the gateway to understanding the past by discussing the enduring problems of the present to conceive a plan for the future.

A Note about the Facts

Since November 3, 1979, people around the world have learned about the Greensboro Massacre through accounts in thousands of newspaper articles, books, a nationally touring play, and television and film documentaries. Initially, the available facts were incomplete, but over time and through the tireless work of the survivors, other activists, researchers, journalists, and filmmakers, most of the details of that tragic day have come to light. In 2004, when the Greensboro Truth and Reconciliation Commission embarked on its mission, its goal was to refresh the facts with the history, context, and personal stories surrounding the event and trials, in order to make its judgments and recommendations.

This book, then, contains little original information about the events of November 3. For that, readers are encouraged to turn to the many articles, books, and other documents listed in the bibliography. To do so is to get immersed into the United States history of social action, political forces, race struggles, and labor movements.

Of all the documents, the one most used to situate the events and history contained in this volume is the Greensboro Truth and Reconciliation Commission's Final Report that is available in its entirety at www.greensborotrc.org and cited throughout here as Final Report, 2006. Quotations from the testimonies provided at the TRC's public hearings are referenced throughout this book and are available at the same Web site.

DEMOCRACY, DIALOGUE, AND COMMUNITY ACTION

CHAPTER I

The Greensboro Massacre, November 3, 1979

NOVEMBER 3, 1979. Radicals with the Communist Workers Party (CWP)[1] were taking their positions at their long planned and well-publicized anti-Klan rally. The event was designed to recruit new textile mill union members residing in Greensboro, North Carolina's low-income neighborhood of Morningside Homes who lived with low wages and poor working conditions at the mills. The CWP believed that once they had built strong and vibrant unions, they would have in place the structure for an even larger movement, one powerful enough to overthrow the government and the capitalist system that left poor and black people with so little. Their strategy was to use the support of local labor unions to agitate mill workers who opposed the Ku Klux Klan's (KKK) messages of hate and separation of the races. The CWP wanted to bring an end to the exploitation of workers for the profit and well-being of textile mill owners who were the state's largest employers. To do that, they had to shut down the influence of the Klan.

What made the KKK so powerful was not its membership numbers that had declined through the years, but its documented history of violence and spread of terror among African Americans and their white supporters. The KKK ignited fear and condemned multiracial cooperation of any kind in order to promote a message of white supremacy. The CWP considered the KKK's intimidating practices and vile speech as major obstacles to its union building campaign.

The Communists believed that the lingering racism that the KKK promoted and the extreme class stratification that marked the South were both intolerable conditions caused and sustained by the capitalist domination of the masses. For the CWP, the solution was to seize the economic and political power away from the reigning city leaders—those who had tolerated and according to the CWP even encouraged Klan activity—and put it into the hands of the working class.

The CWP members were largely university-educated activists, deeply influenced by Marxist theory, and avid readers of Marx, Engels, Lenin, and Mao Tse-tung. Their leader in Greensboro was Nelson Johnson who had established roots and a reputation as a prominent black student leader at North Carolina Agriculture & Technical State University before becoming a community grassroots organizer. Johnson was a thorn in the side of local law enforcement officials who found themselves the target of many of his campaigns against police brutality. Johnson's high profile in previous nonviolent and violent protest actions led the city's police to consider him reckless in his radical pursuits.

By the late 1970s, Johnson's activities were noteworthy as well to fellow civil rights activists including Sandi Smith, Willena Cannon, Joyce Johnson, Claude Barnes, Ed Whitfield, and Signe and Jim Waller, all of Greensboro. Others from Durham, North Carolina joined with the racially diverse CWP coalition—Marty and Mike Nathan, Sally and Paul Bermanzohn, Dale and Bill Sampson, and César and Floris Cauce.

Earlier that year, the WVO/CWP along with local residents in the small, rural community of China Grove, about an hour's car drive from Greensboro, faced-off against the Klan. Following that July confrontation, the CWP redoubled its efforts to challenge and defeat the power of the Klan. They applied for a Greensboro city parade permit for November 3 and staged a press conference just days before on the steps of city hall. The WVO/CWP publicly taunted the Klan to come to Greensboro using insulting, inflammatory rhetoric as a tactic to disgrace the Klan and agitate parade supporters.

On Saturday morning, November 3, 1979, the CWP members and their supporters gathered on the east side of Greensboro shouting, "Death to the Klan!" It was the same aggressive rally cry the CWP had used in door-to-door canvassing efforts and on flyers posted all over town to build interest in the demonstration. The crowd numbering forty or fifty, urged residents to come out of their homes and go to the march starting point at the corner of Carver and Everett Streets. As they waited to begin the march there, the demonstrators sang songs and chanted slogans—"People, people have you heard? Black and white is the word" and "Death to the Klan." The air was filled with anticipation, camaraderie, and righteous anger against the Ku Klux Klan's vicious and racist practices. A white-sheeted effigy of a Klansman swung from a rope with a sign that read, "KKK Scum." Among the adults were half a dozen children wearing khaki colored, military-like uniforms and red berets. The protest march organizers were busy with the last minute duties of fastening flyers to their flatbed truck equipped with a large speaker, attending to the needs of the media, and passing out placards for people to carry. Across the street, news crews were setting up their equipment to report on and televise the event.

Then, a caravan of nine cars slowly drove up, one of the first sporting a rebel Confederate flag on its front license plate. The cars were filled with thirty-seven Ku Klux Klan and American Nazi Party members, many holding shotguns in their laps. As they neared the spot where the crowd stood, a Klansman in the lead car yelled out, "You wanted the Klan, you Communist son-of-a-bitch, well you got the Klan!" A demonstrator cried out, "Here comes the Klan!" and with that, the television camera crews jumped into action to record what would happen next.

The Klan and Nazis leaned out the car windows, slinging racial epithets and slurs while the marchers—communists, supporters, and neighborhood residents—screamed back with insults of their own. The shouting escalated, and in a matter of moments, the scene turned violent. The marchers used their sign sticks and feet to hit and kick the cars. From the caravan, a single gunshot was fired. More gunshots followed as the white supremacists clad in jeans and flannel shirts, and smoking cigarettes, jumped out of the cars to unload more weapons and take aim at the protestors. The marchers fled. Some took cover to dodge the bullets while others grabbed guns of their own to fight back. Spray from one thousand projectiles filled the air—the shots came from shotguns, semi-automatic rifles and pistols—before the nine-car caravan of Klansmen and Nazis drove away.

Eighty-eight seconds after the first shot was fired, five of the protestors, all union organizing leaders, lay motionless on the ground. Four died instantly: César Cauce, Dr. James Waller, Sandra Smith, and Bill Sampson. A fifth, Dr. Michael Nathan, survived two more days in a local hospital before he too died. Ten others were injured, including eight protestors, one Klansman, and a local news photographer.

As the carnage unfolded, people shouted for the police who

seemed to be absent from the scene. What people could not know at the time, but learned later, was that undercover police officers were in fact in the thick of the action. They had photographed the caravan members stowing guns in their cars and then followed behind in an unmarked car, communicating with some police officers by radio transmission. Detective Cooper, one of the officers in the police car behind the caravan, failed to intervene. He explained he was just one officer in plainclothes, in an unmarked car that surely would have not survived the ordeal without back up.

In addition, there was a paid Klan informant, Eddie Dawson, at the lead of the caravan who had earlier provided details of the group's activities and plans to his "handler," Detective Cooper.[2] Cooper, in turn, had reported this information to select ranking officers in the Greensboro Police Department. Finally, not present but also fully aware of the Klan-Nazi plans that day was an undercover agent employed by the federal Bureau of Alcohol, Tobacco and Firearms (BATF), Bernard Butkovich, who had attended the pre-march meetings of those groups to gather information surrounding their violent actions.[3] Considerable intelligence work had been completed, yet not a single warning from the police was issued to neighborhood residents or protestors, nor was any action taken to intercept the violence.

No police assistance came until after the caravan had sped off, when a two-man police unit located five blocks away drove toward the melee and was able to catch the final vehicle in the caravan, a golden-yellow cargo van. The officers arrested twelve Klansmen and Nazis who had in their possession four shotguns, a bloodied hunting knife, three revolvers, two sets of brass knuckles, a five-foot length of chain, and ammunition.

As the demonstrators emerged from their hiding places alongside journalists who had likewise sought cover from the gunfire, fear and anger intermingled. "Stunned protestors wandered around the intersection, hovering over the bodies of their loved ones, trying to tend to the wounded" (Final Report, 2006, 186). And then, a rage took over that was focused on the absence of the police. Floris Weston [then wife of deceased Cauce] recalled, "I immediately knew that we had been set-up. I didn't have any facts. All I had was my gut and my belief that something was wrong and that someone had helped this to happen" (Final Report, 2006, 186).

Nelson Johnson, cradling Jim Waller as he took his last breath, said, "I knew in the depths of my soul that we had been set up" (Final Report, 2006, 188). He stood up and started shouting those sentiments at the police. The police ran over and demanded that Johnson stop. When he refused, the police wrestled Johnson to the ground, stomped on his neck to keep him pinned down, and then arrested Johnson for inciting a riot.

Media accounts of the rampage filled the airwaves and eyewitness newspaper accounts were distributed all over the world. The mass media stories detailed in graphic and written forms the seemingly unthinkable: how two extremist, racist groups had fired upon the protestors in broad daylight, leaving for dead the leftist revolutionaries who had challenged the Klan and Nazis to show up at what would be recorded in City of Greensboro documents and remembered widely as a *shootout*.

The repercussions were vast. City officials braced themselves for more unwanted hostility and violence by declaring a state of emergency for that zone of the city. Doing so allowed them to conduct searches for weapons, close access to certain neighborhoods and college campuses, step up surveillance efforts, enact a neighborhood curfew, establish a "rumor control center" that fielded three thousand phone calls in a three-day period, and solicit support of uniformed troops from the National Guard. City officials broadcasted warnings on radio and television for citizens to stay away from CWP organized activities, including a funeral march scheduled for a week later.

To maintain its standing as a business-friendly and family-oriented place, Greensboro's city leaders immediately launched an aggressive campaign to ward off the inevitable negative publicity. Business and civic leaders demanded the local media tone down the event coverage in order to bring calm back to the city. They further proclaimed that what happened on November 3 could have happened anywhere for the attack was waged by outside groups. The city's leaders declared the City of Greensboro was the innocent victim caught in the middle of the extremist groups' ideological warfare. Greensboro, said then mayor Jim Melvin, took the high road by holding the hand of civility, bringing to light the prowess of the local police to keep order in a difficult time, and thereby united the entire community in the aftermath of the tragedy.

In consideration of the severity of the racially charged dispute, the city received assistance from the Community Relations Service (CRS) from the U.S. Department of Justice that had been established by the 1964 Civil Rights Act. A CRS "conciliation" team was dispatched to Greensboro to work side by side with the city's leaders to calm feelings of fear.

In the mills, some workers failed to show up on the following Monday, worried of what might erupt in the aftermath of November 3. Mill owners, too, were apprehensive and so posted additional security guards at the textile mills. The guards were in place to protect key management officials, not the workers.

Black community leaders attempted to assuage the widespread panic by speaking out in their congregations about the misconduct of the police, and by extension the city, in protecting the interests of African American residents. There was no further violence, yet the residents of Morningside Homes were traumatized and then made to feel responsible for the violence by having to abide by strict curfews, explained resident Candy Clapp. The lack of proactive action by the city added to black community mistrust.

The CWP widows' attempts to bury their husbands and friends were thwarted when all the area funeral homes declined to manage the arrangements. Eventually, white Presbyterian minister Z Holler, who did not know the survivors, intervened to help and a funeral procession was planned.[4] CWP members planned to carry weapons for self-defense at the funeral march asserting that the police were unable to protect them on November 3. Demands and pressure from both the CWP and the police with differing positions ensued until a compromise was struck and the CWP agreed to carry unloaded rifles.

City officials responded to the CWP funeral plans with security procedures of their own. Five hundred National Guardsmen were called in to supplement four hundred state and local law enforcement personnel stationed along the funeral route. A twenty-four-hour state of emergency was declared and an influx of FBI agents arrived in town. All cars with out-of-state license plates were searched, as well as vehicles considered suspicious. A thirty-five-member CWP contingent from Durham faced arrest for possessing weapons during that state of emergency, charges later thrown out by judicial ruling. In total, crowd estimates at the funeral march ranged from five to eight hundred, along with nearly one thousand law enforcement officials and two hundred reporters (Waller, 2002).

Just over a month after the shootings, the Klan held a fundraiser for the legal defense of the men charged in connection with the deaths. Approximately one hundred Klansmen and their families raised $217. Renee Hartsoe, whose husband was charged with murder, expressed confidence that the Klan would get a fair trial because "people in Greensboro are pretty much on the Klan side . . . It is bad that it happened but white people need to wake up" (Final Report, 2006, 232).

The national outcry by antiracist activists was swift. More than three hundred organizations rallied around Greensboro to address the enduring racism and unrest there. The Congress of Racial Equality (CORE), the nation's largest civil rights organization at the time, the Southern Christian Leadership Conference (SCLC), the Interreligious Foundation for Community Organizations (IFCO), and the National Anti-Klan Network, among others, sponsored and mobilized marchers for a February 1980 rally in Greensboro. That event, with crowd estimates of 7,000 to 10,000, is credited as the catalyst for establishing new collaborations and hate-group watchdog groups such as the National Anti-Klan Network and Klan Watch (Wise, 2005).[5]

Greensboro's citizens likewise were outraged and demanded answers. How could November 3 have happened? Where were the police? What was the city doing to protect its citizens? In response, five reports were issued in the year following the shootings to help explain what had happened.[6] The historical record was being written, but without the knowledge, details, and depth of the undercover and informant operations, that historical record would be distorted from the very beginning.

The first report was a ninety-two-page Greensboro Police Department's Internal Affairs Division Administrative Report that was completed less than three weeks after the event. Six months later, two more reports were issued. One was twenty-one pages long, prepared by the Citizens Review Committee appointed by the city's Human Relations Commission. The citizen group conducted an investigator-less examination of the shootings. The other report was an assessment of the planning and operations of the Greensboro Police Department by an independent consulting firm, McManis Associates, hired by the city. The fourth report came out in October 1980, and contained a twenty-eight-page summary analysis by the Human Relations Commission that looked at the contents of the earlier Citizens Review Committee and McManis Associates reports in order to present its own findings and recommendations.

The U.S. Commission on Civil Rights and its North Carolina Advisory Committee released the fifth and final report in November 1980. Titled "Black White Perceptions: Race Relations in Greensboro," the fifty-one-page report included the views and comments of twenty-five citizens including Klansman Virgil Griffin and National Socialist Party of America (Nazi Party) leader Harold Covington. The report concluded that Greensboro was a polarized city with two distinct societies, one with economic and political power, and one with neither. White citizens who were interviewed for the report generally recognized Greensboro as a city that was making progress with regard to race relations in terms of a decline in violence, desegregation of schools, and increased social and cultural interactions. Black citizens pointed out the persistent problems of inequity.

The Trials

At the same time as the reports were being assembled, the groundwork was being set for what would eventually be three court trials. In December 1979, six KKK and Nazi Party members were indicted for first-degree capital murder. In the spring of 1980, the CWP protestors were in trouble as well when six were charged with inciting a riot and/or resisting arrest, charges that were eventually dropped. In August 1980, charges against fourteen KKK and Nazis were brought to trial in the North Carolina State Court.

Based on the television videotapes that showed Klansmen and Nazis shooting and killing the protestors, as well as eyewitness accounts, nearly everyone believed that some or all of the Klan-Nazis would be held accountable for the deaths of the protestors. The all-white jury listened to testimony and viewed videotapes in a courthouse located in downtown Greensboro. They did not hear testimony, however, from any of the CWP survivors who were convinced that the trial was a sham by the state of North Carolina intended to protect the law enforcement officials, and not the November 3 protestors. The survivors, who had wanted but were denied a private prosecutor to assist with the case, expressed concerns that the Greensboro district attorney's office in charge of the prosecution had made legal strategy decisions and public comments that belittled the position of the survivors. Further, that same office had pending charges against some of the demonstrators. That is, District Attorney Mike Schlosser was in charge of prosecuting the Klan in one case and prosecuting the CWP protestors in other actions. During the trial, the prosecutors did not call on government-paid intelligence agents Eddie Dawson or Bernard Butkovich, which was another example to the CWP of the effort to cover up government complicity in the shootings. The prosecution team countered that Dawson and Butkovich were deemed hostile witnesses who could have hurt the case. Six months after the trial began, the jury deliberated for seven days before issuing their unanimous verdict. They found the Klan and Nazis not guilty of murder, rioting, or any crime.

The critical issue considered by the jury in that first trial was whether the Klan and Nazi members acted in self-defense when they fired into the crowd. An FBI analysis that examined the gunshot sound waves taken from television footage concluded that the first two shots fired came from the Klan. But the analysis could not ascertain where shots three, four, and five originated from, ultimately leaving the jurors to think that those shots may have come from the protestors. According to Assistant District Attorney Jim Coman, who like the other members of the prosecution team had an adversarial relationship with the survivors, the verdict was a surprise in light of the videotape evidence, but one that pointed to the CWP's culpability:

> There would have never been this incident if it weren't for what they [the CWP] did: for inviting the Klan into a housing project and to pass out guns and have kids there in the middle . . . To me, the conduct of the CWP—as reprehensible as the Klan was—that they won't even admit they did anything wrong, for me, they bear much more responsibility for what happened. (Coman, 2005)

The jury's decision seemed to reflect their view that the CWP protestors were the first aggressors who hit the Klan/Nazi cars with their signs and sticks, which in turn provoked the gunshots.

Lead prosecutor and district attorney Mike Schlosser blamed the

verdict on the survivor's lack of cooperation when they refused to tes-
tify at the trial and further, disrupted the proceedings with reckless
abandon. On the first day of the trial, widow Marty Nathan stood,
introduced herself, and began shouting that the trial was a sham and
a farce. After she was gagged and removed by the bailiff, widow Floris
Cauce likewise began shouting and released a vial of foul-smelling
skunk oil onto the floor. Both were sentenced to thirty days in jail
(Waller, 2002). Schlosser said the main instigator of all that CWP
action, was Nelson Johnson. "Nelson Johnson is the wheel spoke and
hub. He is a plague on this community" (Schlosser, 2005). To wit,
Schlosser had defended the bond amount that was set for Johnson for
his role in inciting a riot on November 3, a bond amount double what
was set for any of the Klan or Nazis who had killed people that day.

The verdict sent shockwaves throughout Greensboro. A fire was
set downtown by citizens furious with what they considered the protection of racist murderers. Protests were waged in nearby Chapel Hill
and Durham, North Carolina, as well. A wave of opposition to the verdict surfaced in newspaper letters to the editor, resolutions from
churches, and public meetings.

With this swell of community outrage, efforts were launched for
federal intervention. Initially, the U.S. Justice Department stated it had
no jurisdiction in the case, which created another layer of suspicion
among the CWP survivors and citizens in Greensboro who were not
convinced that justice had been served. With growing public protest,
federal officials begrudgingly initiated a Grand Jury investigation in
1982 that heard testimony from 150 witnesses, including the survivors
who had previously been silent. The November 3 survivors remained
angry and convinced that the Justice Department could not impar-
tially investigate the activities of FBI agents and government-paid
informants who the survivors said were provocateurs in the events of
November 3. The survivors' position on this point led them to collect
more than 1,100 petition signatures and a request for a special prosecutor, but their contention of a conflict of interests was denied by a
federal district judge in Washington, D.C. (Waller, 2002).

In January 1984, the federal criminal trial began with a secret jury
selection, an unusual move that was requested neither by the defense
nor the prosecution but enforced by the judge so that potential jurors
could speak freely and without fear (Final Report, 2006, 287). Once

again, the jury was all white, a situation made possible, as was the case in the first state criminal trial, because preemptory challenges allowed then were used to dismiss blacks, without cause, from serving on the jury. In the federal criminal trial, the attorneys for the protestors relied on law that would prove racial hatred was the prime motivation for the crimes that took place. In this case, unlike the first state trial, the jury heard from Greensboro detective Jerry Cooper, who followed the Klan-Nazi caravan to the parade and Eddie Dawson, a defendant in the case, on his role as an informant with the Greensboro Police Department.

Three months after the second criminal trial began in 1984 and amid a climate of anticommunism rhetoric, the jury found the nine accused Klansmen and Nazis again not guilty, this time because the jurors did not believe that racist ideology was the impetus for the confrontation, but that hatred of communism was the cause. In addition the jurors believed that the caravan would have moved through the area without incident if the CWP had not made the first hostile move.

The last opportunity for justice, reasoned the CWP survivors, was to pursue a federal civil rights trial that they had filed originally in 1980, before the start of the second criminal suit. The civil trial had been delayed until the criminal proceedings concluded and then it was mired in a motion to dismiss, judicial inaction, and a stay of all discovery. Finally, in 1985, the trial began, focusing on several complaints:

- The defendants violated the plaintiffs' (survivors') right to assemble, to life, and to equal protection of the laws.
- Law enforcement and their informants officially encouraged and participated in a conspiracy to cover up the incident.
- The city had a policy and practice of improperly controlling informants and of encouraging the violation of equal protection of the laws.
- Wrongful death, conspiracy, and assault and battery claims.

In essence, the claims boiled down to two major issues. The sixty-three defendants—nineteen Klansmen and Nazis, thirty-six Greensboro police officers and other Greensboro officials, four Bureau of Alcohol, Tobacco and Firearms agents, three FBI agents, and the City of Greensboro—were accused of *conspiring* to deprive the victims of equal protection to protest, and then they *concealed* those very actions.

At the heart of the civil trial was the argument that the CWP members and their supporters were not protected by law enforcement for expressing their unpopular political, economic, and social views surrounding labor organizing and racist violence. The suit sought monetary damages on behalf of sixteen plaintiffs including the surviving spouses and wounded protestors. In this case, a different standard of proof was in place for the jury, known as "the preponderance of the evidence" rather than the requirement of "beyond a reasonable doubt" used in criminal proceedings. That is, the jurors would need to decide if the evidence they heard was more likely to be true than not.

The protestors' six-member legal team assisted by dozens of law students, lay activists, and nonprofit civil liberties organizations collected more than two hundred depositions and analyzed 100,000 pages of documents that were bound into twenty volumes. For the first time, the public heard from witnesses under oath about the detailed activities of the Greensboro Police Department, the FBI, and the Bureau of Alcohol, Tobacco and Firearms, even though the organizations' covert associations with the Klan and Nazis had been exposed back in 1980. Eddie Dawson testified that after he obtained the anti-Klan parade permit from the Greensboro police, he and other KKK members planned their attack. He admitted inciting the demonstrators with his shouts, and he revealed how the police department kept him from testifying at the state criminal trial when Dawson threatened to expose department officials.

Meanwhile, public opinion remained decidedly against the Communist Workers Party. In a survey commissioned by the survivors' legal team, two-thirds responded that they would not award money to the victims even if the KKK and Nazis were found to be at fault and/or if the police were culpable (Final Report, 2006, 305).

The federal civil rights trial lasted three months. Deliberations by the jury lasted 11.5 hours with a verdict handed down on June 6, 1985. This time, the jury was comprised of one African American and five whites, one that was not a native southerner. Though the decision was far from what the survivors thought adequate, the jury found Greensboro police detective Jerry Cooper and his boss, Lieutenant Paul W. Spoon, along with police informant Eddie Dawson, and three Klansmen and two Nazis liable for conspiracy to commit assault and battery leading to the death of Dr. Michael Nathan. In November of that year, the City of Greensboro agreed to pay the full jury award of $351,000 on its behalf and that of the Klansmen and Nazis to Michael Nathan's estate for his wrongful death (Final Report, 2006, 307). An additional $40,000 was awarded but never paid for the injuries sustained by three victims: Dr. Jim Waller, Dr. Paul Bermanzohn, and Thomas Clark (Final Report, 2006, 308).

Despite the judgment, the police did not admit wrongdoing. No reprimands were issued, nor were policies of police action reevaluated.

The judicial proceedings connected to November 3 took a toll on Greensboro, stretching out more than five years. In three separate trials, the focus had been on assigning guilt and meting out punishment. The outcomes of all three trials were by the end barely acceptable, in large part because they lacked the vital human need for people to talk with one another. There was constant media coverage, a string of political activism projects, interviews, and courtroom drama. Yet, the greatest deficiency in the managing of the events of November 3 was the near-absent conversation among residents in Greensboro about what had happened, their feelings about labor and racial inequities, and their vision for the future based on community and government cooperation. The residents of Morningside Homes suffered without the benefit of counseling or the opportunity to speak of their trauma. The survivors, intent on making political advances, faced obstacles in telling their complete stories, obstacles from outside their control and also of their own making. Even city officials were adversely affected. In being ever vigilant about image control, they steered themselves away from an open, honest examination of what happened on November 3 and what changes should have been considered for the future to ensure the safety and well-being of the community. The cumulative impact, then, was the painful lack of substantive discussion and deliberation about this significant episode in Greensboro.

Amid the political rancor that preceded and followed November 3, there was little mention as well of the people who were gunned down that day. The CWP Five, as they would be known among the protestors, were accomplished young adults whose lives were noteworthy. The Truth and Reconciliation process thus had among its goals to reclaim the humanity of those who died on November 3 as well their spouses and friends who survived.

CHAPTER 2

Grave Consequences

We in the CWP were black, we were white, we were Chicano, we were Asian, we were recent immigrants, we were native born Americans, we were native Hawaiians. Some of us had a little money, were rich. Some of us were poor. Most of us were young intellectuals who brought our communities together.

—JOYCE JOHNSON

WHEN THE EIGHTY-EIGHT seconds of shooting were over on November 3, the consequences were fatal. Taking into account the lack of police intervention, unreported actions of provocateurs, lingering inequality among classes and races, and heightened agitation between activist and white supremacist groups, the fatalities lost significance in the sea of accusations. The bullets shattered individual lives to be sure, but also a community's sense of safety, and a city's image in managing racial tensions, economic conditions, and class warfare. In the unapologetic appropriation of the disaster to finger pointing and blame, there was little to no way to understand the protestors' deep convictions for social justice or the complex economic and racial situation in which the drama was situated. Contained here are some of the activists' stories.

The people who died on November 3 are sometimes regarded as heroes, other times as martyrs, and still other times as domestic terrorists. They were black, brown, and white, both men and women, struggling to communicate what they believed to be unethical and unjust practices in the workplaces that offered ample benefit to the textile mill owners but not so to the lower-wage workers. With the exception of Sandi Smith,[1] they were buried in Greensboro's city-owned Maplewood Cemetery, only a few blocks from where the five were gunned down. According to retired *News & Record* reporter Jim Schlosser, they may be the only whites buried there (personal communication, August 23, 2005).

The CWP Five

A year after the Greensboro Massacre, a tombstone was placed at the cemetery where the slain CWP members were buried. The proposed inscription was, however, opposed by the members of the city council who cited a new ordinance prohibiting political messages on monuments in city cemeteries (Waller, 2002). With intervention from the North Carolina American Civil Liberties Union, the widows successfully argued that any prohibition of specific content on the grave marker amounted to a deprivation of the survivors' free speech rights.

With the way cleared for the widows to inscribe what they wanted, engraved on the headstone for the five people killed on November 3, 1979, is the political decree in all capital letters, "LONG LIVE THE COMMUNIST WORKERS PARTY 5." The large granite monument stands out in height and width among the other more modest markers in the graveyard. A lengthy message on one entire side is also notable for its distinct, piercing, and strident condemnation of U.S. capitalism. It reads:

> On November 3, 1979, the criminal monopoly capitalist class murdered Jim Waller, César Cauce, Mike Nathan, Bill Sampson, and Sandi Smith with government agents, Klan, and Nazis. Heroically defending the people, the 5 charged gunfire with bare fists and sticks. We vow this assassination will be the costliest mistake the capitalists have ever made, and the turning point of class struggle in the U.S.
>
> The CWP 5 were among the strongest leaders of their times. Their deaths marked an end to capitalist stabilization (1950s–1970s) when American workers suffered untold misery, yet as a whole remained dormant for lack of its own leaders. In 1980, the deepest capitalist crisis began. The working class was awakening. The CWP 5 lived and died for all workers, minorities, and poor; for a world where exploitation and oppression will be eliminated, and all mankind freed; for the noble goal of communism. Their

deaths, a tremendous loss to the CWP and to their families, are a clarion call to the U.S. people to fight for workers' rule. In their footsteps, waves of revolutionaries will rise and join our ranks.

We will overthrow the criminal rule of the monopoly capitalist class! Victory will be ours!

November 3, 1980   Central Committee, CWP, USA
FIGHT FOR REVOLUTIONARY SOCIALISM AND
WORKERS' RULE

Each year on November 3, commemoration activities are planned at the gravesite to pay tribute to the young lives lost in 1979. The corner of Everitt Street and Carver Drive in Morningside Homes where the tragedy occurred no longer exists after the area was bulldozed and made over anew into a $76 million mixed-income, mixed-use community called Willow Oaks. But for those who memorialize November 3, the site remains hallowed ground that holds the final memories of five activists whose lives were cut short.

César Vincente Cauce, twenty-five, was the son of Cuban immigrants and a naturalized American citizen who moved to North Carolina when he was five years old. "His father had been Minister of Education in the dictatorial Batista government before it was overthrown by Fidel Castro and the Cuban Revolution" (Waller, 2005, 7). Once in the United States, the family struggled to make ends meet. Still, Cauce attended and graduated magna cum laude from Duke University with a degree in history. As a student, Cauce learned what was required to become a campus leader in the anti-Vietnam War movement. It was an education he would continue to build upon with his organizing activities after graduation. While employed as a data terminal operator at Duke University Hospital, Cauce led efforts to unionize his fellow workers with the American Federation of State, County and Municipal Employees. He was also active in campaigns to organize poultry factory workers in Durham, North Carolina, as well as other union struggles around the state. Cauce documented the labor struggles throughout the South in his articles for the Workers' Viewpoint Organization newspaper. Cauce married Floris only six months before he was shot in the chest then clubbed on his head and died. Floris would later remarry Larry Weston and when their first child was born in 1982, they named him César.

Michael Ronald Nathan, M.D., thirty-two, was born to a poor Jewish immigrant family and was raised in Washington, D.C. (Waller, 2005). He eventually became the head pediatrician at Lincoln Community Health Center in Durham that served poor and black children. Standing over six feet tall, it was not uncommon to see him dressed in Mickey Mouse socks and a Sesame Street tie for his pediatrics work. Nathan attended Duke University on scholarship, where he was an antiwar and civil rights activist. He was a member of the Medical Committee for Human Rights (MCHR) and the Communist Progressive Labor Party (PLP). Nathan's former wife, Sally, would later marry November 3 organizer Paul Bermanzohn. In 1978, Mike and Marty Nathan married and in April 1979, they gave birth to a baby girl. The following November 3, he was shot in the head and died two days later.

William Evan Sampson, thirty-one, grew up in the South where, "As a child, he witnessed a cross being burned near his home" (Waller, 2005, 9), an event that propelled Sampson into antiracist activity for the rest of his life. He was an antiwar activist and president of the student body at Duke University where he graduated summa cum laude. Sampson continued his educational pursuits and received a master's degree from Harvard Divinity School in 1971 before enrolling in the University of Virginia's medical school. In Virginia, he organized health-care workers to support the liberation struggles in South Africa and was a member of the New American Movement (NAM), which built a broad base of support for Marxist ideals. Sampson's interest in social change drove him to leave medical school one year shy of earning his degree in order to engage in union organizing at the White Oak textile mill in Greensboro operated by Cone Mills (Waller, 2005). In North Carolina, he married Dale, a social worker, and became a shop steward with the Amalgamated Clothing and Textile Workers Union. With support from both black and white textile mill workers, Sampson was readying himself to be elected president of the local union when he was shot in the chest and killed.

Sandra Neely Smith, twenty-nine, was an African American woman raised in South Carolina. By the time she became student body president at Bennett College for women in Greensboro, she was fully aware of the struggles being waged against economic and racial injustices. At Bennett, she was a founding member of the Student Organization for Black Unity (SOBU). Later, she became a community organizer for the Greensboro Association of Poor People (GAPP), where Nelson and Joyce Johnson mentored her. From her activity in the Black Liberation Movement, she met and married Mark Smith, but the marriage did not last long (Waller, 2005). Smith led a march of over three thousand people in Raleigh, North Carolina's capital city to protest for the release of the Wilmington Ten, desegregation activists who had been unfairly charged with arson and conspiracy, and considered prisoners of conscience by Amnesty International. She had planned to pursue a career in nursing but she opted instead to first work at the Cone Mills Revolution Plant where she formed, with others, the Revolution Organizing Committee (ROC) to unionize the textile factory. There, Smith experienced firsthand the sexual harassment, low wages, and unhealthy conditions about which the WVO/CWP was concerned. She was an employee at Cannon Mills in Kannapolis, North Carolina, and a leader with the Workers' Viewpoint Organization when she was shot in the head and died.

James Michael Waller, M.D., thirty-six, was raised in a middle-class Jewish family in Chicago where he survived the outbreak of polio. He received his medical degree from the University of Chicago, with specialty training in pediatrics. He was an early white member of the Student Non-Violent Coordinating Committee (SNCC) and active in the Medical Committee for Human Rights in New York. In 1973, he set up a clinic at Wounded Knee, South Dakota to aid American Indian Movement activists who were under siege by the FBI. Waller moved to North Carolina in 1975 to accept a postdoctorate fellowship at Duke University Medical School. There, he conducted research and coordinated screenings for brown lung disease (byssinosis) with Paul Bermanzohn and others for a condition that was spreading among workers in the state's textile mills. He put his medical career on hold to organize black and white rural workers at the Cone Mills Granite Finishing Plant where he was elected president of the local union. In 1978, Waller led a strike of the Amalgamated Clothing and Textile Workers Union involving some two hundred employees at Cone Mills Haw River plant to get higher wages for the employees. He "was fired shortly afterward, but he continued training workers to run their own union local" (Waller, 2005, 11). That same year, he married philosophy teacher and fellow activist Signe and became a stepfather to her two children before he was shot in the back and killed.

Ten Who Were Injured

The ten who were wounded on November 3 recuperated from their injuries, some almost immediately, and others in time. The scars left behind, however, were deeply seared into their skin and psyches.

Eight demonstrators were wounded. Paul Carl Bermanzohn, M.D., thirty, was shot in head and right arm, leaving him permanently paralyzed on the left side. Tom Clark, who tried unsuccessfully to resuscitate Bill Sampson, was treated and released from the hospital that day for a head wound from shotgun pellets. Nelson Johnson, thirty-six, suffered butcher knife wounds to his arm and hand from an attack by a Klansman. Rand Manzella, twenty-six, received shotgun wounds to his legs. Frankie Powell, eight months pregnant at the time, sustained a head wound after being sprayed with shotgun pellets over the back of her legs (Bermanzohn, 2003). Claire Butler had less serious injuries and was treated and released from the hospital that same day. Don Pelles endured shotgun wounds all along the left side of his body. Jim Wrenn was shot in nine places, lost several teeth, and required a plate surgically inserted into his head.

In addition to the eight demonstrators shot, two others sustained injuries. Klansman Harold Dean Flowers, thirty-two, received shotgun wounds to his legs. David Dalton, cameraman for Channel 12, WXII, also suffered shotgun wounds to his legs.

The Survivors

"We came out of the 60s," explained Nelson Johnson, "and we were good organizers around a lot of progressive issues" (personal communication, July 14, 2009). In fact, Johnson's childhood prepared him for a life of activism. The great-grandchild of slaves, he grew up discussing the implications and stigma of race with civic-minded parents; his father and other black landowners formed a chapter of the National Association for the Advancement of Colored People (NAACP) in the early 1950s and registered black people to vote (Bermanzohn, 2003). Then, when Johnson was fifteen years old, he and two friends held their own sit-in in 1958 at the local drugstore in Littleton, North Carolina. One afternoon, the three nervous young boys bought sodas and sat down at one of the two tables in the shop before a white man screaming racial epithets derailed their plans. Johnson recalls:

> So we stood up—and got crushed. What would have happened if we didn't get up and leave? We instinctively knew the police would have come in and beat us. If we resisted, the cops would have killed us, and that would have been that . . . We could have held our ground, hoping that circumstances and history would bail us out, like at Woolworth's in Greensboro two years later. But it wouldn't have happened in Littleton, it's too small a place. If we had held our ground, we would have been hurt. There are so many people who did lifetime jail sentences because they tried to have a little bit of dignity. (Bermanzohn, 2003, 22)

The next year, Johnson tried again to assert himself by sitting in the front of a bus as Rosa Parks did before him in Alabama. He was on the way to a state student government convention with his friend. The two rode in the back of the bus, as was custom until they reached Charlotte, North Carolina. There they walked to the front of the bus, took their seats, and sat quietly as white people hurled wads of paper at them. Moments later, a white man approached and delivered a knock-out punch to Johnson's head that caused him to fall over and then to retreat to the back of the bus. The response from the black bus driver and all the other bus riders was silence, a silence upheld as well by Johnson's high school principal who warned that to say anything about the incident would garner trouble for everyone (Bermanzohn, 2003).

Johnson's civil rights training was honed at North Carolina A & T State University where he attended college after serving in the United States Air Force. Later, his immersion into the philosophies of the Black Nationalist movement, African liberation, and Marxist studies led him to consider for the first time that it was not white people at fault for the black condition, but perhaps more fundamentally, the economic state arising out of capitalism and U.S. imperialism (Bermanzohn, 2003). One of his fellow WVO study partners and November 3 survivor Signe Waller explained:

> Injustice done to black people is usually subsumed under the rubric of racism, that is, prejudice based on skin color. But the

WVO analysis treated racism as also a manifestation of something deeper—a consequence of underlying economic structures
and historical developmental relationships. (Waller, 2002, 119)

Thus, on November 3 Johnson says, "We decided we would have a conference because we were dealing with racism and other issues that challenged our organizing efforts" (personal communication, July 14,
2009). For him, what transpired was a kind of counterdemonstration
organized primarily by the Greensboro Police Department, with the
FBI and the Bureau of Alcohol, Tobacco and Firearms. He asserts, "In
some sense, you could make the argument that you had a state-
supported death squad" deployed on November 3, 1979.

For survivor Willena Cannon, November 3 was not the first time
she had experienced collusion between the Klan and law enforcement.
At age nine in Mullins, South Carolina, where she was born, Cannon
witnessed the Klan burn a black man alive. It was a traumatic event
that would have an everlasting impact on her view of the world, white
people, law enforcement, and the need for a civil rights movement.

> The man was black, the woman white. They had been going
> together. They both consented to the relationship, and black peo-
> ple in Mullins knew that. The men chasing them were from Orry
> County, known to be Ku Klux Klan country . . . When the Klan
> found the couple, the girl didn't cry rape . . . and she got beat bad.
> I didn't know the man, but I knew of his family. The Klan threw
> him in a barn, an old abandoned tobacco barn. They locked him
> in. And then the sheriff came . . . He should have stopped that
> murder, but he didn't . . . he acted like he knew the Klansmen and
> agreed with what they were doing. After the sheriff left, the Klan
> threw kerosene on the barn with the man in it and set it on fire.
> The barn was old and burned real fast. The man hollered and
> hollered; his scream got deeper and deeper. And then silence.
> Nothing . . . the barn burned down to nothing . . . There was no
> newspaper, no report. That man just disappeared. And nobody
> was supposed to talk about it. (Bermanzohn, 2003, 3–4)

Following that wretched episode, Cannon says she learned that "it was
dangerous to talk" about the Klan in front of white people who might
retaliate against someone in the family. She learned to be quiet. She
did not hear the stories of her elders. Instead, "Everything was so secre-

tive. Nobody ever talked about things" (Bermanzohn, 2003, 8). Cannon eventually left that small town, enrolled at North Carolina A & T State University, joined the civil rights struggle, and found what she had been looking for—deep discussion, not silence, about unequal social conditions in need of change.

Survivor Signe Waller likewise found herself engaging in deeper study to question world events, principally the Vietnam War and civil rights activity. From 1967 to 1971, she was teaching philosophy at Southern Massachusetts University, raising two children with her husband, and participating in antiwar teach-ins, mass rallies, and demonstrations. At that point in time, Signe considered herself a follower, rather than a leader, and saw herself engaging in what she called a "ladylike style of sixties protesting" (Waller, 2002, 6). By 1971, her husband accepted a position in the art department at the University of North Carolina at Greensboro, and so with her family, she moved south. When she did, she founded the Greensboro Peace Center where she accelerated and deepened her activist activity. By 1974, she joined Nelson and Joyce Johnson's countywide coalition against the death penalty.

Signe was also involved in several study groups, some led by members of the Workers' Viewpoint Organization. By the mid-1970s, her marriage was falling apart, due largely to her political activity. Still, Signe continued her self-education and came to believe:

> Communism—a political theory predicated on eliminating classes in society and using the social wealth accumulated from everyone's labor to satisfy the human needs of all—appeared to be the only medicine strong enough to cure society of the ills of capitalism. Nothing short of a revolutionary transformation of society would get to the root of social and economic problems . . . The goal was a victory for the multiracial working class, a basic power shift. (Waller, 2002, 32)

Signe would teach for two years at the historically black women's Bennett College before shifting gears and becoming a factory worker at Greensboro's Revolution Mills where she put to work in earnest her political passions and communist party organizing skills.

November 3 was a catalytic point for civil rights action, but the activists' work and reflection both preceded that day and continued thereafter. Nelson and Joyce Johnson, Signe Waller, Willena Cannon,

Marty Nathan, Sally and Paul Bermanzohn, and other survivors were among the progressive contingents in their respective communities to advance social change. They saw themselves as everyday activists focused on education, affordable housing, labor rights, poverty, cultural warfare, and racial justice.

Paul Bermanzohn, the son of Holocaust survivors, took seriously the charge to be politically active in confronting discrimination. Listening to the stories his parents shared, Bermanzohn proclaimed to the TRC, "I became a certified anti-Nazi by the time I was three years old" (2005). In college, he was active in antiwar demonstrations and by the time he entered medical school Bermanzohn says:

> I became more radical as I saw how poor people were treated. How no expense was spared in taking care of upper class people and how if you were poor, and especially if you were poor and black you were treated as a lesser creature. I was shocked to hear poor black people routinely called "teaching material" in the clinics. Poor white folks weren't treated much better. (Bermanzohn, 2005)

Bermanzohn admitted his mistakes in 1979 when he taunted the Ku Klux Klan to come to Greensboro: "I think we were too brash" (Barry, 2003, A14). Even so, he remained convinced that the young activists held up the right ideals in their efforts to transform the world. After the trials surrounding the massacre ended in 1985, so too did Bermanzohn's political activity until 1999, on the occasion of the twentieth anniversary of November 3. It was then that Bermanzohn once again stepped into the political scene, this time to rally against genetically engineered food and biotech corporations he argued were harming the fate of the world's food supply (Bermanzohn, 2003).

The lingering trauma for Sally Bermanzohn lasted long after the event and trials, even as she raised two daughters and pursued a master's degree in urban studies at the City University of New York (CUNY). Because she could, she kept quiet about her involvement in Greensboro while living five hundred miles north in New York City (Bermanzohn, 2003). As it would turn out, though, keeping silent about such a life-altering event gnawed at Sally Bermanzohn's sense of self. So when Sally was admitted into a political science doctoral program at CUNY in 1988, she "came out" to a trusted advisor who responded with care—enough to jump start her research about the lives of other survivors, including how they coped in the aftermath of the tragedy (Bermanzohn, 2003).

Marty Nathan dispersed the monetary award she received at the conclusion of the federal civil trial to the other survivors of November 3. In turn, they donated back what they could as seed money to form the Greensboro Justice Fund, which since then disbursed over $500,000 in mostly small grants to grassroots organizations in the South working for racial and economic justice, civil liberties, peace, and protection from homophobic violence. For her, the fund was a form of reconciliation in tribute to her slain husband, Mike Nathan, and the others who lost their lives on November 3. Her career eventually took hold as a family practice physician in a low-income clinic as she settled into life in Massachusetts with her husband, Elliott Fratkin, her daughter, and two more adopted children from Ethiopia. On the occasion of the thirtieth anniversary of November 3 in 2009, Nathan turned over the Greensboro Justice Fund's remaining assets to the Beloved Community Center and the Tennessee-based Highlander Research and Education Center to fund scholarships and other projects for community organizing.

Greensboro's story of November 3 and the commitment to truth and reconciliation afterward showcases the cumulative effort and actions of social change makers who challenged the prevailing social mores to forward what they conceived of as more just forms of community. Though the City of Greensboro and its leaders did not value the work of the survivors, other organizations bestowed honors upon the survivors, offered cash awards, hosted the survivors for talks and seminars, and visited the survivors to learn from them.

Notably, in 2005, Nelson and Joyce Johnson were recognized by the Ford Foundation's Leadership for a Changing World Award with $100,000 for their longtime efforts to address difficult social issues, including the work surrounding the truth and reconciliation effort.[2] With a portion of the award money, the Johnsons funded a twenty-three-member delegation from Greensboro to go to South Africa in November 2007. There, Naomi Tutu, daughter of Bishop Desmond Tutu, accompanied the participants, ages seven to eighty, to learn up close the lessons of the South African Truth and Reconciliation process. Upon their return to Greensboro, the delegation hosted an evening discussion and offered recommendations compiled by Guilford College student and delegate James Lamar Gibson about ways in which to enrich the community activities and future directions suggested in the TRC's Final Report.[3]

In 2008, the Johnsons received two more awards. First, they were one of six recipients of the Defender of Justice Award sponsored by the North Carolina Justice Center. Second, they received $10,000 and a Purpose Prize for Innovation from Civic Ventures, a national think tank on baby boomers, work, and social purpose.[4]

Looking back, the survivors contend 1979 was a watershed moment that made clear the consequences of not attending to the deep economic, racial, and social rifts evident in Greensboro. As a result, Greensboro would lose ground on virtually every economic and social indicator in the decades following.

CHAPTER 3

An Unfolding History of Social Unrest

We should face up to unpleasant truths about ourselves, but we should not take those truths to be the last word about our chances for happiness, or about our national character. Our national character is still in the making.

—RICHARD RORTY

IN 1979, GREENSBORO, North Carolina, was in crisis amid deep social class and race divisions. Vestiges of paternalism and the subordination of blacks led to a civil yet stifling culture where white elites "helped" those blacks willing to abide by the "pervasive discrimination" in the social structure (Chafe, 1980, 16). The tenuous situation persisted, and was enough to rouse feelings of anger, distrust, suspicion, antagonism, and exasperation that ultimately led to the Greensboro Massacre and later, the initiation of the United States' first Truth and Reconciliation Commission. This chapter traces the roots of that unrest and protest action.

The day-to-day reality for blacks and poor people in Greensboro was dismal in 1979. The result was that an otherwise beautiful city was trapped between competing sociopolitical philosophies and irreconcilable differences over matters of race and labor. Even for those sectors of the community that believed prosperity was within reach, a cohesive response from citizens was necessary to carry out citywide plans for renewal; that response was one the community simply could not muster. For those in despair, mired in lack of opportunity, Greensboro was home to heavy-handed leaders unsympathetic to their plight. Cynicism from all sides prevented meaningful dialogue and problem solving.

To have a city where the conditions were staggeringly poor for some, yet ripe with opportunity for others, left a gaping hole in the very heart of the community. Each sector, concerned deeply with the welfare of their community held tight to their own, differing ideas of how to address the demands of the time.

Even as it held on to its traditions, the people in Greensboro struggled to loosen the grip of racism and paternalism that had shaped its southern identity. Indeed, the actions and beliefs of the past century had left an indelible mark on the lives of whites and blacks as evidenced by the poor quality of their discourse and economic inequality. The grip of conformity manifested itself in mores of fitting in, getting along, not causing trouble, and preserving the status quo. That cultural system is what the American South historian William Chafe would famously describe as the "progressive mystique," the undeniable practice of civility to showcase the New South's façade of tolerance that in effect destroyed the opportunity for authentic communication among races and about race, thus leaving racism intact despite a rhetoric that spoke otherwise (1980). In Greensboro, white city leaders learned to deflect conflict with a strategy of encouraging "moderation" in all things to silence unruly voices and temper any genuine possibility of addressing the inequalities that continued to disproportionately affect poor people and blacks.

As a result, the economic and social conditions of the city worsened. Glenda E. Gilmore, author of *Defying Dixie,* was a young white girl growing up in Greensboro in the 1960s. She says of the city and the South:

> Within those [southern] borders, racial oppression reigned supreme, controlling not only public space but political conversation and private conscience and narrowing the political imagination of even its most defiant subjects. Those who openly protested white domination had to leave, one way or another. (2008, 3)

Gilmore points to the South as the location where class struggle, labor activism, and racial tensions were unleashed alongside the more radical promises of communism to overturn white supremacy and capitalist structures during the Cold War. All this, she argues, gave rise to a civil rights movement imbued with a more complex consideration of social justice than is often noted in history books—one which could be sustained only by the persistent efforts by organized black and white people to change society (Gilmore, 2008).

Uncomfortable truths of racial and economic injustice look and sound unpleasant in the South, and thus the preference was not to talk about them, opting instead to move the conversation toward forward-looking, constructive attempts to dismantle prejudice. Yet, the sting of the past remained real for a great many. For them, silence was not an option. Historically, some of the most prominent protestors of white domination, besides the blacks themselves, were members of the Communist Party:

> Communists gave Southerners a vision and a threat. . . . It was Communists who stood up to say that black and white people should organize together, eat together, go to school together, and marry each other if they chose. (Gilmore, 2008, 6)

Jim Crow laws that codified the separation of people by races were challenged—repeatedly—but the laws themselves called attention to how physical separation of the races was only the most overt of the problems. More devastating was that blacks were at the mercy of whites that would "assert and reiterate black inferiority with every word and gesture, in every aspect of both public and private life" (Chafe et al., 2001, 1). In that climate, white supremacy reigned within the hearts and minds of its people to give shape to Greensboro's identity.

Greensboro's history, similar to other southern cities, is deeply connected to slavery, the Civil War, tobacco, and textiles. As a site where African Americans were bought and sold as property, then later exploited again for their labor, African Americans in the South continued to live there but without many basic human rights. They were unable to vote freely, purchase a house in neighborhoods of their choosing, shop in various stores, obtain meaningful employment, or in other ways pursue their own paths to happiness and well-being. In other words, African Americans experienced a de facto second-class citizenship (Chafe et al., 2001).

When *Civilities and Civil Rights* was first published in 1980, author William Chafe detailed Greensboro's unbridled adherence to civility

since the 1940s as a powerful weapon of social control to trump any
substantive regard for civil rights. He noted that by leaning on consensus as a decision-making model, white Greensboro officials ensured
that attempts to change existing policies and structures that ignited
conflict, were doomed to fail, thus keeping the status quo intact. A
white hegemony prevailed that kept schools segregated and black
workers earning less than their white counterparts at factories. Indeed,
"According to the 1979 census, North Carolina had twice as many black
households as white households living below the poverty line" (Final
Report, 2006, 39). Wage disparities continued between the races, even
though civil rights legislation had been enacted. Unfit housing conditions and lack of enforcement of the housing codes meant that the
poorest parts of town located in black communities left thousands living in substandard, slum-like conditions.

In response to these inequalities, black and white activists throughout the South, and certainly in Greensboro, sought change. The routes
to change were varied and evolved over time to address a range of issues.

The emergence of the civil rights movement in the late 1940s and
into the 1950s and 1960s is perhaps the most well known and documented of these social change efforts. *Brown v. Board of Education* in
1954 asserted that segregated public school instruction was unconsti-
tutional. Greensboro was one of the first cities to proclaim that it
would champion school integration. However, the high-minded talk
failed to deliver on its promise. Finally, a federal court in 1971
demanded the immediate integration of Greensboro schools, which
only by court order occurred two months later. In the end, Greensboro
was not only *not* one of the first to integrate, but in fact was one of the
last cities to comply with the federal standard. Lewis Brandon III, a
community activist and local historian, remarked, "Change doesn't
come because of the goodness of the people in the community. People
have to struggle, people have to fight to get change in this community"
(Final Report, 2006, 43).

On February 1, 1960, Greensboro was the site of what would become
known as the Sit-In Movement. Four black freshman college students
from North Carolina Agriculture & Technical State University, frustrated
and saddened by the racism they could not escape, decided to take
action. Ezell Blair Jr. (later Jibreel Khazan), Franklin McCain, Joseph
McNeil, and David Richmond walked to the Woolworth's Department

Store on Elm Street in downtown Greensboro to sit at the lunch counter where they knew they would be refused service. The store sold goods to all people, but the lunch counter was open only to whites. This double standard stood for the lifelong racial indignities experienced by the Greensboro Four and other blacks in the South. The resolve to act crystallized among the four young friends with determination and courage in what would become a worldwide, nonviolent protest action for racial justice (Chafe, 1980).

Several times over the next six months, the sit-ins in Greensboro were suspended after negotiations with city and business leaders held out promises of change. But the rhetoric was empty, and so sit-in action resumed with shifts of college and high school students taking over the counter seats. Finally, the economic repercussions from the lost revenue at the lunch counter threatened the viability of the store, and that is when officials conceded to the demands for integration (Wolff, 1990). On July 26, 1960, the Greensboro Four were cheered for acquiring for all people the equal status they had sought, and what thousands of supporters in town demanded, and what the 70,000 people in more than fifty-five cities and thirteen states across America insisted upon with other sit-in actions (www.sitinmovement.org/history/greensboro-chronology.asp).

The collective work of the Greensboro students, joined by others nationwide, gave rise to new methods and language to address racial inequities (Chafe, 1980). Young people around the country began talking more, dissatisfied with what they deemed only modest progress and efforts of the existing black-led organizations like the National Association for the Advancement of Colored People, Southern Christian Leadership Conference, and Congress of Racial Equality.

Students not only discussed the need for social change, but they also put their bodies on the line to get it. In Greensboro, picketing efforts amplified at food establishments and movie theaters. By 1963, "some demonstrations exceeded 3,000 people a night" (Final Report, 2006, 46). The police took action as well, arrests mounted, and students filled Greensboro's city jail to capacity. More were taken to a former polio hospital, unfit as it was without even adequate bathroom facilities. The black community in town responded by taking the jailed students food, clean sheets, and pledging support in other ways.

At the same time, massive voter registration drives were underway in Greensboro and throughout the South. Mobilizing blacks was the goal with Greensboro's students at the forefront of that action.

Young people were anxious for deeper change and more inclusive organizing efforts. In the summer of 1960, the Student Non-Violent Coordinating Committee was formed in nearby Raleigh. Under the direction of Ella Baker, the organization grew rapidly by sending organizers door-to-door to invite working-class black residents' stories and experiences into the planning efforts for subsequent protest actions.

The Black Power movement that began in the 1960s was by the 1970s also activating more direct, collective action, demonstration, and strikes. Influenced by anti-Vietnam War sentiment, the Marxist critique of class divisions and economic inequities, and antiapartheid actions, the thrust of the movement's work had turned to self-determination and self-defense in the face of continued racism. In Greensboro, under the leadership of Nelson Johnson and the influence of Black Power, Students Organized for Black Unity formed in 1979. The Malcolm X Liberation University, established that same year in Durham, moved its operations to Greensboro a year later where a strong activist community supported the Black Liberation and Marxist ideological foundations of the school. After two more years, the university closed due to lack of financial resources, ineffective collaboration with other civil rights organizations, and internal conflicts (Belvin, 2004).

At the hub of much of the Greensboro activity was the eloquent organizer, Nelson Johnson. With a $27,000 grant from the Ford Foundation in 1968, "Johnson created GAPP [Greensboro Association of Poor People], which was one of the first independent anti-poverty organizations in the country" (Final Report, 2006, 48). GAPP grew to include three offices, including one located across the street from where the November 3, 1979, shootings occurred. GAPP provided ombudsmen services to Morningside Homes residents and other blacks throughout the city, "fighting for people's welfare money, going downtown to protest official intimidation whenever local blacks felt aggrieved" (Chafe, 1980, 177). Two GAPP board members even lived in Morningside Homes.

More tensions in black-white relations in Greensboro surfaced in 1969. "In March of that year, Nelson Johnson led the A & T Cafeteria Workers Strike as an intentional means of bringing community and student concerns together" (Final Report, 2006, 49). The cafeteria workers' wages increased and working conditions bettered as a result of the action. "However, the strike was also a watershed in the violent confrontations with the police and concerns about 'Negro militants' . . . According to police, students marched in the streets, stoned cars, and exchanged gunfire with police" (Final Report, 2006, 50).

Several months later, another event would erupt in violence—the Dudley High School Revolt in May 1969. When school administrators first took honor student Claude Barnes's name off the ballot in the race for student body president and then disallowed him from taking office once he won in a write-in victory, Barnes and several others walked out of class in protest (Chafe, 1980). Barnes, active with GAPP and SOBU, sought support from the organizations' members, including Nelson Johnson. With their assistance, subsequent protests with 300–400 people effectively shut down Dudley High School and once again, violence ensued.

> Shortly after, white vigilantes also began prowling the city and the [Dudley] students retreated to the A & T campus. The police responded to the situation by calling in National Guard tanks to attempt to storm the A & T campus and knock down the doors of A & T dormitories . . . The violence culminated with the still-unsolved fatal shooting of student Willie Grimes on the A & T campus. (Final Report, 2006, 53)

Nelson Johnson's involvement in the 1969 protests left white political leaders fearful of the danger he and his followers posed to the City of Greensboro. For black activists, the events surrounding the Dudley Revolt reinforced their anger over reckless and deadly police actions.

Despite what Chafe concluded was an overreaction of local and national officials in the Dudley Revolt, it was Nelson Johnson who was the scapegoat that suppressed opportunities for meaningful conversation and social change:

> By organizing poor people, public-housing tenants, cafeteria workers, and high school students to reject the definition of their proper "place" handed down by white authorities, Nelson Johnson and his associates were undercutting the very foundations of white power. (Chafe, 1980, 197)

During the 1969 holiday season, GAPP and Nelson Johnson persisted in their efforts, supporting a labor strike and advocating for area renters. Workers at the National Industries of the Blind wanted better wages, better working conditions, and improved safety guidelines. The renters petitioned the city council for improved housing conditions, rent control, and strict code enforcement to ensure safe and healthy housing.

GAPP continued its activism into the 1970s. In 1972, GAPP supported a community call for an independent Citizen Review Board to investigate police brutality charges. In 1974, GAPP spoke out against Duke Power rate increases. It also, "organized a 'Stop the Test' campaign against the high school competency test" (Final Report, 2006, 56). The competency test was a requirement for a high school diploma but African Americans and poor white students were failing without programs put in place to help the situation, according to GAPP activist and November 3, 1979, survivor Willena Cannon (Final Report, 2006, 57).

By the end of the 1970s, Nelson Johnson and Sandi Smith were experienced grassroots organizers who had long been involved in youth civil rights movements. They "shifted their emphasis from race to class and began trying to build multiracial coalitions in the [textile] mills" (Final Report, 2006, 58).

> The mainstream of Greensboro's white community was in denial about the poor black community's experience of inhumane living conditions, racial discrimination in health care, wages, working conditions and education. The unwelcome bearers of this message were often seen as a violent threat. (Final Report, 2006, 60)

It is within this context of organizing efforts on behalf of blacks in Greensboro, that a "clash was inevitable" (Final Report, 2006, 61).

The hostility toward blacks was matched at the time by a disdain for unions that threatened employer growth and profits. The American South in the late twentieth century and early twenty-first century established itself as antiunion territory.

In Greensboro and the surrounding areas, the textile mills had strong ties to the local political power that was held by business people, elected officials, and church leaders. Mill owners would make land and other donations to the cities in which they operated in order to curry favor with the local officials. Thus, when mills wanted to "stretch-out" workloads—requiring employees to work longer hours without more pay—to boost the company's production schedule and profits, they had the backing of friendly politicians, the benefit of local court rulings to thwart union activities, and even the resources of the National Guard when needed (Final Report, 2006, 68).

Labor organizers attempted to build alliances of black and white workers, but doing so ran up against the cultural tide of racism. The Truth Commissioners highlighted this dynamic: "Though many organizing efforts attempted to eliminate the racial gap, it remained virtually unbridgeable throughout the South, including in North Carolina. Instead, unions took on the conventions of the culture, segregating along racial lines" (Final Report, 2006, 72).

In effect, mill owners tapped into racial fears as a means by which to keep segregation alive in order to divide and weaken union activity. The strategy was simple, but effective. If the workers could be pitted against one another by race, then they would be unable to assert a collective voice. By the mid-1970s, in the midst of an economic recession that found the textile industry in trouble, placing blame on the backs of workers was common. With the workers fearful of losing their jobs, there arose "fertile recruiting opportunities for a resurgence of the Klan, growing after years of decline" (Final Report, 2006, 75).

Simultaneously, the textile workforce saw a growing number of workers' rights violations. From 1957 to 1980, there was a 750 percent increase in reported violations according to a review of NLRB records in a 2000 Human Rights Watch report (Compa, 2000).

Along with labor union drives, another rallying location emerged for workers, this time surrounding a critical health matter. Brown lung disease or byssinosis was sweeping through North and South Carolina textile mills. The irreversible condition was caused by cotton dust that blocks the airways in the lungs, eventually leading victims to suffocate to death. In response, the Carolina Brown Lung Association was formed in Columbia, South Carolina, in 1975 to seek workers' compensation arising from the disease and to help mill workers in other ways, primarily through screening clinics, education, lobbying, and legislative reform. By 1977, a relatively new Occupational Safety and Health Administration (OSHA) verified what mill workers already knew about the disease, and began measures to require the reduction of contaminants and worker exposure to cotton dust. At the same time, Paul Bermanzohn and Jim Waller, WVO members and physicians, volunteered with the lung association by screening mill workers. The association eventually chastised the two, however, for promoting radical political activity and union membership during the health screenings. Those actions, said the association, exceeded the organization's health imperatives and cultural values of group decision making and cooperation (Final Report, 2006, 85).

Communist doctrine had been familiar in U.S. labor union organizing since the 1920s, reaching out to blacks and whites to promote an agenda of self-determination and the elimination of poverty, inequalities, racism, and capitalism. However, once World War II erupted, U.S.-based communist organizations and their sympathizers faced growing opposition and threats as they were confronted with McCarthy hearings, intimidation, laws, and practices intended to squash their influence. The 1970s Mao Tse-tung inspired groups, of which the WVO/CWP was a part, appealed to some, but certainly not a majority of union workers. At Cone Mills, at least two other related groups were active and visible— the Revolutionary Communist Party and the Revolutionary Workers' League. The WVO[1] distinguished itself by emphasizing its anti-Klan posture, using particularly aggressive tactics that espoused "hard line communist ideology" (Final Report, 2006, 93), and making no secret of its ambition for revolution. Ironically, the WVO/CWP relied on strict hierarchical leadership (Bermanzohn, 2003) that limited the possibilities of collaborating with other local or national union organizing efforts.

The WVO/CWP, in order to activate a sufficient worker base, had to spotlight the oppressive practices of the mill owners and area law enforcement that from their vantage point was colluding with the Klan:

> the capitalist class deployed the Klan when it was threatened by a potentially powerful and united workers movement *and* out of fear of African American activists linking up with communists who were outspokenly promoting socialist revolution. (Waller, 2002, 204)

The Ku Klux Klan, the white supremacist organization best known for its ritual burnings of thirty- to sixty-foot wooden crosses encircled by a membership clad in white robes and hoods, experienced the height of its popularity in the 1920s with four million members. In the 1950s and 1960s, membership had significantly declined yet civil rights activity prompted a renewal of recruitment efforts to support traditional southern values, promote the separation of the races, and preserve states' rights. In 1965, Klan rallies drew 150 to 3,000 people to each event in North Carolina according to State Highway Patrol crowd estimates (Final Report, 2006, 100). Their rallies constituted "the largest political gatherings of any kind in the state at the time" (Final Report, 2006, 101).

North Carolina's public leaders claimed the KKK's activities were unsustainable and would eventually fade away without a government crackdown. State officials eventually yielded to pressure to contain the KKK after North Carolina was identified as the state with the highest Klan activity in the nation. The governor and the FBI's counterintelligence operation (COINTELPRO) coordinated police and investigations that for a time seemed to work. However, in the mid- to late 1970s, the Klan was rebuilding under the national direction of David Duke. By early 1979, confrontations were common between Klansmen and their opponents throughout the South and North Carolina specifically. A February 1979 KKK exhibition at a library in neighboring Winston-Salem brought protest from the NAACP, the Jewish Defense League, and the Revolutionary Communist Party (Final Report, 2006, 103). A month later, protests continued against the showing of the 1915 silent film, *The Birth of a Nation,* in that same city's convention center.

On May 26, 1979, Klan provoked violence erupted in Decatur, Alabama. There, the Southern Christian Leadership Conference was marching in protest of the conviction of Tommy Lee Hines, a mentally handicapped black man who had been accused of raping several white women. Hines's family claimed he was incapable of driving the car that was used in the assault. The marchers, including members of Greensboro's WVO, were attacked by 150 Klansmen calling for Hines's lynching. In the fray, twenty-three shots were fired from both sides of the clash, injuring two Klansmen and two demonstrators. No Klansmen were charged. Black demonstrator and civil rights leader Curtis Robinson, however, was charged *and* convicted of shooting a Klansman who had beat the car carrying Robinson's wife and children (Final Report, 2006, 104).

WVO members Paul and Sally Bermanzohn, Nelson Johnson, Roz Pelles, and Jean Chapman were at the Decatur march, an experience they say heightened the WVO's resolve. As it would happen, the KKK shortly thereafter announced another screening of *The Birth of a Nation,* this time in China Grove, North Carolina, to be held in July. The highest-grossing film of its day, the silent, epic-length movie by D. W. Griffith, features technical and creative innovations in portraying blacks as barbaric and subhuman while valorizing the Klan. The WVO decided to meet with residents of China Grove to organize a protest aimed at stopping the film's screening.[2] The WVO advocated for a program of "armed self defense" to show that people need not be intimidated by racist terror (Final Report, 2006, 128). Reactions from China Grove residents were mixed. Some were appreciative of the support offered by the WVO, pointing out how infrequent it was for white people to stand side by side with blacks. Some older residents, however, objected to the WVO's militant tactics, fearing it would provoke retaliation by the Klan.

On the day of the film's showing, July 8, 1979, one hundred WVO members and local residents carried signs, chant sheets, and sound equipment as they marched up to the porch of the China Grove Community Center. The Klan and Nazis stood holding shotguns, rifles, and handguns. The two groups faced each other and traded insults. The protestors waved clubs in the air and held onto broken bottles, pipes, and sticks. Some were illegally carrying concealed weapons according to WVO member Signe Waller, who was fearful and yet resolute about the need to confront the Klan that day (Final Report, 2006, 131).

Eventually, the Klan and Nazis retreated into the building, a move seen as a victory by the protestors—the Klan had backed down. In response, the protestors burned the Klan's Confederate flag, nearly burning the U.S. flag as well before a China Grove community leader intervened. Afterward, WVO leaders envisioned expanding their efforts to a statewide anti-Klan movement and with that, plans were put in motion for the November 3, 1979, educational conference and march in Greensboro.[3]

The Klan and Nazis were also hard at work planning their next moves. In September, Nazi Party leader Harold Covington sent a letter to the other Greensboro-operating communist organization, the RCP, apparently confusing the RCP with the WVO. He wrote, "we had it all worked out with the cops that if you were dumb enough to try to attack the [China Grove] community center we'd waste a couple of you and none of them would see anything" (Final Report, 2006, 148). Later that month, the Nazis and Klan met and agreed to combine resources in the United Racist Front coalition and attend the November 3, 1979, march.

Klan informant Eddie Dawson emerged as an important figure in the weeks before the march. He spoke at Klan rallies and meetings, urging confrontation on November 3 in Greensboro. Just two weeks prior, on October 22, Dawson reported his activities to the Greensboro Police Department and of plans by roughly eighty-five Klansmen to bring guns and challenge the communists on November 3. For the information, Dawson was paid $50. Later, Dawson made a second call to retired Greensboro police officer, Lieutenant Ford, telling him that thirty-five to fifty Klansmen were going to attend the march, possibly with guns. The concerned Lieutenant Ford relayed this information to the Greensboro Police Department and offered to arrange a meeting with Dawson. But a meeting was unnecessary since Dawson was already in contact with his handler within the police department, Detective Jerry "Rooster" Cooper. A few days later, on October 26, Dawson informed the police that the Klan and Nazis would meet at the home of a fellow Klansman on November 3, drive together to the parade, heckle the marchers, and throw eggs. According to Dawson, Klansman Virgil Griffin was going to ride the parade route the night before in order to identify a spot for a confrontation (Final Report, 2006, 152).

Meanwhile Bernard Butkovich, the undercover agent with the Bureau of Alcohol, Tobacco and Firearms, was reporting information to federal authorities, but not to local law enforcement officials. He confirmed what Dawson had reported and added what he knew from being present at a meeting of the Nazis—that the Nazis intended to take a pipe bomb to the march on November 3 (Final Report, 2006, 160).

Just as officials were infiltrating the Klan, they were also investigating activist organizations, like the WVO/CWP, using strategies developed in earlier days. COINTELPRO, under the direction of then FBI director J. Edgar Hoover, operated from 1956 to 1971 to "expose, disrupt, misdirect, discredit, or otherwise neutralize" individuals and political organizations thought to be subversive (Final Report, 2006, 110). COINTELPRO relied on covert operations and agent provocateurs who would pose as group members to spread rumors and dissolve group cohesiveness. COINTELPRO named groups a threat to national security if they criticized the practices and policies of the U.S. Government. Groups targeted were communist and socialist organizations, antiwar groups, Black Nationalist groups, women's groups, student protestors, civil rights activists, and the NAACP. According to some sources, as much as 85 percent of COINTELPRO's operations were devoted to infiltrating for the purpose of eliminating these groups. The remaining 15 percent of their operations were aimed at white hate groups including the Ku Klux Klan and Nazi Party, who were lawless and unpredictable, perhaps, but not subversive according to Hoover's FBI (Final Report, 2006, 112).

COINTELPRO formally ceased operations in 1971 after a group of activists broke into FBI offices, stole classified memos, leaked these documents to the media, and put the program at risk of public exposure. The remnants of COINTELPRO remained, according to critics.[4] As evidence, the November 3 survivors pointed to the lack of FBI disclosure on the details of their surveillance of the WVO in 1979, and the use of agents, quite possibly as provocateurs, to encourage or at the very least know and not report the risks posed to protestors on November 3 by the Klan and Nazis.

Like the FBI, the Greensboro Police Department was troubled by the activities of communist groups in the city. They kept "pretty active" intelligence files on Nelson Johnson, as well as Sandi Smith, though neither had pending criminal charges (Final Report, 2006, 123).

The Days Leading Up to November 3

Two weeks before the planned November march, Nelson Johnson went to the downtown police station to apply for a parade permit. He met with Captain Larry Gibson, who accepted the application contingent upon an agreement that marchers not carry weapons and that stick sizes be restricted. Johnson protested this unusual condition for approval, but complied. The parade starting point as written on the permit was the intersection of Everitt Street and Carver Drive to begin at 12 noon. Police asked about the posters that advertised the event beginning at the Windsor Community Center at 11:00 A.M., to which Johnson explained that the community center was an easier gathering spot for out-of-town participants who would then be shuttled to the actual parade starting point as indicated on the permit application.

The permit application was not approved in a timely fashion, according to Johnson, who became frustrated with the delays that to him were indicative of police attempts to disrupt the WVO/CWP's plans (Final Report, 2006, 155). He announced a press conference for November 1 on the outdoor steps of the police department to publicly condemn the police for their "slimy tactics" (Final Report, 2006, 155) including the removal of WVO posters, and the intentional spreading of rumors of impending violence. Though the police finally issued the permit thirty minutes in advance of the press conference, Johnson blamed the police for fanning the flames of fear in the community. The church hosting the educational conference canceled the event there, Johnson said, when police told church leaders that violence was certain.

Also on November 1, Klansman and Greensboro Police Department informant Eddie Dawson requested a copy of the parade permit that outlined restrictions against weapons as well as the parade assembly point and route. Since the permit was deemed public information, a copy was given to Dawson.

That evening, WVO members met to discuss security issues surrounding the march. They wanted to arm themselves out of concern for potential police brutality and the Klan reputation for violence. Thus, they printed and distributed flyers that night calling on neighbors along the parade route to arm themselves on their front porches with weapons. Johnson said he was not in favor of taking guns to the march, calling it a "great mistake" to carry weapons after he signed the permit agreeing to its terms. He argued that to carry or display weapons would invite further harassment from the police (Final Report, 2006, 159).

Across town, BATF undercover agent Bernard Butkovich was watching the local television news with Nazi Party members. When the story on Johnson's press conference aired, Butkovich saw one of the television watchers point a gun at the television and say, "I've been experimenting with pipe bombs in the woods and it would work good in a crowd of Niggers" (personal communication, Lewis Pitts, March 15, 2011).

By Saturday, November 3, everyone was taking their respective places as plans turned toward action. The police held several briefings, the Klansmen and Nazis met early at a Greensboro home, and the protestors in town set up check-in points for the out-of-town supporters driving to Greensboro.

POLICE PREPARATIONS

At the 6:00 A.M. briefing that day, assignments were made, the parade route was reviewed, and a strategy to keep a low profile was discussed. The officers spoke of how the Klan and Nazis would likely be disrupting the march. Lieutenant Spoon said the Klan and Nazis might bring guns, which meant the officers should anticipate trouble (Final Report, 2006, 170).

At 10:00 A.M. the tactical units, to be used as backup, were briefed. Detective Cooper reviewed his latest conversations with Dawson earlier that morning and his observations of guns being loaded into the Klan-Nazi cars. He alerted the officers that Klan leader Virgil Griffin was in town, someone known to be "a hot head with a short fuse" (Final Report, 2006, 171).

Then, decisions were made that would baffle the community for years later. First, because commanders said they did not know how long officers would need to be on duty for the parade, they instructed everyone at 10:30 A.M. to take a break for food and report to their positions by 11:30 A.M. That the police made this decision in spite of the information they had received from the undercover informants, would later add to the community's mistrust of the police. "To protect and to serve," the accepted U.S. police motto, was set aside, said community members when the police took no action and issued no warning that day of the possible violence.

Second, two police officers in the neighborhood responding to a domestic disturbance call were ordered to leave the area as soon as possible, just before 11:00 A.M.

At 11:16 A.M., police unit officers were advised that nine cars of Klansmen were heading toward the parade route. However, because they were on lunch break, many officers were several miles away. Detective Cooper, following the Klan-Nazi caravan, radioed multiple times to provide updates on the caravan's path to Everitt and Carver, which it finally reached at 11:20 A.M.

PROTESTOR PREPARATIONS

By 10:00 A.M., early arrivals were at both the Windsor Community Center and at Morningside Homes positioning sound system speakers on the flatbed truck and attaching signs to the required 2x2 sticks that marchers would carry during the parade. The signs proclaimed "Death to the Klan" and "Celebrate the Founding of the Communist Workers Party" (that day the WVO planned to publicly announce its name change). Most demonstrators arrived later, between 10:45 and 11:00 A.M.

In response to the previous night's planning meeting, activist "marshals" were appointed to defend the others on the chance there would be trouble. Five demonstrators carried weapons and others had billy clubs and sticks. Bill Sampson, killed that day, had several "long guns" in cases locked in his car (Final Report, 2006, 171).

When the police arrived at the Windsor Community Center, shortly after 10:15 A.M., the demonstrators shouted antipolice chants and refused to speak to the officers, frustrated they said with previous police tactics. Sergeant Comer, the officer in charge, had just left Everitt and Carver where he reported seeing no signs of group activity. He deduced that the march was to begin at the community center. Nelson Johnson and other demonstrators would later challenge this claim, since the parade permit clearly indicated that the intersection of Everitt and Carver was the march starting location.

MEDIA PRESENCE

The media began to arrive shortly after 10:00 A.M., expecting the parade to begin at 11:00 A.M. Journalists first went to Windsor Community Center but were directed by parade organizers to Everitt Street and Carver Drive. Journalist Laura Blumenthal said one of the demonstrators told her where the parade starting point was, but instructed her to not tell the police. Four television crews and numerous reporters from local newspapers were on hand.

KLAN AND NAZIS GATHER

Nearly three dozen Klansmen and Nazis were at Klansman Brent Fletcher's Greensboro home by 10:30 A.M. Nine had semiautomatic weapons, rifles, and shotguns. In addition, others had nun chucks, hunting knives, brass knuckles, chains, tear gas, and mace. According to Klansman Mike Sherer:

> By the time the Klan caravan left Fletcher's house, it was generally understood that our plan was to provoke the Communists and blacks into fighting and to be sure that when the fighting broke out the Klan and the Nazis would win. We were prepared to win any physical confrontation between the two sides. (Final Report, 2006, 174)

Klan informant Dawson organized the white supremacists into their cars, trucks, and van, and descended upon the protestors. The plans were completed, shots were fired, people were killed, and the march was brought to a halt before it ever began.

Fissures in the Community

November 3, 1979, did not create, but did highlight the fissures in the community that persisted: race and class divisions, and an enduring, existential lack of trust. The swelling gap between the rich and the poor paralleled the divide between whites and blacks. Lush country clubs and gardens sat then and remained years later not so far from sparse, subsidized housing. Academically rich K–12 schools turned out both scholarship rich students and dispossessed students who dropped out too early to earn their high school degrees. In response, the city's complexion changed as whites fled from the city's center to take refuge in the suburbs.

Though the city's pride as the seat of the Sit-In Movement is symbolized today in its $27 million International Civil Rights Museum, the city remains conflicted about other episodes that sought to bring attention to the injustices experienced by blacks, including the Greensboro Massacre of November 3, 1979. And that, survivors argued, is why a Truth and Reconciliation Commission convened by the people was so profoundly needed in Greensboro, North Carolina.

CHAPTER 4

Truth and Reconciliation Commissions Seek Healing, Not Vengeance

Neither truth nor justice alone, but a democracy that does its best to promote both, is the bedrock of any worthy truth commission.

—AMY GUTMANN AND DENNIS THOMPSON

TO BETTER UNDERSTAND why Greensboro initiated its truth and reconciliation process, this chapter discusses when, how, and where around the world these nonjudicial bodies for truth seeking have operated. The goal is to provide the contextual frame for the work of restorative justice that is the foundation of truth commission activity. Restorative justice, unlike retributive justice that seeks to punish individuals held responsible for misdeeds or crimes, aims instead for reconciliation by highlighting the strengths and shared solutions that arise from the interconnections among people.

Reconciliation using restorative justice principles thus focuses on the community as a precondition for the well-being of individuals. In Africa, that tradition is known as "Ubuntu." In the United States, Ubuntu is most closely related to conceptions of dialogic ethics and ethics of care. This chapter thus considers if and how Ubuntu, dialogic ethics, and an ethics of care provide the moral suasion necessary for truth and reconciliation in the United States.

It has been only since the 1980s that TRCs have acquired legitimacy as a means to address human rights violations. Initially, these commissions were fueled by ambitious hopes but not always useful processes and thus many proved ineffective at documenting past crimes or gaining public trust (Hayner, 2001). By 1995, many of the earlier insufficiencies had been corrected when the South African Truth and Reconciliation Commission was launched. It remains the most well known and stands out as the preferred archetype for truth seeking and reconciliation among the more than fifty TRCs that have functioned in all regions around the globe. The South African TRC was both hailed and critiqued as a political compromise that eventually included the collection of 20,000 statements, fifty public hearings over the course of 244 days, seventeen truth commissioners, and sixty staff members. Its work concluded with a five-volume Final Report handed to then president Nelson Mandela nearly three years afterward.

TRCs are temporary bodies generally established by a new or transitional government. Operating independently of government influence, they seek to bridge unjust pasts with more promising futures based on truth, tolerance, and equality. TRCs hope to mend factions and restore faith for a more peaceful coexistence (Verdoolaege, 2008). Critics notwithstanding, truth commissions offer an alternative justice-seeking method that advances direct democracy by providing a meaningful public platform for citizen speech, deliberative processes, and public policy changes.

TRCs most often arise from the need of victims and survivors who have been silenced to be included as legitimate bearers and makers of history.

> Truth commissions link together complex ideas about suffering, justice, human rights, accountability, history and witnessing. Alongside legal practices they involve and invoke memorial and narrative practices that have important effects in shaping understandings and sculpting new social possibilities. (Ross, 2003, 1)

In other words, the very personal stories of pain are used "to answer troublesome questions and be clear about yet unresolved doubts" that enrich and complicate archived documents and legal proceedings (Magarrell and Roehm, 2003, 2).

Priscilla Hayner, author of *Unspeakable Truths: Confronting State Terror and Atrocities,* asks if any society can "build a democratic future on a foundation of blind, denied, or forgotten history" (2001, 5). History teaches us that the answer is simply, no.

In Latin America, commissions were introduced upon regime changes following periods of oppression and violence in Argentina, Bolivia, Brazil, Chile, El Salvador, Ecuador, Guatemala, Haiti, Panama, Peru, and Uruguay. In Africa, truth commissions targeted national reconciliation in Chad, the Democratic Republic of Congo, Ethiopia, Ghana, Kenya, Liberia, Morocco, Nigeria, Rwanda, Sierra Leone, South Africa, Uganda, and Zimbabwe. Other truth and reconciliation commissions operated in East Timor, Fiji, Germany, Nepal, the Philippines, Serbia and Montenegro, South Korea, the Soloman Islands, Sri Lanka, the United States (in Greensboro, North Carolina), and more recently, Canada.[1]

In accounting for the surge of TRC activity around the world, proponents argue that our understanding and decisions surrounding human rights issues are better when people speak openly of their painful experiences (Amjad-Ali; 2008). Thus, TRCs invest great effort to create supportive environments at their public hearings, absent the adversarial tension more common in courtrooms. When this is accomplished, survivors communicate publicly what injustices they experienced or witnessed. Their stories contribute to a coauthoring and rewriting of an historical record. Similarly, perpetrators may be better able to admit and atone for their actions in a setting free of harsh, impersonal questioning.

Dialogue is thus a key feature of the TRC process. Among academic scholars, dialogue is most often regarded as communication's deliverance. Dialogue is understood to be a distinctive form of communication premised on values of authenticity, freedom, inclusion, and respect that together demonstrate our common fate in a common world (Buber, 1955). Where the excesses of persuasion and other forms of talk have distorted, maligned, manipulated, and forced, dialogue offers a communication experience more compassionate than what dispassionate debate on public policy can elicit.

Dialogue is rooted in the concrete, lived experience. It comes by invitation, not demand. Dialogue scholars agree, however, that we can increase the frequency of dialogue when we engage and express genuine listening, caring, concern, and respect for the other person (Anderson et al., 2004; Peters, 1999; Bohm, 1996; and Stewart, 1995). Those communicative practices comprise the common mandate by which TRCs conduct their business, bringing together survivors, perpetrators, and the community to talk. In advance of the public hearings, for instance, staff often provides guidelines and assistance to help the participants adequately prepare their written testimonies. After testimony is delivered at the public hearings, it is typical that the commissioners ask appreciative, follow-up questions to prompt more talk by the participants. The audience plays an important role, albeit a generally silent one, to bear witness to the proceedings. In sum, TRCs aim for inclusiveness as a "superstructure" principle necessary for telling the truth (Verdoolaege, 2008).

South Africa established its own parameters for a truth and reconciliation process to promote national unity and reconciliation relying on Ubuntu to demonstrate respect for human dignity, express compassion, and maintain a community focus. Ubuntu's moral strength is steeped in its high regard for dignity and respect in the relationship between self and others (Tutu, 1999). With its origins in Bantu languages of southern Africa, Ubuntu has been translated by Liberian peace activist and Nobel Peace Prize winner Leymah Gbowee as, "I am what I am because of who we all are."

Ubuntu is an expression of helpfulness that former South African president Nelson Mandela said is communicated in our everyday interactions with others:

> A traveler through our country would stop at a village, and he didn't have to ask for food or for water. Once he stops, the people give him food, entertain him. That is one aspect of Ubuntu. Ubuntu has various aspects. Ubuntu does not mean that people should not enrich themselves. The question therefore is, are you going to do so in order to enable the community around you to improve? (www.youtube.com/watch?v=ODQ4WiDsEBQ)

A person's own moral, ethical, and spiritual life, then, are in large part shaped by relationships with others (Massango, 2006).

Taken beyond its consideration and enhancement of individual human well-being, an Ubuntu ethic for the community highlights the political dimension of sociality:

> In its politico-ideological sense it is a principle for all forms of social or political relationships. It enjoins and makes for peace

and social harmony by encouraging the practice of sharing in all
forms of communal existence. (More, 2004, 157)

Ubuntu as a worldview entered the public sphere when Archbishop
Desmond Tutu touted its spiritual and political dimensions during the
South African Truth and Reconciliation Commission's proceedings.

Ubuntu embraces hospitality and connection that "preserves the
integrity and fabric of the society" (Murithi, 2006, 25). Likewise, dialogic ethics considers the same communicative actions as vital for a
civil society. Emmanuel Levinas (1988), in advancing dialogic ethics,
says *being for the other* is the ethical imperative and communicative
stance for peace. In a stark departure from "me first" thinking, Ubuntu
and Levinas's dialogic ethics recognize the deep interconnections
among all and points to similarities as well with Buddhist thought
(Lama, 1999; Hanh, 1988). Seen this way, justice evolves as much from
nurturing relationships—an ethic of care—as it does from firm, universal conceptions of right and wrong (Gilligan, 1982). Ubuntu, like
an ethic of care, considers ethics to be a prescriptive guide for how we
ought to speak and act to prevent harm and presupposes care as a natural and universal expression of all people that crosses gender, ethnic-
ity, and cultural differences (Noddings, 1995/1984).

Ubuntu requires a full participatory framework in the political
arena, and thus is rightly considered a demanding and involved
approach to justice. When there are no easy answers to questions of
what is just, right, and fair, as is the case in the work of TRCs, struggling
with the fine points as well as the larger contextual frames are essential
to the process. With a different orientation, one based on retributive
justice, this process of grappling with more than the specific incident
might be viewed as a distraction to expediency and a violation of dispassionate reason.

In Greensboro, as in other locales, that meant the TRC had to hold
difficult, sometimes contradictory or incomplete pieces of information
together in order to allow a new path to reveal itself. For example, the
account of November 3 that circulated in the media in the aftermath
of the tragedy reduced the information to a gun battle or shoot-out
between opposing extremist groups. The details, including the context
in which that event took place, were regarded as superfluous to the

main point that Greensboro did not want further violence. Therefore, at least initially, the role of the police and the lengthy backgrounds of community involvement by the protestors were overlooked. An approach grounded in an ethic of care or Ubuntu would place these community facts in the forefront to allow a complex situation to remain as such. It is this latter approach that TRCs take. They honor the particulars in their investigations and throughout their multifaceted layers of community outreach.

Putting principles of Ubuntu to work in cultures where individual rights are sacred requires sustained time and commitment to transform the focus from self-preservation to an outward-based concern for others and a communal model for justice. Thus, TRCs are carefully crafted to solicit and then allow stories to unfold privately before introducing them in public for community consumption and discussion. In this way, TRCs provide raw narrative materials for the entire community to consider as it discusses the pain, fear, skepticism, and hope embedded in those experiences. With a trajectory toward healing, Ubuntu points individuals and communities to consider how they should relate to one another in the currents of everyday life (Nabudere, 2005).

A central communicative skill to enacting a dialogic ethic or Ubuntu is listening in ways that actively engage with and welcome others into our domain of understanding, what Lisbeth Lipari terms "listening otherwise" (2009). As is the case with Ubuntu, listening otherwise calls upon us to *feel* the suffering of others so that we are "awakened and attuned to the sounds of difference rather than to the sounds of sameness" (Lipari, 2009, 45). Listening otherwise is an act of compassion that notes the silence, too, that may point to what is difficult, unfamiliar, and even strange (Lipari, 2004).

In these philosophies—Ubuntu, dialogic ethics, and ethics of care—what we say, to whom we say it, in what terms we say it, and for what ends we say it, matter deeply. It is through this ethical frame that TRCs conduct their business.

The next section of this chapter offers a working definition of restorative justice and an overview of its role in truth and reconciliation processes. With roots in legal scholarship and faith-based principles (Ubuntu), restorative justice enjoys measured interest among peace and conflict advocates.

Restorative Justice

John Braithwaite, an Australian criminal lawyer, is among the most often-cited experts on restorative justice, defined as an approach to restoring dignity to the victims, offenders, and the community that has been violated (2002). Restorative justice is holistically focused in its efforts to bring together the three parties through a process of initiating dialogue, offering apologies, and making amends to repair or build the relationships therein. Within this paradigm of justice, punishment is not forgotten, but it is not the central focus of the crime's aftermath. Restorative justice is a foundational principle for TRC operations (Kerber, 2003).

South Africa's TRC, for instance, emphasized in their processes that restorative justice had to involve the community. Accordingly, the stories shared at public hearings were structured to detail the harms done, but also to discuss the impact of those harms on the community.

According to Howard Zehr, a professor of restorative justice who has mentored organizations and individuals, including 2011 Nobel Peace Prize winner Leymah Gbowee, South Africa's approach to violence and wrongdoing depended upon the development and deepening of relationships.

> Restorative justice is a process to involve, to the extent possible, those who have a stake in a specific offense and to collectively identify and address harms, needs, and obligations, in order to heal and put things as right as possible. (Zehr, 2002, 37)

South Africa's process was intended to transform the lasting shame into productive possibilities for change; trust, they reasoned, had to be rebuilt among people and between people and their government.

Restorative justice examines the past, but it also looks forward and in so doing can also be considered "pro-storative" in building relationships anew says theologian Guillermo Kerber (2003). Faith-based organizations, Kerber asserts, should be active in promoting restorative justice for they are experienced in accepting confessions, offering forgiveness, and guiding people toward acceptance of responsibility to rebuild communities.

Dr. Peter Storey, Duke Divinity School professor, South African

Methodist church leader, and a member of the selection committee for the South African Truth and Reconciliation Commission, concurs, and explained at a 2005 Greensboro gathering that restorative justice and reconciliation are nonnegotiable obligations for people of faith:

> When we acknowledge each other's permanence, when courageous people take the crucial first step, when we really engage with each other and listen to each other's stories, when we truly seek to do justly to each other . . . then we make space for God's "new thing" of reconciliation to happen.

Storey emphasized that restitution comes in changing those circumstances that hurt people and harmed relationships.

Despite its promise to rebuild damaged communities and broken relationships, restorative justice has had a hard time gaining traction in the United States because fear, not trust, is promulgated and punitive measures doggedly pursued (H. Zehr, personal communication, April 23, 2010). Further, restorative practices are not part of legal training. A focus on restorative justice, though hard to embrace, contributes to a fresh dialogue that reminds us that our relationships with one another are paramount to the possibility of a free, democratic civil society, says Zehr.

Some legal commentators remain skeptical of restorative justice efforts. They ask how truth and reconciliation commissions with their focus on restorative justice can be useful in countries like the United States where in theory the democratic principles TRCs depend upon are already in place. Democracies, they argue, operate according to the rule of law that provides redress in the judicial system for those who have been hurt.

Critical legal scholars, however, have long countered that rule of law does not provide a guarantee of justice. Instead, all too often, the hierarchical social structures in democracies protect the status quo and are reproduced in and through cultural conditioning including the prevailing legal doctrines. The result, say critical scholars, is that many people are in fact alienated from their democracies, and legal maneuverings operate to persuade citizens to consent to seemingly inevitable, inhumane, and unjust social orders (Gabel and Harris, 1983). In this way, the legal systems can fail citizens. The courts, for instance, could not assuage the depth and extent of slavery. Progressive legislation introduced through the years helped the situation, but the lingering impact of slavery on the African American population remains palpable in the United States with the disparity of health care, wages, housing, education, and virtually every other quality-of-life marker. Likewise, women, immigrants, Native Americans, and people with disabilities to name only a few of the minority groups in this country who have experienced persistent bigotry and inequities reinforced in systemic practices have struggled long and hard to gain modest advances in their rightful access to the most basic human rights.

TRCs then can illuminate the shortcomings surrounding the sanctity of legal action. Like democracy itself, rule of law is a great ideal sometimes left unrealized, as was the case in Greensboro. TRCs offer a different, even corrective approach to discipline-based justice that invites the entire community into the proceedings.

TRCs should not be considered a panacea for injustice, yet their structure and processes offer a measure of hope. And hope, says Benjamin Barber, is what sustains a democracy. He comments that the American Dream of equality for all remains a story both untrue and also capable of propelling the nation toward more just practices. "To be an American is not to have secured equality and justice, but only— with the help of a story of unprecedented aspiration—still to hope and to struggle for them" (Barber, 1994, 77).

Truth telling surrounding racial incidents is a tangible step in the direction Barber suggests; it can provide relief, such as in the case of the lynching of four young African Americans in Moore's Ford, Georgia, in 1946.[2] Cities throughout the United States—Detroit, Boston, Minneapolis, and Portland, Maine, to name a few[3]—see that truth and reconciliation commissions that scour the past with an eye for truth rather than cover-up can restore hope where racial inequities have persisted. In the South alone, more than a dozen programs for truth and reconciliation have been identified by University of Maryland law students[4] (Ricks et al., 2007).

Still, employing restorative justice practices requires a collective orientation largely absent in traditional Western thinking. George Lakoff, a cognitive linguist, concludes that much of our political discourse and subsequent decision making derive from moral systems that we develop during childhood, not from reasoned discourse with others in our community (2002). A conservative worldview, for instance, emerges for individuals who complied with their fathers' authority and his insistence on self-reliance as the foundation for good moral development. In this "strict father model," competition, discipline, hierarchy, rules, and adherence to the chain of command are esteemed (2002). In contrast, people raised by what Lakoff calls a "nurturant parent model" will be more likely to adopt an Ubuntu approach since the development of moral character came from an appreciation for equity, empathy, fairness, collaboration, social responsibility, and open-mindedness.

The competing values and metaphors—pull yourself up by your bootstraps versus how can you consider an alternative path—means our society has "no universally shared sense of foundational truth" (Pearce and Littlejohn, 1997, 26). However, it is this feature of public life—talking through seemingly intractable differences—that truth commissions address in the hopes of promoting peace among disparate groups, rather than settling for polarized views and violence.

In the democratic tradition advanced by Richard Rorty and Benjamin Barber following John Dewey, communication is regarded as the primary social process by which the political decisions are made that determine how we are to live together (Pearce and Littlejohn, 1997). Engaging in public discourse thus is crucial in order to listen and consider other views and deliberate among competing claims to choose the path forward. Yet, many constraints endemic in modern society challenge our ability to interact with others respectfully.

First, public discourse has suffered from disinterest in reconsidering the past. People in contemporary society prefer instead to embrace the narrative of "progress" and the immediate rewards it presents. If time is money, as the twenty-first-century zeitgeist implies, then the past is best disposed of quickly, so that the newest and the latest life offering in a "liquid modern society" can take center stage in a perpetual succession of new beginnings (Bauman, 2005, 3).

Second, mass media, as it has evolved into corporate-owned structures pushed to pursue profits more than to uphold its civic duty, has shirked its responsibility to foster meaningful public discourse according to its critics. News stories, limited in space or time, routinely fail to present sufficient context and details surrounding complex matters. News organizations then hide behind a code of objectivity that assumes facts are literal and nonpartisan, rather than understanding that news emanates from the political grounding in which the facts are embedded (Lakoff, 2002). Self-proclaimed experts, pundits, and news personalities who host call-in talk radio shows and television "news" segments stream inflammatory opinions, oftentimes absent salient facts and a critical historical perspective, yet too often are accepted as reasoned discourse.

Third, the hegemony of experts has hijacked public discourse with its presumption to know what is best for the citizenry. The abuse of power by politicians and even special interest groups trumps the polyphony of public voices (Pearce and Littlejohn, 1997).

Fourth and finally, corporations whose money buys votes, influence, and policy threaten our democratic ideals. Asserting First Amendment rights, corporate "persons" have the upper hand to ensure their candidates are voted into office, to pass laws and establish policy that benefits the corporate donor keeping the candidate in public office.

Thus modern society presents TRCs with two dilemmas. First, can a TRC rally sufficient public support to launch a long-term process that requires thoughtful deliberations and dialogue? Second, will government institutions and mass media provide the necessary information and guidance that can reveal submerged truths so that people can learn, understand, and carve a new restorative path for its community?

In what Martha Minow (1998) calls "overlapping aspirations," truth commissions use acknowledgment and public rituals to prompt community and institutional changes such as sweeping away communal and official denial of past wrongs with public admissions; uncovering facts that help meet the victims' right to know as well as build a more accurate historical record; transform violence and aggression into institutional practices of respect and dignity; establish democratic practices that respect human rights; promote reconciliation across social divisions; restore dignity to survivors; and, express and act on the aspiration of "never again" will such a tragedy occur (88).

When adequate efforts are then devoted to including as many people as possible to work for justice, democracy is enacted as the bedrock of truth and reconciliation commission activity (Gutmann and

Thompson, 2000). The goal, however, is not consensus. As long as there remains a focus and concern for the community well-being, such as addressing the injustice of apartheid in South Africa or the requirement of police protection for protestors in Greensboro, there may very well be disagreement and continuing dialogue over what the facts suggest, the best routes to achieve desired changes, and the scope of change needed to satisfy the public. That is, TRCs offer people a full range of testimonies, investigation efforts, and analysis of that history. In doing so, their deliberative processes target three conditions of life that advance democracy: discovery of the truth, forgiveness, and reconciliation.

TRCs ponder the fate of the human condition just as philosophers have long done, particularly in light of our capacity for harm, torture, greed, and oppression.[5] Though these philosophical writings have focused on the conditions that influence one individual to restore a relationship with another,[6] more recently the rise of TRCs has prompted a consideration of how cities, groups, and countries can enact a future absent the past violence and infused with a just government or set of practices (Minow, 1998).

Because reconciliation cannot be guaranteed or enforced, TRC observers the world over question if the emotionally wrenching testimonies bring about the desired healing or do those acts of reliving abuses reinjure the survivors all over again? A series of other questions follows. Do the TRC findings and final report offer sufficient justice for a community if the perpetrators are not punished for their criminal charges? Do testimonies, free from biting cross-examination, offer ample evidence of the truth? Is acknowledgment of past abuses an adequate standard by which reconciliation can be forged? Indeed, "none of them [TRCs] have delivered instant gratifying results, nor have they brought about 'closure,' the word so often seen in relationship to them" (Phelps, 2004, 119).

Indeed, TRCs operate at their best when they open doors to the past, rather than close them. To do that, African scholar Timothy Murithi says attitudes and behaviors of cooperation and collaboration —Ubuntu principles—need to be practiced to address lingering pain from past abuses:

> This notion of Ubuntu sheds light on the importance of peace-making through the principles of reciprocity, inclusivity and a

sense of shared destiny between people . . . It provides an inspiration and suggests guidelines for societies and their government, on how to legislate and establish laws which will promote reconciliation. In short, it can culturally re-inform our practical efforts to build peace and heal our traumatized communities. (Murithi, 2006, 29)

Thus, sustaining positive relationships in the community is a collective task in which all have a stake and a responsibility for the outcome.

It follows that for Western cultures, Ubuntu affords a fresh perspective on ways to overcome hostilities between races, to encourage more collective engagement by its citizenries, and to promote sustainable futures in recognition of our individual dependence upon the well-being of all. More specifically, Murithi (2006) points out four lessons Ubuntu offers to cultures and communities worldwide. First, public participation is critical for lasting peace. Second, victims need to be supported as perpetrators are encouraged to speak throughout the admittedly difficult process of truth telling and fact finding. Third, there is value in acknowledging wrongdoing and expressing remorse, as well as granting forgiveness to achieve peace. Fourth, for reconciliation to occur there must be an overriding and constant expression of the essential interdependence of humans as communicated in empathy for others, sharing of common resources, and invoking a spirit of cooperation to resolve common problems. These lessons are ones that can resolve conflict, shape public policy, establish new, more democratic forms of governance, institute structures for racial equality, and establish economic parity among all people (Murithi, 2006).

Critics of Ubuntu, John Hatch points out (2008), note that its rhetorical force arises from community, and thus could forsake the possibility of individual liberation necessary for a pluralistic society. Indeed, while the caution is worthy of our attention, the pendulum would have to swing mighty far in a direction to which we have rarely even taken small steps. Still, if difference is to be upheld as a marker of our culture's strength, we would be well advised to consider how distinctions are preserved and nurtured within the context of communal well-being. That is, we must accept our inevitable interconnectedness as a natural expression of our individuality that benefits us all (Krog, 2008).

In sum, applying the principles of Ubuntu, dialogic ethics, or an ethics of care to contemporary Western matters is possible, but admittedly difficult. Like restorative justice, the African moral philosophy of Ubuntu has promise and challenges for acceptance in the United States. South Africa's TRC lifted the idea of Ubuntu to new heights as a redemptive force in promoting if not achieving the restoration of peace in that country. Greensboro's TRC hoped that it too could find a way to initiate and complete a process intended to reclaim history, encourage understanding, and instigate social change.

Making the Case for a TRC in Greensboro

Why a TRC for Greensboro and why then, people asked? Supporters and commissioners defended the need for a TRC for multiple reasons.

Most significantly, race remained a central issue and concern in Greensboro. Though people interacted with different races every day, the subject of race and the evidence of racial disparities were hidden from public discussion. In college classrooms, students found few courses that openly discussed the subtle forms of discrimination affecting interpersonal relationships and systemic practices. It was no wonder then that in a survey of six hundred library users, 90 percent indicated they wanted to talk about a current social issue in their book reading programs, but that they did not want to discuss race.[7]

In addition, the people in Greensboro believed the time was right for a truth and reconciliation commission because the city was waning economically. Gone were the textile mills and company villages that once provided homes and jobs to thousands of blue-collar workers. The final chapter in the story of the textile mills was written in 2010 when Greensboro's Guilford Performance Textiles (formerly Guilford Mills) announced its closure along with the layoff of all remaining 150 workers. The company, established in 1946 with two knitting machines and six employees, grew to become a Fortune 500 company by 1988 with $539 million in sales. In the late 1990s, more than 700 employees worked at the plant before layoffs began in 2000 in response to poor profits, the move of operations to Mexico, and the phasing out of the apparel-fabric business (Patterson, 2010).

Gone as well were many of the farmers and craftsmen who once harvested tobacco and made furniture. And gone with them was the way of life that kept families and commerce closely connected.

Gone are the separate (and unequal) entrances to theaters, golf clubs, neighborhoods, and schools. And gone are many of the southern ways that kept whites exclusively in the seats of power.

Greensboro's demographics rapidly changed, though its overall annual growth in population remained fairly static (a mere 1.1 percent growth since 2005). Like the rest of the United States of America, the rise in the minority population translated into cultural changes that were both positive and negative. In Greensboro, new ethnic restaurants and small businesses opened. At the same time, there was a surge in school suspension and incarceration rates for minorities.

In 1960, Greensboro was a primarily white town, with only 25 percent identifying as African American or black. By 2006 the demographic portrait was more complex with Greensboro home to 55 percent whites, 37 percent blacks, 4 percent Hispanic, 3 percent Asian, and 1 percent Native American or "some other race" (American Community Survey, 2006). By 2010, there were more changes and for the first time, Greensboro's minorities were more numerous than white residents, 51.6 percent and 48.4 percent, respectively (U.S. Census, 2010).

From 1994 to 2009, the immigrant population in Greensboro grew by nearly 400 percent, the largest percentage coming from Latin American countries (Debbage et al., 2008). The largest migration was of Mexican nationalists who moved to Greensboro to fill jobs at poultry processing plants, the remaining agricultural jobs, and construction and service work.

As Greensboro moved from its roots as a major textile mill city to one more recently welcoming entrepreneurs and large corporations focused on computer imaging, transportation, and medical technology, some of its citizens were left behind. Without the requisite skills or education to move into the new sectors of employment, the median household income failed to keep pace with both the national average and the surrounding region. The official unemployment rate in 2006 was 6.6 percent with the impact felt most acutely by the 9.8 percent of the blacks who were without jobs as compared to the 4 percent of whites (American Community Survey, 2006). In January 2011 in the country's worst economic recession since the Great Depression, Greensboro's unemployment rate grew to 10.9 percent,[8] putting the city near the bottom of every labor force chart highlighting just how bad the economic downturn had become.

The poverty rate in Greensboro was and remains disturbing to a great many people as well. At 17.5 percent in 2010, it surpassed the national average of 15.3 percent, which ranked Greensboro as one of ten metropolitan areas with the highest poverty rates in the nation.[9] Women and children in this bleak situation were deeply impacted. "In Greensboro, women heading households with children under the age of 18 have an astonishing poverty rate of 46.9%" (Greensboro State of Human Relations Study, 2008). In 2010, Greensboro and Guilford County in which it sits had the nation's fourth-highest rise in poverty and the South's second-highest rise in unemployment (www.partners endinghomelessness.org). That same year, there were 1,064 homeless people on any given night according to the point in time study conducted by Partners Helping Homelessness (Fernandez, 2010). Of those homeless, the vast majority identified themselves as African American, reminding us that race and class are uncomfortable partners. Regrettably, the homeless represented one of the faster-growing populations of the city.

Educator and Greensboro TRC commissioner Muktha Jost along with activist Ed Whitfield and Mark Jost (2005) suggest that "sometimes the rules are fair but the game isn't" to make the point that the legacy of discrimination continues in the present day despite important advances. They use the game of Monopoly as a teaching moment for future teachers of America. The prospective teachers are divided into groups with the first group moving game pieces around the board and acquiring property, before the other groups are allowed to join in the action. Soon thereafter, someone generally cries "foul play" noting that those who started later are at a distinct disadvantage, at the mercy of those holding property. The point of the simulation, the educators explain, is to demonstrate that blacks in America too have been struggling to catch up, with little assistance or even understanding from their white brethren regarding the enormous odds stacked against them to keep pace in a game that was never fair to start.

Dr. Lawrence Morse, retired economics professor from North

Carolina A & T State University, saw the potential in Greensboro to assert a new paradigm in race and labor relations by using the TRC proceedings to demonstrate the benefit of vigorous, truthful relationships he believed would be attractive to businesses. The sitting mayor at the time, Keith Holliday, did not agree. Holliday feared the story of Greensboro's history would lead companies in California and elsewhere to label the city "red neck" (personal communication, May 8, 2003).

The time was right for a truth and reconciliation commission in Greensboro as well in light of the USA PATRIOT Act[10] that was limiting civil and human rights. Many TRC supporters generally regarded it as a knee-jerk reaction to the bombing of the World Trade Center in 2001. They noted civil liberties were being systematically compromised by secret searches of homes and businesses, unfettered government access to tax and medical records, indefinite detentions of immigrants, and unrestrained domestic and foreign intelligence. The trajectory was for a more regressive government, not a democratically inspired one, Greensboro's citizens proclaimed. Former mayor Carolyn Allen would later comment that this shift at the national level had a distinct impact on local politics, fueling the rise of reactionary politicians.

There was a strong moral argument for a TRC as well. Many people—blacks and whites—held firmly that justice had been denied in Greensboro so many years earlier. For Dr. Morse the TRC process was long overdue:

> The project should have been done 10 years ago. It is clear that we need to go back to it [November 3]. The folks in the city don't know what happened. Most people back then read the newspaper and watched the networks, which objectified the protestors as communists and claimed it was a shoot-out as opposed to an assault. (personal communication, May 5, 2003)

Greensboro sought to elevate grassroots organizing to a new level, funded by community members and national and international foundations that recognized the importance of self-governing enterprises in local communities.

At the same time, a national movement was afoot to reinvigorate high school and college youth civic participation. To counter the trend of declining involvement in politics and civic activity, colleges and universities were using service-learning courses to pair students with community partners to address local concerns. The AmeriCorps/ VISTA program grew as a federally funded pathway for youth employment and public service. Other efforts, including the American Association of State College and Universities' Democracy Project, Learn and Serve America, Constitution Day, USA Freedom Corps, and the President's Council on Service and Civic Participation all supported the effort to integrate young people into community initiatives.

Greensboro touts seven colleges and universities as the foundation of a growing creative class and economy for its roughly 250,000 residents (Florida, 2002). The institutions of higher education—the University of North Carolina, Greensboro; North Carolina State A & T University, Bennett College, Guilford College, Greensboro College, Elon University School of Law, and Guilford Technical Community College—are, as well, among the largest employers in the city along with health-care services, transportation and warehousing operations, and computer industries.[11]

Advocates for the TRC in Greensboro noted that the time was right for the process because the people involved with November 3 were still alive and active in a range of political issues. History could come alive in the concrete details and stories that had not been previously revealed in the same way.

Greensboro's TRC, then, would follow the path charted by South Africa and other nations to seek redress for past human rights violations. At the same time, Greensboro's process was unique in not having government support as did all the other TRCs. Instead, Greensboro had only its residents to organize a commission and its duties, raise funds, and promote the findings of the process to affect change in the community. Everyone wondered if it could be done. Would it be successful? What would a truth and reconciliation commission for Greensboro mean in the long run?

CHAPTER 5

Greensboro's Truth and Reconciliation Commission: Principles and Processes

Now they would be able to tell their stories, they would remember, and in remembering would be acknowledged to be persons with an inalienable personhood.

—DESMOND TUTU

WHAT FOLLOWS IS an overview of how an alliance of blacks and whites mobilized to form the Greensboro Truth and Community Reconciliation Project, a grassroots organization that would eventually lay the foundation for the United States' first Truth and Reconciliation Commission. Without government support, people organized themselves to accomplish what until that time had never been done in the world. This chapter discusses how ordinary people worked together, over a period of more than five years, to accomplish their goals. They selected truth commissioners who in turn relied on a small, dedicated staff and a bevy of volunteers to complete the necessary investigative and public work. In total, it was the concerted effort of more than one thousand people who brought to fruition the first TRC in the United States, in Greensboro, North Carolina.

Throughout, those who supported the truth and reconciliation effort were guided by the central question, what are the possibilities for participatory democracy in Greensboro that arise from this process? They recognized that the truth and reconciliation process was not simply to bring resolution to what happened on November 3, 1979, though that was indeed an important goal. Emphatically, the citizens in the community supportive of truth and reconciliation were the

same ones working on a host of other community initiatives—
neighborhood preservation, safe and affordable housing, homeless
services, education reform, intercultural understanding, intergenerational communication, sustainability, and more. To them, what was
distinctive about the truth and reconciliation process was its *process*
that promised to highlight and nurture deeply democratic possibilities.
Social trust, a bedrock principle for democratic action, required that
Greensboro citizens look honestly at the past, engaging all stakeholders
in important conversation, using dialogue to unearth hopes and fears,
and collectively asserting a vision for the future.

To transform what had been the long-standing traditions in
Greensboro to allow government officials to operate at their own pace
and in their own ways, the TRC stood out as a dignified democratic
process that enabled people to "become fully free to claim their moral
and political agency" (Moyers, 2008, 92). Through an extended process
of communication, the grassroots organizers and their supporters
moved the community toward practices of collective action, relying
on a sensibility for peace and justice, not confrontation and fear.

Greensboro's TRC reinvigorated the deliberative processes in the
community that had been all but forsaken. The goal was not to cast the
finger of blame on any one person. The Greensboro TRC, affirming the
humanity of all people, sought to acknowledge mistakes and misdeeds
in the hopes of changing future patterns of interaction among social
classes and races, and between institutions and the people.

Prior to the launch of the TRC, mistrust in the community was
rampant. Thus, a cloud of suspicion, from the beginning, surrounded
the grassroots organizers. Ulterior motives, critics argued, were surely
at the heart of the undertaking. Slowly though, many of those suspicions fell away as time after time, the TRC process dedicated itself to
inclusive practices and full transparency in its operations.[1] Theirs was
a program of hope in a city where hope had been chipped away by the
forces of globalization and the rancor of unresolved conflict.

At the beginning of the twenty-first century some of Greensboro's
citizens were feeling the squeeze of the economic recession and many
more were troubled by a seemingly unresponsive local government.
Racial strife and labor unrest were back in the headlines as the city
groped to find its identity amid a declining textile industry base. To

the least prosperous citizens and their allies, there appeared to be a lack of diligent concern on the part of city leaders for basic human rights. Black city councilwoman Claudette Burroughs-White, representing some of the community members who lived near or in the part of town where the tragedy occurred, explained:

> I've heard from people in the neighborhood who say they still don't know what happened or who the people were who were involved. I don't want to get into blaming or looking into reopening the court situation, but I do want people to have an open dialogue. (Steadman, 2003, A-1)

By 2001, the Beloved Community Center under the guidance of Nelson Johnson and the Greensboro Justice Fund directed by survivor Marty Nathan had established sufficient community interest for a truth and reconciliation process. The grassroots organizing committee, the Greensboro Truth and Community Reconciliation Task Force, as well as a National Advisory Board were established and operating with funding provided by the Andrus Family Fund, a grantor focused on community reconciliation programs. Part of the grant included a contract with the International Center for Transitional Justice (ICTJ) to provide ongoing consulting services to Greensboro's project.

The National Advisory Board held its first meeting on March 16, 2002. Three high-profile co-chairs were selected to lend their wisdom and experience to the effort (Magarrell and Wesley, 2008): Dr. Vincent Harding, the first director of the Martin Luther King, Jr. Center for Nonviolent Social Change; Dr. Peter Storey, a member of the selection committee for the South African Truth and Reconciliation Commission and before that a prison chaplain to Nelson Mandela; and Cynthia Nance, professor of law at the University of Arkansas specializing in employment and poverty law.

Not long after, the Local Task Force convened, co-chaired by former Greensboro mayor Carolyn Allen and retired Presbyterian minister Z Holler, who in 1979 persuaded a funeral home to make arrangements for those who died on November 3. Later, Baptist minister Reverend Gregory Headen was appointed the third co-chair.

For the next year, the two groups met to draft three guiding documents. The Declaration of Intent was completed first, and signed by thirty-two Greensboro leaders. That document was a public manifesto published in the local newspapers on January 11, 2003, that laid out the reason and purpose of the group's action with the expressly stated intent of involving "all sectors of Greensboro and with a cross section of national and international leaders to forge a broad and effective Greensboro Truth and Community Reconciliation Project" (Final Report, 2006, 454). The Mandate for the Greensboro Truth and Reconciliation Commission was next written to provide a framework and focus for the TRC's work. Finally, the Nomination and Selection Processes for the TRC were developed "to make the selection of the Commissioners the most democratic process and community-wide initiative possible" (Final Report, 2006, 455–456). Representatives from fourteen groups of wide political, racial, and economic persuasions composed the Selection Committee, which chose its own chairperson, Judge Lawrence McSwain, an appointee of then mayor of Greensboro, Keith Holliday. The Selection Committee met in private, and without oversight from the grassroots Local Task Force, to cull through sixty-seven community nominations before selecting seven individuals to serve as truth commissioners.

On June 12, 2004, more than five hundred people assembled on the occasion of the swearing in of the commissioners for the United States' first Truth and Reconciliation Commission. Held at Greensboro's newly renovated train depot where historic signs remained to show where segregation once dictated "colored" entrances and seating areas, the ceremony boasted rows of seats occupied by people of all different colors, ages, and races, intermingled, not separated in any way. Formal proceedings and speeches were followed by a colorful display of multicultural costumes, songs, music, art, and performances to bring a celebratory tone to the event where attendees signed their names and offered best wishes on five-foot tall, oversized canvases, marking the momentous start of the Greensboro Truth and Reconciliation Commission.

As the TRC's work commenced and staff was hired, auxiliary events were planned to keep the public informed and involved. In November 2004, more than one thousand people celebrated the twenty-fifth anniversary of November 3 at a series of events under the banner, "Transforming Tragedy into Triumph," which included a march, workshops, spiritual services, and presentations.

In February 2005, the first community dialogue entitled, "What is Truth? What is Reconciliation?" was organized by faculty and students at the University of North Carolina at Greensboro and held at the city's downtown library. That event introduced the truth commissioners to the wider community.[2] In March, the Local Task Force presented a petition containing more than five thousand signatures to the Greensboro City Council requesting that it endorse the work of the TRC, which was summarily rejected. In April, an afternoon "Faith, Prayer and Reconciliation Service" was held with guest speaker Dr. Peter Storey and comments from Mayor Keith Holliday. In June, socials at a local coffeehouse began and an Interfaith Spiritual Reflection Community Service was hosted. Then, in July, a cable television show, "TRC Talk," began airing and the first public hearing was held. For the remainder of that year, two additional public hearings were hosted, a benefit concert was organized, university faculty from half a dozen schools met to discuss "Teaching through the TRC," and Archbishop Desmond Tutu met with TRC commissioners. That fall, a daylong community reflection on all three public hearings was held to solicit citizen recommendations for community reconciliation.

The TRC delivered its final report to the community on May 25, 2006, at a ceremony attended by more than four hundred people at Bennett College. According to Commissioner Mark Sills, the day was symbolic not only in celebrating the completion of the work by the country's first Truth and Reconciliation Commission, but also by virtue of who was at the ceremony, including city council members, police officials, Klansmen, media, supporters, and curious others. He said:

> And when you think about it being on a small campus, a black college campus on the east end of town, to have the kind of folks that were there—yeah. I thought it symbolized in many ways the success of what we had accomplished, that that diverse a group would come together to receive our report. (Magarrell and Wesley, 2008, 33)

Individuals from various faith-based, nonprofit, civic and community groups met as well for many more months, committing themselves to discussing the report in preparation for the next phase of the TRC process, which commenced in December 2006 with a year-long community dialogue series.

Greensboro's TRC revealed the character of this community, with all its promise, challenges, hopes, and flaws. In a community consumed by a history of Jim Crow racism and of the subsequent economic inequalities that emerged anew in the twenty-first century as Greensboro continued to struggle from significant manufacturing job losses (Debbage, 2008), the time was right, many reasoned, to at last address the legacy of race and class policies that all but ensured winners and losers in this societal structure. To do so, the community had to acknowledge the anger and pain felt by those situated at the bottom of the social class structure. At the same time, the community had to wrest power away from the political elites in order to assert more progressive ideals. From the TRC process emerged a portrait of hope for a community-directed and sustained democracy. Ascertaining the truth of the past was central to that hope.

Doxtader (2003) claims the process of truth and reconciliation is directed at re-constituting community, an act that is inherently rhetorical and based in the acts of speech. When communities experience harmful opposition, combatants seek a space of recognition, where at least the beginning of resolution may emerge. Truth and reconciliation projects are valued because of their ability to encourage people to speak to each other, instead of continuing with aggression and hostility (Doxtader, 2001). In Greensboro, the truth commissioners shouldered the lion's share of the responsibility to get people to speak.

Seven Commissioners Convene for Two Years

The seven truth commissioners included five women—three African American, one naturalized U.S. citizen from India, one white retiree—and two white males. Five of the commissioners resided in or very near Greensboro, one made her home an hour away in Durham, North Carolina, and one resided in the state of New York. These demographic features of gender, race, and geography were important determinants to the fourteen Selection Committee members who wanted to honor the diversity of the city and ensure that both people of Greensboro and also outside of it could deliberate together. Supporters assumed the truth commissioners' differing cultural and political perspectives would be negotiated to reach agreement surrounding the tasks before them.

The Greensboro Truth and Reconciliation Commission members, as distinct as they were, remained collectively dedicated to the project throughout its duration. They entered into their responsibilities without the benefit of knowing how deep their commitment would be tested, but every single one stayed the course of the process. None would relinquish his or her responsibility to serve. None was paid for time and service. Each had known from the start that the work would be difficult; still, all conceded that the time and emotional energy required to accomplish their work far exceeded what they had originally considered. Their words and actions reflect what Emmanuel Levinas describes as the impossibility of releasing oneself from the ethical obligation of responsibility:

> the impossibility of canceling responsibility for the other, impossibility more impossible than jumping out of one's skin, the imprescriptible duty surpassing the *forces of being*. A duty that did not ask for consent, that came into me traumatically, from beneath all rememberable present, anarchically, without beginning. That came without being offered as a choice ... (Levinas, 2006, 7)

As Levinas describes, the truth commissioners found they could not abdicate their responsibilities—they recognized the significance of their work and their accountability to a community that had entrusted them with such an important task.

Commissioner Pat Clark of Nyack, New York, said that as the only commissioner not from North Carolina, she experienced unique benefits and challenges. As a Greensboro TRC commissioner, Clark recognized that she alone had the luxury (as she called it) of not needing to address the barrage of comments and questions on the importance and impact of the process that came from the media, friends, and workplace associates. At the same time, she noted this was also a limitation in that Clark did not have the opportunity for the spontaneous conversations in the community that illuminated the deep challenges people raised with other commissioners. Clark's career included being the executive director of the U.S.-based Fellowship of Reconciliation, and on staff with the American Friends Service Committee and the Southern Poverty Law

Center before that. From those experiences, she had seen many transformative examples of truth-telling processes. Thus, for Clark among the most promising results of the TRC in Greensboro was having people speak of their experiences *as* the first step toward reconciliation: "I experienced this with people who were afraid to talk, didn't want to dredge up the past but given the opportunity surprised themselves with how much they had to say and how much confusion and fear remains for them today" (Final Report, 2006, 400).

For two years, the commissioners planned regular multiday meetings to pore over transcripts, watch videos, hear testimonies, meet with national and international experts in restorative justice, and grapple together to reach agreement about what would be included in the Final Report. In the end, they addressed all five principal areas that Hayner (2001) argues are the purview of truth commissions: clarifying and acknowledging the truth; responding to the needs and interests of victims; contributing to justice and accountability; outlining institutional responsibility and recommending reforms; and promoting reconciliation to reduce tensions arising from past violence.

Greensboro's truth commissioners returned often to the words of their official mandate for guidance and focus in fulfilling their responsibilities to the community. Conclusions needed to be supported by "adequate documentation," for instance, which meant that despite common-sense or intuitive appeal, some facts and interpretations were not included in the report if there were insufficient records, stories, or other corroborating evidence (Magarrell and Wesley, 2008). Bringing facts to light that had been buried or disregarded from the community's collective memory was one of the TRC's most important accomplishments to disavow lies and distortions from the public discourse (Amstutz, 2005).

Despite clear guidelines, the commissioners still faced disagreements and tensions surrounding varied interpretations of the foundational documents. According to Commissioner Dr. Muktha Jost, a native of India and Greensboro resident employed as an assistant professor in the School of Education at North Carolina A & T State University, the mode by which the research process would unfold was contested. To her, the research process needed to account for facts, but also had to address the emotions and feelings circulating in the community. She asked how the commissioners could best examine and describe the "cultural memory, hurt in our bones. How do we capture that in our research?" (Magarrell and Wesley, 2008, 89).

The commissioners' differing worldviews provided rich opportunity to consider the mounds of material from many vantage points. However, as the commissioners would find, reconciling those views was time consuming, and at times extremely difficult. Commissioner co-chair Cynthia Brown recounted:

> If you can imagine, in 47 years I have never been in a physical fight. I have often thought of myself as a nonviolent peace-lover. While I never used the word pacifist to describe myself, that would probably have been an appropriate term until I found my personal inclination in stark contrast to the historic and current realities facing many people living in poor, oppressed communities. This contradiction became more pointed as I vigorously debated my sister Commissioner, a self-described pacifist, about my emerging belief in the *necessity* of armed self-defense. (Final Report, 2006, 396)

Brown, who since 1982 has assisted grassroots organizations in asserting their collective community power, used her opportunity as a commissioner to closely examine the events of November 3 that in 1979 she neglected to do. Then, she was a college senior at Bennett College, and though she remembered the shootings, Brown says she did not participate in any post-November 3 discussions, perhaps due to "youthful ignorance and indifference" or maybe due to the "fear and silence about issues related to the tragedy" that were simply not discussed (Final Report, 2006, 394). Brown was not alone in having to assert her views in ways that would influence the findings and recommendations of the entire Truth Commission.

Commissioner Angela Lawrence, born and raised in Greensboro, and a witness to the November 3 shootings as a girl, at times felt like she alone had to advance a point that none of the others could see, due in part to her lower social-class status:

> My commitment to this process was informed by truth, life and survival not by degrees, paychecks or common organizational structure. There were many times when I felt like I stood alone

and advocated for a different perspective that was not the status quo. (Final Report, 2006, 406)

Lawrence was a former residents' council vice president of Ray Warren Homes' public housing community that like Morningside Homes in 1979 was operated by the Greensboro Housing Authority. She viewed November 3 as "just one of millions of acts of violence perpetuated by racism, hatred and greed" (Final Report, 2006, 407).

Commissioner Mark Sills summed up the varied and diverse backgrounds of the commissioners in this way—it was a group that had its challenges, but it was ultimately that diversity that made possible the requisite sensitivity, technical knowledge, and skills to overcome the hurdles on the path to accomplishing their task. He said the commissioners pursued the work "with mutual respect and a vibrant willingness to share responsibilities according to each of our unique abilities and skills" (Final Report, 2006, 419).

Thus, the task before the truth commissioners was to construct a history that could connect the accumulated narratives and facts. Doing so in a way that addressed and transcended the interpretations of individual truth commissioners was the challenge.

Near the beginning of their tenure, the truth commissioners drafted "Guiding Principles of the Greensboro Truth and Reconciliation Commission."[3] There, the commissioners collectively asserted their beliefs that truth was multilayered; creative outlets were needed for community members to share their stories and feelings; fairness and impartiality were ideals to uphold; no testimony should be rejected and all should be respected; and that community trust could be restored and hope rekindled in Greensboro.

Reverend Dr. Mark Sills was the former head of the city's largest homeless shelter, Greensboro Urban Ministry, and later executive director of Faith Action, an interfaith center fostering community across cultures. He explained that what was needed in the truth and reconciliation process was a "comprehensive truth shared by enough people" that could in turn lead to the desired reconciliation (personal communication, February 24, 2005). The commissioners had to do this work knowing that some useful information would be simply unavailable. For instance, the police were uncooperative in 1979 in providing documents, as they were again during the TRC process. The upshot was that the truth commissioners would need to fill in the gaps where they could, a process not uncommon to the work of all Truth Commissions. As Martha Minow concludes from her extensive work examining the possibilities and limitations of these bodies:

> Truth commissions undertake to write the history of what happened as a central task . . . Yet, just as no historical account can fully grasp the entire truth of events, a commission report will be limited . . . The most distinctive element of a truth commission, in comparison with prosecution, is the focus on victims. (1998, 60)

Indeed, it was this focus on the victims—the survivors and the community—that was the guidepost for the work of the Greensboro TRC.

Commissioner Barbara Walker, a retired manager from Wrangler Corporation and community volunteer with the YWCA, League of Women Voters, Family and Children's Services, and the City of Greensboro's Commission on the Status of Women, was touched by the stories in her community that the TRC process revealed:

> Several spoke of their relief at finally being able to talk freely and safely about a scar on their souls. The fear they expressed is hard for me, a white woman living in my white privilege, to realize and understand. Their stories clutched my heart in a vise I think will never be released. (Final Report, 2006, 423)

The experience of being a truth commissioner brought up for Walker both negative feelings of depression and anxiety and also more positive ones she considered momentous, enriching, and rewarding.

Personal and professional tolls aside, the commissioners proclaimed the experience to be overwhelmingly positive for the community. Commissioner co-chair Robert Peters brought forward legal questions to the commission based on his more than forty years of work as a corporate attorney with AT & T before retiring, and wrote a "Concurring Opinion Summary" in the TRC Final Report. Two years after the release of the Final Report, he concluded that the city had made progress as exemplified by the African Americans occupying top leadership positions in the government, police, workplaces, and schools. He noted, however, in an October 25, 2009, e-mail to TRC supporters that achieving racial equality needed to remain a priority and focus of citizen action:

> Progress is still required in the areas of education (especially pointing out the dangers of racism, violent language and actions), economy, housing, justice, and fundamental fairness. If we are not structurally blinded by the past, but instead use lessons learned from it to move forward, we will make a better future for all.

The commissioners embodied the spirit of hope, even as they confronted the realities of despair.

Greensboro's truth commissioners were active in the community prior to their service, but not considered among the city's top leaders. This fact led to some initial criticism and concern that the truth and reconciliation process would not be taken seriously without prominent leaders at its helm. The supporters of the TRC process countered with the claim that the process was a citizen-initiative, not a leader-initiative. Their hopes were firmly pinned on the qualifications and dedication of the commissioners who were vetted by the Selection Committee. The commissioners as a group had some members who were outspoken while others were reserved. Some were involved in social justice and others were unaware, personally, of daily acts of discrimination. In other words, they were people just like the people of Greensboro.

TRUTH IS THE COMMISSION'S TASK

The commissioners fully recognized that "the truth" had been called into question ever since November 3 in 1979 and that through their analysis, a clearer view of what happened back then could be determined. They relied on archived documents, stories of those involved, and an examination of the context in which the events took place to find as Commissioner Mark Sills said, that they "*essentially* agree[d] on so much. Surely no one of us agrees with every word in our final report . . . Yet, there is sufficient agreement among us that all of us felt comfortable signing our name to this historic report" (Final Report, 2006, 420).

Knowing that more than one version of the "truth" would surface, the commission saw its work as harmonizing the stories where possible, verifying facts, removing false or misleading information, and constructing or reconstructing the details into what they believed would be a truth closer to the "whole truth" that was reflective of the veracity and clarity that comes from close examination of disparate pieces of knowledge. The telling and understanding of the truth they argued was a precondition for the possibility of reconciliation.

The commissioners' stance on truth was clear, but contested. Those who opposed the process questioned how this body could ascertain "the truth." The local newspaper editorial staff also questioned the value of a truth-seeking process when no new information was on the horizon. Even among the TRC supporters, there were differing views.

In an e-mail exchange in the fall of 2005, one active Local Task Force member expressed his concern that a focus on the truth was diverting more important conversations and action for reconciliation. He said,

> Even the wonderful folks . . . the survivors of November 3rd cannot yet accept the possibility for different "truths" . . . they are still looking for "The Truth." Human community interactions are not informed by rigid truths and hard science but are infinitely complex . . . How the CWP, the Greensboro Police, the media, the Klan, and different parts of the community all viewed November 3rd has much to do with the ideological framework with which each observed and interacted that day.

The writer asserted that "the" truth may not be achievable and that a better use of time and resources would be for the commission "to turn its direction and place emphasis on forgiveness . . . the goal of the process should be forgiveness and letting go the anger of November 3rd, 1979."

Responses were immediate and forceful by other supporters who saw the e-mail writer's remarks as troublesome, arrogant, and even heretic to the truth and reconciliation process itself. One volunteer worker said she was disappointed by what she viewed as a disingenuous engagement with the process. "It seems like you are trying to discredit the truth and reconciliation process. . . . you do an injustice to everyone . . . by not honestly engaging in the dialogue that is taking place." Lewis Pitts, the November 3 civil trial attorney and Greensboro resident was also disturbed by the comments. He said,

I value your commitment and know of your many years of active involvement in many causes. I appreciate all of that. . . . but I feel that your recent email and its distribution, as well as other similar ones from you, purport to claim a higher moral ground or authority than those of us who might see things differently . . . it feels like an attack on the commission and many who have struggled for its existence . . . The balance between truth and reconciliation is no doubt a difficult task . . . Saving souls is very important; creating a constitutional, participatory democracy with accountability for wrong-doing is a different endeavor. I think the latter endeavor is being approached by the Greensboro Truth and Reconciliation Commission with both the moral and civic dimensions it deserves.

Of note is that even as the community members squared off on what role truth should play in the truth and reconciliation process, they did so with respect for the maintenance of community, pointing out that "wonderful folks" were involved in the project, that they valued the commitments of one another, and that they wanted honesty and dialogue to guide the process. Interestingly, the exchange pointed out something even more important. While civility is crucial in community conversations to maintain relationships, the same civility can be used to conceal, disregard, gloss over, or too quickly dismiss truths such as in this case the police, government, and media complicity in crafting an understanding of a story that thrust blame on the victims of November 3. For Pitts, it was the fear of once again having civilities trump civil rights (Chafe, 1980) that led him to challenge the purported wisdom of encouraging reconciliation without a full accounting of the truth. More e-mails followed over a ten-day period, finally including the call for face-to-face conversation on the matter (though that did not ever transpire). Each communication attempted to honor the other person while holding onto a position believed important, similar to Martin Buber's call for all us to walk the "narrow ridge" in order to understand each other, while also honoring our values in what could be described as a dialogic encounter that allows for different views to emerge respectfully (Arnett, 1986).

The truth commissioners may or may not have read the e-mail exchange, but throughout the process they did not waver from their view that the truth was to be the basis for future, positive changes in the community. Commissioner Barbara Walker explained her views at a public meeting:

> The dictionary says truth is a fact. That's well and good for a dictionary. But there are many truths. Our job or my job as I see it is to listen to as many truths as there are out there, try to learn from those, and get as close as I can to *the* truth. If lots of people participate in the give and take of talk, then maybe reconciliation can happen. (personal communication, February 24, 2005)

Collectively, the commissioners saw truth as the starting point for community conversation: "We hope that our findings will foster meaningful community dialogue around issues relevant to these historical events and to the issues the community still is facing" (Final Report, 2006, 24).

The truth commissioners' processes and beliefs surrounding the necessity to reveal the truth would later be reflected in a document, "Toward an Inclusive Vision," drafted by the Local Task Force as a proposal for how citizens would carry out the recommendations of the Greensboro Truth and Reconciliation Commission. It said, in part:

> Many mistakenly think of the truth and reconciliation process as being mainly about the past; it is not, rather it is mainly about the future . . . With our past as an inspiring gift from which we all can learn, let us go forward together determined to carve out of the disasters and disappointments of yesterday a compelling vision of compassion, justice and hope for tomorrow. (Greensboro Truth and Community Reconciliation Project, 2007)

For the TRC commissioners, ascertaining the truth and documenting that in the Final Report was of foremost importance. For too long, they argued, an incomplete narrative of the history of November 3 circulated in Greensboro in ways that denied the relevance of police actions and the significance of social activists in sustaining a healthy democracy.

The TRC commissioners in Greensboro thus recognized their role to establish a new tradition of compassionate listening and reasoning in the struggle for justice as an alternative to the discourse of blame, contempt, and cynicism that marked much of the community's public discourse surrounding November 3, 1979, and other, more contemporary concerns (Magarrell and Wesley, 2008). To do this, the commissioners organized and hosted three public hearings, held on three different college campuses in the city.

THE PUBLIC HEARINGS ARE THE VOICE OF THE GREENSBORO TRC

On July 15, 2005, a line of people, numbering about forty, walked in silence for a mile from the Beloved Community Center, located just east of downtown Greensboro, North Carolina, to the site of the first public hearing of Greensboro's Truth and Reconciliation Commission. Many had waited over twenty-five years to break their silence, have their say, and hear the complete accounts of friends and adversaries.

In the auditorium of one of the area's high schools, the chairs began to fill with the widows and survivors and their friends who had stood by them, many since 1979. There were others present, too, people not in Greensboro in 1979, but who had learned about the events since that time. The Greensboro police, absent from public view on November 3, 1979, were on hand in full force at this public hearing and the other two that would follow during the next two months. In attendance were also Klansmen who had appeared previously in made-for-television documentaries that aired on the History Channel and A & E Network's City Confidential Series. They were there with fellow Klansmen flanked on both their sides. Students from the area colleges, including Steve Flynn, a doctoral student and adult activist protesting school testing policies that limited the creative potential of children, occupied some of the auditorium seats. There were a few public officials present, though not many. Lining the sides and stretched across the back of the auditorium was an abundance of video equipment, cameras, reporter notebooks, and media representatives. Scanning the room, you could see a handful of professors from the area's six colleges and universities. Greetings were exchanged among the many activists who were involved with peace and justice movements ranging from economic reform to antiwar vigils and affordable housing campaigns. There were a host of others there, too, who were as curious about how seven truth commissioners would sort through the inevitably conflicting accounts of November 3.

The truth commissioners' seats were up on the stage, to the audience viewing's left and situated behind long tables where water glasses and microphones were strategically placed. On the right side of the stage was a single long table with a few chairs for the people providing testimony or their accounts of November 3.

This first public hearing—spanning two full July days—was focused on "what led us to November 3rd?" The second public hearing, held one month later at North Carolina A & T University, was organized around the theme, "what happened that day, November 3rd?" and the third, final public hearing, held two months later in September 2005 at the University of North Carolina at Greensboro, featured answers to the question, "what were the consequences of November 3rd?" Among the most highly anticipated speakers were Klansmen Gorrell Pierce and Virgil Griffin.

Gorrell Pierce, a lifelong resident in rural Buies Creek, North Carolina, spoke of his humble roots to explain how he was attracted to the Klan as a young man. Pierce grew up on farmland, in an impoverished part of the state,[4] where his ancestors had lived since 1753. He told the truth commissioners that when he was growing up, people sat on their front porches, talking about the Civil War, Reconstruction, and relatives who had served in the Confederate army. When he graduated from high school, Pierce was interested in politics, but not the Republican Party. He read about the John Birch Society, which seemed more in tune with his conservative beliefs, anticommunist sentiment, and pro-American stance. He explained that life in Buies Creek was without much entertainment for a young man with his interests, "so it was kind of easy for me to wind up on the side of the Ku Klux Klan" (Pierce, 2005). He moved up the ranks quickly, according to his testimony, and became Grand Dragon or leader of his area's organization, the Federated Knights of the Ku Klux Klan. Pierce was forbidden to attend the November 3 march by his superior, but admitted he did go to pre-march planning meetings with the Klan and Nazis where he identified Bernard Butkovich as a federal agent. Looking back, he recounted the November 3 tragedy as one in which everyone was culpable:

> We could have had five dead Klansmen in place of five dead Communist Workers Party [members]. And the good part is that it wasn't five children or some woman washing her dishes and a stray bullet goes through the window. You know, everybody that

was out there was engaging in a riot, a ruckus. As my grand-mother said, when you run through the briars naked, boy, don't squall when you get scratched. I guess we were all asking for it.

Pierce confessed that being in the Klan was not something he was proud of anymore, but hoped his testimony could help explain why and how he got involved, and how he wanted to be remembered:

> When I leave from here, I hope this thing is over. I'm done with it; I'm satisfied to live my life . . . like I told Reverend Johnson, I'm done with it, and nice to see you and shake your hand. It ain't going to get no better until everybody else throws their sword down. (Pierce, 2005)

Like Gorrell Pierce, fellow Klansman Virgil Griffin was willing to speak to the truth commissioners. Unlike Pierce, Griffin remained active in the Klan, and thus his remarks jarred the audience with ideas and views many had thought no longer existed in America.

Griffin, Imperial Wizard of the Cleveland Knights Ku Klux Klan since 1985, was Grand Dragon of the organization in 1979 and in Greensboro with the Klan/Nazi caravan on November 3. He started his testimony with pointed criticism:

> Well first, I'd like to say I don't think this Commission's going to solve anything. I think it's a total waste of time . . . If you've got the interest[s] of Greensboro and the city and the citizens of Greensboro [in mind], I think you'd shut this thing down right now and tell the media to get out of here and never bring it up again. Now I'll answer any questions you've got. (Griffin, 2005)

To explain how he got involved and why he remains in the Klan, Griffin said:

> I joined the Klan back in the '60s when I was 18 years old. I joined it because I believed in what they stood up for: against Com-munism, drugs, integration. I don't believe in mixed marriages, I don't believe in integration. I don't believe in drugs, I don't believe in the Communist Party. And, another reason, the blacks has [sic] the NAACP speaking out for their rights, have Louis Farrakhan's organization speaking out for their rights, Jesse Jackson and the Rainbow Coalition, and Al Sharpton and others. The white people need someone to speak out for their civil rights.

For Griffin, the events of November 3 unfolded as they did because the communists provoked the Klan:

> The reason I came to Greensboro, [is because] they put the poster out, Death to the Klan, said we's hiding under rocks, we were scum. I'm not scum. I'm as good as any man walks on this earth. I'm as good as anybody . . . I'm not ashamed to say I'm Imperial Wizard of the Ku Klux Klan, and I'm not afraid of no man. And I don't hide. That's why I'm here today. If Paul Bermanzohn and Nelson Johnson hadn't put that poster up, it wouldn't have happened. And now they can sue me if they want to, they can stand in line. I don't care. I don't care if you want to sue me . . . So, they have the right to do it. That poster is the only reason I came to Greensboro, and it is clearly the Communist Party's fault that poster was put out. I don't put out a poster callin' [out] the Communists—I don't agree with 'em, I disagree with 'em, don't believe they have no right in this country period.

Griffin insisted that he would not have gone to Greensboro had he known violence would erupt. At the end of his testimony, he politely said of the experience, "it's been my pleasure."

During the TRC public hearings, a deep respect for the process was expressed repeatedly. Greensboro Massacre survivor Yonni Chapman summed up the feelings many in the audience could relate to:

> I am particularly glad that Gorrell Pierce and Virgil Griffin, both participants in the Klan-Nazi caravan that confronted demonstrators on November 3rd, have chosen to testify. Let me be clear. I have not forgotten nor forgiven these men for their part in the assassination of my friends and comrades. Nevertheless, the greater good demands that everyone have the chance to tell their stories. (Chapman, 2005)

This recognition that every party to a story has a unique perspective was given a preeminent position in the TRC hearings.

At the public hearings, fifty-four people in all provided public testimony. Another seventy-eight statement providers were listed in the Final Report along with mention of "many more" who requested their identities not be revealed (Final Report, 2006, 520).

At the second and third public hearings, the commissioners and audiences of 300–500 people listened attentively to more survivors, police officers, the judge in the first state trial, attorneys from all three trials, former residents of violence-torn Morningside Homes, children of WVO/CWP members, ministers, current city and county elected officials, professors, journalists, historians, faith leaders, and activists in labor and community organizing. The truth commissioners recognized that on the subject of November 3, there were many voices that needed to be heard.

ENGAGING THE COMMUNITY

The truth commissioners and their staff solicited input and involvement from a wide range of community members to prompt talk by individuals and among groups of people. Among the methods used to encourage community participation were educational events, mobilization of community residents to submit statements, offering of a supportive and nonthreatening environment for people to speak, welcoming all perspectives and stories, and encouraging public dialogue about the process. In addition, small and larger events—artistic performances, spiritual gatherings, lectures, and informal coffees—drew together people to discuss November 3, its impact, and the lingering effects of race, economics, political power, and culture on the current condition of the community. The varieties of discourse events were deliberately designed to encourage different modes of participation, celebration, and response. The truth commissioners acknowledged that if they had had more time and resources, they would have scheduled even more conversations with individuals and groups for it was by talking that trust about the TRC process was built in the community and a greater knowledge base was secured by the truth commissioners and their staff.

To tap into the youth population, alliances were forged with local colleges and universities to provide internships, classroom instruction, volunteer opportunities, and other experiences to young people. As it would turn out, a student majoring in communication studies at the University of North Carolina at Greensboro (UNCG) would develop the project's logo and Web site. Another student in the business school at UNCG would launch a fundraising campaign that collected more than $1,000 early on from community members to support the effort. Students from that school and others, including Guilford College, Elon University, Bennett College, Greensboro College, and North Carolina A & T State University, organized youth forums, collected surveys, created art and visual displays, recorded music, and conducted interviews.

The TRC staff worked with nearly 150 mainstream media outlets locally and nationally. Further, the commission established its own Web site, blog, public access television show, and weekly electronic newsletter sent to more than eight hundred recipients. The newsletter, *Ubuntu Weekly,* debuted on February 22, 2005, and continued until its sixty-fourth issue was released on May 16, 2006. At its peak, distribution reached 857 contacts including community members, media outlets, and peace and justice organizations.

A month after the last public hearing, the TRC hosted a day-long "community dialogue" in which more than one hundred community members participated. Keith Holliday, then mayor of Greensboro, attended in part. Together, people were asked to reflect on the truth and reconciliation process, begin discussion on what reconciliation might look like in Greensboro, and offer views of what categories of information they believed the truth commissioners should include in their Final Report. The structured small group discussions with trained facilitators and note takers yielded bountiful ideas that were included in the Final Report (2006, 469–474).

The last major outreach effort by the TRC before it issued its Final Report was to contact "public bodies" as instructed by the Mandate to receive and read the report. In all, more than fifty religious and civic organizations, schools, book clubs, and other local organizations agreed to be designated "Report Receivers." In doing so, the organizations committed to read the executive summary or Final Report as a group and then engage in dialogue surrounding the TRC's recommendations in order to promote reconciliation in the city. Advance appreciation and instruction for the report receivers were provided at a special evening reception to brainstorm the various ways in which groups might organize their tasks. The ambiance was hopeful and excited as young and old, black and white people shared ideas they believed would improve the quality of public life in Greensboro.

UBUNTU PUT INTO PRACTICE

Indeed, in 2006, nearly three decades after the Greensboro Massacre, and during the truth and reconciliation process, four survivors of November 3, 1979, met with the most unlikely of persons. Signe Waller, whose husband, Jim Waller, died on November 3, traveled with her son Alex Goldstein, who was only a child in 1979, and the Reverend Nelson Johnson to meet with former American Nazi Party member Roland Wayne Wood. Wood, a principal November 3 attacker, was by 2006 confined to a wheelchair in an assisted living facility. He begged forgiveness as he recounted the events and his role on November 3 and then in one room together the four prayed—two Jews, a black man, and a former Nazi. It was a moment no one expected and one Waller later said gave rise to her hope that community transformation is possible through the process of revealing the truth and engaging in acts of reconciliation. Her heavy heart, she says, was lightened by the visible prospects that the past did not have to dictate the future. For Roland Wayne Wood, who said he could not forgive himself for the events of that day without the forgiveness of those in the room, a soul's call for mercy was answered. Reverend Nelson Johnson called it a moment of grace where the wall came down that had for so many years defined and divided their relationship to one another (Earnhardt Pirkle, 2009).

Acts of forgiveness were among the ways in which the people of Greensboro embraced Ubuntu in the TRC process to consider difficult, sometimes contradictory or incomplete pieces of information together in order to allow a new path to reveal itself. Other ways Ubuntu emerged were in the recasting of old narratives of hate into newer stories of hope. For example, the account of November 3 that circulated in the media in the aftermath of the tragedy reduced the information to a gun battle between two opposing extremist groups full of hate. The information originally filtered out of the story of November 3 included the role of the police and the lengthy backgrounds of the protestors who had accumulated long track records of confronting injustice in workplaces, schools, and neighborhoods. An approach to understanding grounded in an ethic of care or Ubuntu made these community facts central. The TRC honored the particulars in its investigations and throughout its multifaceted layers of community outreach.

Invited testimony from Arkansas Tech University professor Jeffrey

Woods and Southern Poverty Law Center investigator Joe Roy, among others, brought to life the history of the South leading up to 1979. They detailed how workers wanting union representation jeopardized a more patriarchal way of life. They explained the activities of liberal whites that aided blacks in their quest for equality. In these educationally rich testimonies, Greensboro's residents learned that the tensions in their city in 1979 were visible all over the South in a trajectory bound to force change.

Reconciliation transforms conflict through a "creative and a flexible human activity that is undertaken for the sake of humanity as a shared community" (Nabudere, 2005, 17). In place of blame or punishment, accountability and "making it right" are the operative guidelines for justice according to the precepts of Ubuntu. The goal is to establish or restore relationships in the community. To do this, the TRC commissioners struggled to hold together a fragile community in the midst of difficult conversations. Dr. Muktha Jost described the process as mired in toxicity among competing claims to the truth.

> We are all torn apart in so many ways and in so many directions because of the past. That we lack a shared understanding of what happened in the past splits us farther apart. Without that shared awareness of the past, we lack the vocabulary or the language that we need to speak together. (Final Report, 2006, 404)

To manage, Jost abided by what she regarded as a personal "first principle"—namely, affirming the humanity of all. She called upon the citizens of Greensboro to reclaim the values of honesty, integrity, fairness, and respect for all people, a vision of her own that illustrates the promise of Ubuntu.

Greensboro's TRC process thus introduced the concept of Ubuntu, the connection of self to others, but did not explicitly use the word in community discourse. That rhetorical decision is not surprising in light of the U.S. focus on individuality and independence as societal norms. Still, the TRC modeled the concepts of Ubuntu in its tasks and built its features into the guiding values of the process, even naming the TRC's on-line newsletter, *Ubuntu Weekly*. Ubuntu, not as a word but as a sentiment, surfaced again and again in the public testimonies, as a release valve to help extinguish smoldering grief.

THE NEXT GENERATION OF PAIN

The public hearings hosted by the Greensboro Truth and Reconciliation Commission included testimony from two children of CWP demonstrators. The two were not yet born in 1979, but they were nevertheless profoundly influenced by the events of that day. Alison Duncan, the daughter of former CWP members Robert and Elaine Duncan and a 2004 graduate of Guilford College, was the first of the two to speak on the second day of the final public hearing. César Weston, also a graduate of Guilford College, and active in local politics and service to the community, followed Duncan. He is the son of Larry and Floris Weston, and was given the name César after Floris's first husband, the slain César Cauce. The words from the two young people, and the vulnerability they communicated, revealed that the pain of November 3, 1979, continued not only for a community, but also crossed time into another generation that bore the burdens of finishing a struggle not completed.

Duncan was unable to hold back her tears when she put into words a life deeply influenced by her parents' quest for social justice. The constant reminder of November 3 was in the namesakes of those who died including her brother and nearly a dozen young people she knew well:

> There was at one time a second generation list serve where children of organizers . . . would send out what things they were working on and it was wonderful to see, it was inspiring and it seemed everyone had been inspired to work for social change or just had politically active parents so they became politically active children. I always went to as many things as I could but at the same time it never felt like I was doing enough . . . one of the reasons I give myself for never doing as much as I feel I could, is the inevitable feeling that if I do this, I could die . . . There were many people's lives that changed that day, changed to not trusting the system that's supposed to protect you, changed to fear many things, but my life never changed, it started that way. (Duncan, 2005)

As Duncan concluded her remarks to the Truth Commission, César Weston began his, but not without first holding his friend Alison and agreeing that his life, too, was a reflection of the lives and work of those who died on November 3, 1979.

Weston admitted his desire to be strong, assertive, and organized when he spoke at the public hearing. Weston practiced, he said, holding his emotions at bay when talking about November 3, though he realized from Duncan's comments how poignant are sensory perceptions, daily experiences, and long-held feelings:

> I wasn't born until over three years after November 3rd, 1979. My father is Larry Weston, not César Cauce, but . . . I came directly out of the physical and emotional wreckage left in the wake of November 3rd, which I still see as the unanswerable instance of state sanctioned murder . . . Another way I have felt the impacts of this event is . . . in the direction and path that I have chosen in my life. I will adopt a path of social justice and service in whatever I do. And this will be the direction of my life now until the end of my days no matter how I meet them. From the time that I could think coherently, the November 3rd legacy has carried with it an unspoken expectation of political activity and consciousness. And growing up under the quiet watchful eye of one, who to me, is a true hero, taught me something of quiet devotions, ideals and from an early age my board was set. Though I have not lived the experience in question myself, I felt enough of the second hand agony, waded through enough of the wreckage to feel some of this trauma. (Cauce, 2005)

Weston and Duncan provided the audience, perhaps more than any other speakers, a close and personal look at the impact of November 3 on people of all ages, not just those who had survived the incident, and not just those who were alive when it happened. The young people, themselves dedicated to social change, advocated for more involvement by all people to be active in the pursuit of social justice.

CHAPTER 6

The Commission's Final Report: Recovering the Truth

The greatest value in our report, we believe is placing this information within a historical context and examining these events with a broader view of history to inform the "truth."

—FINAL REPORT

THE GREENSBORO TRUTH and Reconciliation Commission's 529-page Final Report is well-researched and warrants a complete reading for a full account of Greensboro's TRC process, the history of southern race and labor relations, and the internal workings of law enforcement agencies as well as grassroots, community-action groups.[1] In this chapter I provide a summary of the structure, guiding principles, findings, and recommendations of that report.

Greensboro's truth commissioners designed their Final Report to situate a fact-supported review of a contentious episode in the city's past into historical context. They also issued judgments and recommendations, but with the caveat that their conclusions were to be questioned, extended, and refined as the subject of continued community dialogues:

> We hope that our modest examination of a difficult chapter of Greensboro's history and how those events shape the community today may serve as a profound and timely reminder of the importance of facing shameful events honestly and acknowledging the brutal consequences of political spin, calculated blindness and passive ignorance. While the [Greensboro] TRC recognizes the differences between Greensboro's history and the abuses addressed by other truth commissions, we share a common aspiration: that the

truth about the past will help us build a better, more just and more inclusive future. (Final Report, 2006, 15)

With a focus on restorative justice, Greensboro's truth commissioners wrestled with two recurring tensions in their analysis. First, they saw the need to provide reasoning and judgment that addressed not only the legal standard, but also the ethical imperative for community conduct. To do that, they examined the issues not in isolation from the events of the times as might be the case in legal proceedings, but instead by understanding that the cultural mores and related historical happenings had great influence on the causes and consequences of an event. Second, they grappled with how to hold responsible the individuals and institutions for wrongs committed. The truth commissioners understood that individual acts often arise in response to cultural conditions and organizational constraints. At the same time, the truth commissioners believed that individuals are agents of their own destiny.

The truth commissioners' work was guided by a mandate[2] to examine the context, causes, sequence, and consequences of the events of November 3, 1979, along with five broad questions that the commissioners attempted to answer to make transparent their process.

1. *Are truth and reconciliation opposing values, or are they inextricably linked?*

The truth commissioners acknowledged within their ranks and with outside groups, that there was community disagreement surrounding the priority of truth or reconciliation in the TRC process. They reported on the one hand that African American supporters were generally interested in a focus on truth-telling and truth-seeking goals to bring about the justice missing in race and class relations. On the other hand, most members of the white community who expressed support did so because of their faith in the promise of reconciliation to bridge deep divides in the community.

In the end, Greensboro's truth commissioners saw their work as primarily concerned first with seeking the truth that could secondly, pave the way for reconciliation. Thus, for the commissioners, reconciliation would be left to the community to more clearly define and concretely manage, rather than a task for the commissioners themselves to undertake.

2. *What is the difference between recrimination and establishing accountability? What is the difference between what we are doing and what happened in the three court trials around these events?*

The truth commissioners hoped that people who committed wrongs or made mistakes surrounding the events of November 3, 1979, would admit to that during the TRC process. In the end, that aim was not fully realized. Instead, many people insisted on reiterating what they had long accepted, even in the face of information that would contradict it. Other people refused to participate in the process. In some instances, however, new truth telling did emerge from people who had not previously spoken about November 3. Throughout, the commissioners kept as their goal transformative or restorative justice[3] that could recognize the role of history, culture, and community in influencing individual decisions, while not altogether excusing individual actions.

3. *Who were the victims of November 3, 1979?*

The truth commissioners chose not to use the term "victim" in their report for a number of reasons. First, the family and friends of those who died on November 3, 1979, referred to themselves as survivors, not victims. Second, the truth commissioners found the term victim to connote a certain helplessness that they felt did not properly reflect the attitudes or identities of those involved in the TRC process. Third, the commissioners recognized that the community was not aligned on who was really harmed on November 3, 1979. Though conventional wisdom would suggest that those people who lost lives and loved ones surely suffered the most, there was clearly another view. For some in the community, the people who died or survived with injuries "were perpetrators of the violence at least as much as they were victimized by it" (Final Report, 2006, 22). In place of the term "victim" the truth commissioners identified two categories of individuals and organizations: those who were harmed directly; and those who were harmed indirectly.

4. *How do we frame the "context, causes, sequence and consequence" of the events of November 3, 1979, when the options are limitless?*

Three court trials, numerous newspaper articles, documentary films, books, and other portrayals of what happened November 3 provided the community with significant data and facts. However, the truth commissioners believed that the Final Report could put to rest rumors and misinformation—disguised as facts—that had persisted. Most important, though, the truth commissioners saw their contribution to the "truth" as putting the facts and sequence of events within an appropriate historical context. By way of example, one of the most frequently cited criticisms of November 3 was that the Communist Workers Party chose "Death to the Klan" as its slogan for the march on November 3. During the TRC process, community members learned that "Death to the Klan" was not a slogan conjured up by the CWP; it was an umbrella catchphrase used by anti-Klan groups throughout the South (Green, 2005).

The Greensboro TRC sought to place November 3 within a broader context by examining the timeframe of other labor struggles and race-related events that occurred within the lifetime of those who participated in the 1979 events. These individuals, born in the 1940s and 1950s, were deeply affected by strikes in the South that included racial violence, corrupt or distorted law enforcement policies, and the surge of labor and civil rights organizing. These cultural conditions were of course influenced, the truth commissioners reasoned, by the United States history of constitutional rights that though hopeful were nonetheless inadequate by allowing the persistence of slavery, white supremacy, and worldwide geopolitical conflicts.

5. What does it mean to be an independent commission?

For many in Greensboro, it was difficult to distinguish between the grassroots Greensboro Truth and Community Reconciliation Project and the independent Greensboro Truth and Reconciliation Commission, and more, to believe that the Truth Commission could be free of influence by the advocacy-based project leaders and November 3 survivors. Despite the friendly relationship maintained between the TRC and the GCTRP, the truth commissioners insisted that they were an autonomous body: "We affirm that we have conducted our research and community engagement in accordance with our mandate to operate independently of any external influence, including the GTCRP" (Final Report, 2006, 24).

The Truth Commission's independence from government influence was also evident. A city council vote, along racial lines, to "oppose" the truth and reconciliation process cemented the unenthusiastic view the city council held regarding the TRC process. At that April 19, 2005, meeting, the city council was presented with the more than five thousand city resident signatures calling for the backing of the process and agreement to at least consider the recommendations the truth commissioners would eventually suggest.

The lack of collaboration with government was both a limiting condition and a positive feature acknowledged by the truth commissioners in their Final Report. On the limiting side, financial resources and some statements were impossible to secure from government sources and the powerful leaders who comprised the city's core decision makers. The ripple effect was that securing funds of any significant amount and eliciting cooperation from local individuals, businesses, and foundations proved to be difficult for those entities feared "they would face negative repercussions" by those who held the seats of power in the city (Final Report, 2006, 24). On the positive side, with the Truth Commission free of government control, it was unrestricted in establishing its own moral guideposts, findings, recommendations, and standards of fairness to inspire a community trust that government institutions had repeatedly failed to do, particularly among members of minority and marginalized communities.[4]

The truth commissioners did not set their sights on the impossible task of developing the complete and perfect truth of what happened before, on, and after November 3, 1979. Instead, their work focused on drawing sound conclusions from the available evidence.

The Truth Commission and its staff conducted their own interviews, consulted police records, and reviewed trial testimony from all three court cases, the Grand Jury testimonies, civil suit depositions, and criminal case pretrial interviews. In addition, they perused the civil suit discovery material, including internal records from the FBI and the Bureau of Alcohol, Tobacco and Firearms, as well as the personal files of at least one judge, several attorneys, and others closely involved in the events of November 3, 1979. To answer lingering questions about the influence of the media, the commissioner's contracted with a communication researcher to analyze the print media reports from 1979 to 1985.[5]

Still, there were limitations to the meticulousness of the research tasks. For starters, the Greensboro TRC faced the same restrictive conditions common to truth commissions all over the world: gaps in available evidence; imperfect memory; inadequate time and funding; and lack of sufficient staff to investigate all leads to the maximum extent possible.

Evidence was sometimes hard to collect. When individuals were reluctant to provide statements to the TRC staff either because of fear of retaliation or distrust of the process, the commission consulted trial testimonies from the previous court cases, other recorded interviews, and secondary literature as needed. Certain government documents were also difficult to secure. Information collected under the Freedom of Information Act had much of the content blacked out with redactions. Learning more details of what government agents may have known in advance of November 3, 1979, was thus hampered.

Recognizing that memory deteriorates over time, the Truth Commission favored reading court testimonies of what happened on November 3, 1979. They appreciated however, that TRC public hearing testimonies tendered important details of the long-term impact of earlier events. Where possible, the Truth Commission consulted multiple sources to corroborate the details, facts, and stories they collected. They acknowledged that verifiable facts, or what the South African Truth Commission referred to as "forensic truth," could be compatible with the "narrative truth" comprised of individual perspectives (Final Report, 2006, 28–29). The Truth Commission reasoned, "Exposing some of the differences in experience and perspective provides a human, lived dimension to the framework of fact-finding, and was an explicit aim of our research" (Final Report, 2006, 29).

Bound to a finite timeframe in which to conduct the research, the TRC found itself needing to make choices regarding how far to pursue an investigative lead. A much larger volunteer corps augmented the small staff, but still the voluminous materials requiring attention proved a challenge. The commissioners pledged to assess the significance of the facts by using legal principles and ethical guidelines as their standards. For instance, they considered acts of omission and commission to be inconsistent with democratic ideals and thus ethically, if not legally wrong.

The truth commissioners adopted what they called an "antiracist" orientation, noting that racism is the "unacknowledged 'elephant in the room' that continues to haunt social relations in Greensboro" (Final Report, 2006, 31). As a result, the Final Report specifically addressed racial inequalities in an attempt to provoke public conversation and dialogue about systemic inequalities that may have contributed to the context and events of November 3, 1979.

The Truth Commissioners' Findings

The truth commissioners found, unlike previous juries, that the Klan and Nazis had indeed planned to disrupt the parade, and thereby violated the marchers' constitutional rights to free speech and assembly. They further believed the evidence was clear that the Klan and Nazis intended to provoke a violent confrontation.

The TRC found the police "irresponsible in their deliberate absence from the parade starting point, given the information that the Klan indeed were coming and would likely provoke violence" (Final Report, 2006, 194). This finding was perhaps the most significant of the report, countering the position the City of Greensboro had adopted in 1979 and had continued to uphold—that the city's police acted with utmost professionalism and skill. The mayor in 1979, Jim Melvin, never publicly questioned the competence and performance of the police on that day. Quite the opposite—he praised their actions at every juncture in ways strong enough to influence many, if not most, public officials since that time.

The truth commissioners were adamant that key police planners "made repeated decisions to divert officers away from the designated and agreed upon assembly point" and thus found the "GPD officers were negligent in their duty to protect the marchers and residents of Morningside" (Final Report, 2006, 195). But why would the police act in such a way? The TRC reasoned that the police overstated the threat that Nelson Johnson posed and understated the risks the Klan represented. The police took steps, the commissioners said, to contain the communist activists, yet they did nothing to stop the caravan carrying Klan and Nazis known for racist violence. In fact, the "low profile" the police department officers agreed to take was in the view of the truth commissioners actually "no profile"—there were no marked cars with uniformed officers nearby, there was inadequate planning for foreseeable events, not one single unit was on hand, and there was a failure to stop the cars fleeing from the shooting, thus showing "deliberate indifference to the safety of the marchers and the neighborhood residents" (Final Report, 2006, 200).

Members of the WVO/CWP spoke out against economic injustice, racism, unfair labor practices, and poverty—all-important conditions deserving of condemnation. However, the vitriolic rhetoric employed by the WVO/CWP was in the TRC's view an example of naive recklessness in the face of the violent track record of the Klan and Nazis. The TRC acknowledged as well that the WVO/CWP was likely unaware of the premeditated activities of the Klan since the police had failed to communicate that information to them. The truth commissioners said, "We find police failure to inform the WVO/CWP of known threats to the marchers unconscionable" (Final Report, 2006, 199).

The question in Greensboro that had hung in the air since November 3, 1979, was, didn't both sides—the Klan/Nazis and the WVO/CWP—invite violence that day through their radical rhetoric? The TRC said "no." They argued that "while both groups deliberately engaged in provocative and even violent-sounding rhetoric, the message of racism and violence promoted by the Klan and Nazis outweighed in effect or intent the WVO/CWP's rhetoric of violent overthrow of capitalism and destruction of the Klan." (Final Report, 2006, 191). Records showed that Klansmen advocated the murder of black people—a position the Greensboro TRC claimed to be "immoral and demanding of public rebuke" (Final Report, 2006, 191).

The truth commissioners believed the police resources devoted to investigations of Nelson Johnson and the WVO were influenced by Cone Mills's complaints of union organizing leafleting. In fact, the commissioners, said, "The evidence shows that the concern about the WVO had more to do with their 'revolutionary' rhetoric—which was not only intensely anti-establishment but particularly anti-police—than their actual criminal activity" (Final Report, 2006, 123).

Among the controversies surrounding November 3 was that the neighborhood of Morningside Homes was unexpectedly terrorized by gunfire that day. Some residents claimed the WVO/CWP should have alerted them of the planned march and the advance announcements publicly taunting the Klan to come. In response, WVO members said they did communicate about the march. Dale Sampson, Willena Cannon, and Joyce Johnson all testified that they personally participated in distributing information sheets in the area. Posters were mounted as well all along the planned march route. In fact, the WVO members complained that the posters were being removed by the police who claimed the signs were illegally placed on telephone and streetlight poles. Days before November 3, a catered luncheon was hosted by the WVO and others to discuss the march, though none of the residents of the area came. Evelyn Taylor, president of the Morningside Neighborhood Council in 1979, said the residents failed to show up because "they didn't want to be bothered" (Final Report, 2006, 147).

As terrible as the events of November 3, 1979, were, many argued that what followed was worse—more cover-up about what really happened that day. The truth commissioners agreed. They concluded that the police failed in its duty to adequately reveal the whole story surrounding November 3 with "evidence of deliberate manipulation and concealment of the facts that we can only interpret as intended to sever the Greensboro Police Department from any responsibility" (Final Report, 2006, 212). To support this troubling conclusion, the truth commissioners pointed to multiple specific charges of imprudent conduct.

The commissioners noted that Greensboro's director of public safety in 1979 repeatedly lied in a conscious attempt to mislead the public. He said seven times to the city's Citizen Review Committee in 1980 that the police had no prior knowledge of the incident at China Grove. However, other officers and police records revealed that specific conversations and memos containing this information were circulated throughout the department.

At least six police officers testified that they had advance information that Klansmen, numbering fifty to hundreds, would be driving to Greensboro on November 3, 1979, to disrupt the march. Yet, the Internal Affairs Division summary report prepared in the weeks following the event represented the number of Klansmen as being about ten "with no qualification of the conflicting and better-informed sources" suggesting a far larger threat to the community (Final Report, 2006, 214). The full Administrative Report authored by the Internal Affairs Division was even less informative, concluded the truth commissioners, suggesting that the police only learned on the morning of November 3 that Klansmen *might* be present, without including the depth of intelligence work and conversation taking place in the month prior.

Informant Eddie Dawson and BATF undercover agent Bernard Butkovich supplied select law enforcement officials with details regarding the Klan and Nazis possession of weapons. However, police officers at the parade briefings on security duty were not provided that critical information.

In addition, police officers received reliable information that a Klansman in Winston-Salem had purchased a machine gun for use in Greensboro to "shoot up the place" (Final Report, 2006, 216). Detective Cooper denied knowledge of this yet other officers reported talking to him specifically about that. There was no mention of this was in the Administrative Report.

The Greensboro police maintained after November 3 that they were confused by the WVO/CWP advance publicity about where the parade was starting, and thus not in the proper location to provide protection. Yet, the truth commissioners uncovered at least five separate discussions by police planners between October 19 and the morning of November 3 addressing the poster advertisement of the 11:00 A.M. gathering at Windsor Community Center and the actual parade location beginning at 12 noon at Everitt and Carver. The truth commissioners said the police were fully aware of both locations and times, and thus found it inexcusable that the police failed to provide safety. The commissioners also asserted that "the claim that the officers were confused about where the parade would start is simply not credible" (Final Report, 2006, 217).

Police officers and community members were led to believe that the decision to take a "low profile" was made by Captain Trevor Hampton. Yet, the Final Report found internal police staff minutes showing Deputy Chief Walter Burch made that decision, along with the directive for no armed officers at the parade starting point. Why was this significant? It was another instance, the truth commissioners found, of how facts were knowingly misrepresented. The argument had been made by the City of Greensboro that the police could not have engaged in any wrongdoing when the commanding officer

Hampton, an African American, would have done all he could to protect the black Morningside Homes residents.

The commissioners debunked the claim that the use of alternate radio frequencies was a source of police confusion, as detailed in Elizabeth Wheaton's 1987 book, *Codename GREENKIL*. The truth commissioners did note that officers following the Klan-Nazi caravan chose to use the unassigned Frequency 4 that not all officers would hear while Frequency 3 had been designated for parade transmissions, and Frequency 1 was used for standard patrol information. The truth commissioners concluded that "transmissions should have been on a channel where all personnel tasked with security for the march would be made aware of this increasingly dangerous circumstance" (Final Report, 2006, 221).

The truth commissioners noted further that the police department's Internal Affairs Division Administrative Report altered "the record in a way that omits important elements of police action" on November 3 (Final Report, 2006, 221). Chief William Swing admitted the radio transcript released in their report had deleted information deemed not relevant, including a call to officer April Wise and her partner to immediately leave the Morningside area where they were responding to a domestic dispute just before 11:00 that morning. Wise later made a radio transmission reporting someone in a blue Ford Fairlane (one of the caravan cars) was threatening pedestrians with a shotgun immediately after the shooting—that information was apparently deemed irrelevant and also removed from the official transcript.

Finally, if the Administrative Report intended, as Chief Swing said, "to provide a complete explanation of what happened that day" (Final Report, 2006, 222), the truth commissioners remain unconvinced. There was no information about the Klan informant or the BATF's undercover agent inside the Nazi organization, leading the truth commissioners to assert the Internal Affairs Division deliberately concealed the information.

In sum, the truth commissioners found "that both the Greensboro Police Department and key city managers deliberately misled the public about what happened on November 3, 1979, the planning for it and the investigation of it" (Final Report, 2006, 223). Further, in reference to the police report that contained false information and concealed facts, the truth commissioners said it could "only be interpreted as a tactic to deflect blame away from the police department" (Final Report, 2006, 223).

In addition to calling for police department reform, Greensboro's Truth Commission made clear that November 3, 1979, was a call for action across the city. November 3 was not just an incident to be buried in the past. It was, they said, a deeply textured occurrence that continued a struggle to achieve equity in civil and human rights. That is, despite claims by the city elite that November 3 was significant only to the people directly involved that day, the truth commissioners said:

> Many people in Greensboro, and indeed the community as a whole, were traumatized by the events of November 3, 1979 . . . From the day of the shootings through the end of the three trials and the completion of several government-commissioned reports to the declaration in 2008 of this truth and reconciliation process, there has been evidence of pain that has gone unaddressed. (Final Report, 2006, 228)

Even though they found inadequacy in police operations, the truth commissioners noted a number of more positive efforts that were launched in the aftermath of November 3 as part of a damage-control strategy.

For instance, the City of Greensboro released its opposition in 1982 to a district system for city elections to provide greater opportunity for minority representation on the city council. Another change was made in the city's budget to more equitably distribute resources across the quadrants of Greensboro, providing renewed funds to the black areas of the city. Finally, attempts at dialogue about race and among races were started and continued with support from the city's coffers for public events and employee training.

The positive changes were acknowledged, but the truth commissioners concluded that fear and distrust remained high among many segments of the community in Greensboro. The commissioners noted that the criticisms waged in 1979 against local government policies remained so in the twenty-first century as the activities of the Truth and Reconciliation Commission were launched. As evidence, they pointed to the excessive police force bordering on intimidation that was used when the twenty-fifth anniversary events for November 3 included plans for a march. To the truth commissioners, Greensboro in 2004 was acting as it had in 1979 where only one of two options seemed plausible for parade security—absence or intimidating overkill (Final Report, 2006, 250)—rather than thoughtful and cooperatively planned protection.

There were more incidents as well that pointed to the opposition of the community leaders and officials to embrace the community-grown effort for truth and reconciliation. For example, in advance of the Truth Commission's first public hearing, information was leaked to the press by someone in the police department, the city council, or the city manager's office that Klansman Virgil Griffin was to speak. This act jeopardized Griffin's participation since he had agreed to speak on the condition that his appearance not be announced in advance in order to prevent protestors and press from clamoring. The city council claimed that Griffin's appearance could put the city in danger, an announcement the truth commissioners saw as a tactic to incite fear and keep citizens away from the proceedings.

Later, a Community Dialogue hosted by the TRC upon the completion of the three public hearings was held at Mount Zion Baptist Church. Police officials met in advance with church representatives but failed to include TRC staff in the discussions, citing that as an oversight. Some prospective statement givers and community dialogue participants reported they were discouraged by local officials from participating.

The truth commissioners concluded that the TRC's activities were indeed relevant, important, and for some, even threatening. Attempts to suppress the TRC process included secret meetings, innuendos, intimidation tactics, deliberate efforts to mislead the public, and even a break-in at the TRC offices where file cabinets containing research, financial, and personnel files were ransacked. Rumors circulated and were repeated by some community leaders alleging the commission's operation was only possible because of "outsiders," that there was a less than autonomous relationship with the grassroots Greensboro Truth and Community Reconciliation Project, and that people with views counter to the survivor experiences were being subjected to intimidation tactics. No evidence was ever found to support these claims. Instead, the truth commissioners found intimidation coming from the police when they learned that their staff's executive director, Jill Williams, was the target of police surveillance.

What Greensboro needed, said the truth commissioners, was deeper and continued dialogue about what happened in 1979 to counter the distrust that lingered in the community. The truth commissioners believed the City of Greensboro missed the opportunity to be a thoughtful, protective source upon which its citizens could depend. Instead, it chose in 1979 and throughout the many years later to pursue "stability" by suppressing protest, spreading rumors, focusing on image management rather than problem solving, and dismissing or discrediting citizen critiques of city operations.

In addition to the failings of the police department and city officials, the truth commissioners also exposed the injustices in the justice system. When the two criminal court juries found the KKK and Nazis not guilty of the crimes charged, the community experienced "its own form of trauma, creating its own confusion, fear and distrust over whether our system of law enforcement and justice will protect them" (Final Report, 2006, 258). The questions that quickly began to circulate persisted well into the next many decades:

- How was it possible that the Klansmen and Nazis escaped criminal convictions?

- How could the courts in the criminal trials have convened all-white juries?

- Why did the survivors refuse to speak at the first state criminal trial?

- Why in the civil case was only one victim compensated when five people died?

- Why did the City of Greensboro pay the judgment in the civil case on behalf of individual police officers *and* the KKK and Nazis?

Twenty-five years later, the Greensboro Truth and Reconciliation commissioners disagreed with the first and second jury verdicts that found the Klan and Nazi's not guilty. The truth commissioners cited the presence of the caravan, "accompanied by shouts of 'Show me a nigger with guts and I'll show you a Klansmen with a gun!' and 'Shoot the niggers!'" as the first aggressive move in the massacre. Further, the commissioners noted:

> a commonsense understanding of self-defense would dictate that because the Nazi/Klansmen in the caravan came to Greensboro to provoke a fight, self-defense cannot be invoked by them. . . . the fact that four of the five demonstrators shot to death (one of whom was shot in the back) were unarmed seems to us to make the defendants' argument and the jury's decision of self-defense that much more difficult for the community to understand. (Final Report, 2006, 280)

The commissioners said since the caravan members were the aggressors who used excessive force, at a minimum, they should have been found guilty of voluntary manslaughter (Final Report, 2006, 281).

The Greensboro TRC concurred with Greensboro's many residents who felt betrayed by the justice system. The commissioners pointed out that "the legal system inevitably reflects and also is influenced by the prevailing social and political contexts" (Final Report, 2006, 258) that was so entrenched in anticommunism sentiment and concern for civility that it was difficult for court-appointed attorneys, witnesses, and jurors to see beyond the militant rhetoric of the survivors.

The truth commissioners countered the jury decision in the second trial, noting there was ample evidence of racial animus, or intentions of ill will, based on the explicitly racist language used by Klansmen coupled with the Klan ideology of white supremacy (Final Report, 2006, 290). It was the jury's unwillingness to examine the effects of racism in our culture, said the truth commissioners, that likely undermined any real opportunity for justice:

> it may have been more palatable for the jurors and indeed for the public more generally, to view Nov. 3, 1979 as a "shootout" between extremists for which both sides were equally to blame, than to examine the racist elements of the killings. (Final Report, 2006, 290)

It was only in the third, federal civil trial that the failures of the first two trials were made apparent—biased jury selection, lack of prosecutorial vigor, and lack of adequate witness testimony. What the final trial, by way of contrast, made clear was that for a government-sanctioned march planned and executed according to permit specifications, the government did not provide adequate protection to the demonstrators, the neighborhood, and even the counterdemonstrators. The knowledge was there for all to see that the KKK and Nazis were organizing a violent response to the Communist Workers Party's right to assemble, yet no one in a position of authority responded. Lewis Pitts, attorney for that case, noted in his public testimony at the truth and reconciliation commission hearings:

> We felt it was very significant that a Southern jury found liable, jointly, police officers and the Ku Klux Klan in these acts of violence. I don't know that that had been done. And we wanted to, if you will, celebrate that progress. (Final Report, 2006, 308)

The truth commissioners added that "litigation may have been settled, but the moral issues were not" (Final Report, 2006, 309) since the police did not admit wrongdoing as a condition of the settlement, nor did any reprimands get issued or reevaluation of policies arise in the aftermath of the tragedy.

The truth commissioners noted that it was near impossible for the survivors to get the fair trial they desired, despite three attempts, because of the political context in which November 3 was wedged. The anticommunism sentiment, strong as it was, was inextricably linked to the communists' support for equal rights of blacks in an antiracism stance not fully supported in the South.

The final remedy in the law was never fully satisfactory to the survivors or to the many people of Greensboro, yet the six years of legal wrangling did establish that people together could fight against injustice embedded in the complicated layers of our system and culture. Many believed that November 3 was a window into the goings on of the 1980s where a conservative federal judiciary was put in place by the Nixon and Reagan administrations and civil rights suits were becoming cost prohibitive to wage. Against those obstacles, and more, the survivors of the Greensboro Massacre and their legal team were able to celebrate a victory in establishing by way of verdict for the first time that law enforcement officials together with hate groups were liable for the death and injury of citizens. While long believed in the South that law enforcement was complicit with hate groups, this was the first legal ruling to lend credibility to that claim.

The truth commissioners pointed out that the most unsettling aspect of the judicial process was the paradox of the videotape footage showing the shootings and verdicts that found no crimes were committed. In the words of the commissioners, "When the justice system fails to find people responsible when wrongs are committed, it sends a damaging signal that some crimes will not be punished, and some people will not be protected by the government" (Final Report, 2006, 311).

Reporting the Story: Media Portrayals and the Community's Understanding

In the immediate aftermath of November 3, 1979, and in the many years that followed, confusion reigned among citizens in Greensboro about what happened that day. In part, the media contributed to that condition through its reporting practices. As the Truth Commission reviewed the results of research examining 617 articles from 1979 to 1985, they looked to see what information was communicated and in what ways or "frames." Recognizing that the media represents one (rather large) piece of the cognitive puzzle from which people draw conclusions about social life, there were several important other factors at work that would affect the community's understanding of what happened on November 3.

First, as people were making sense of the news, their prior knowledge, biases, and interpretive frameworks would naturally be factors. For those who believed communism to be a serious threat to our democracy, the CWP's actions would hardly be considered noble. For those who understood hate group violence to be an immediate concern to civil rights, the KKK and Nazis would be viewed as domestic terrorists. For those who had experienced or witnessed suspect activities within law enforcement circles, the view of that authority as a corrupt institution no doubt emerged.

Second, community understanding was affected by what media source(s) people relied upon for information. For example, the daily newspapers, the *Greensboro Daily News* and the *Greensboro Record,* focused their coverage on the culpable actions of the Klan/Nazis and the CWP whereas the weekly *Carolina Peacemaker,* circulated primarily in the African American communities, questioned police department actions and official wrongdoing (Final Report, 2006, 325).

Third, mistrust in the community was rampant in 1979. The questioning of police operations began immediately following November 3, 1979. At the same time, supporters of police action organized a petition to express their satisfaction with the law enforcement arm of city governance. Members of the KKK, the Nazi Party, and the CWP *all* claimed misrepresentation in local newspaper reporting. Many journalists were frustrated as well, particularly with the city's lack of cooperation in providing access to documents and other information and the survivors' refusal to respond to inquiries.

Fourth, the events of November 3 involved a lot of people, many of them with the same names, leading to confusion in even understanding who did what in this tragedy (Final Report, 2006, 325). For example, the bullet fired by (Jerry Paul) Smith may have been read in the newspapers as coming instead from victim (Sandi) Smith. Additionally, district attorney (Mike) Schlosser working for the prosecution on behalf of the survivors was confused, at least at times, with defense counsel (Steve) Schlosser and prosecutor (Rick) Greeson may have been mixed-up with defense team attorney (Hal) Greeson. The last name, Johnson, was the same for WVO/CWP organizer Nelson, federal prosecutor Michael, and police officer T. R. Among judicial officials, federal criminal judge Flannery had a name close in sound and spelling to federal prosecutor Flannagan. And, among those with the surname Matthews were two Klansmen, Horace Greeley and David Wayne, as well as police photographer J. T. Keeping the story straight had to be difficult for many citizens unfamiliar with the individuals named in November 3 news stories.

Fifth, event fatigue surely had an effect. The first news of what happened that day would be countered with ample, often-contradictory pieces of evidence by the time the civil trial was conducted more than five years later. In response, many citizens may have tuned out after initial reports, never fully incorporating into their understanding of what happened, the newer information. In addition, the public (and the jurors) had seen considerable video coverage and learned of multiple versions of sound analyses of the gunshots around which there was little to no agreement about their significance among experts, let alone laypeople.

Finally, the community's insistence on civility as a mode of communication no doubt played an important role in interpreting the

events of what happened on November 3. That form of civility operated in Greensboro to suppress meaningful dialogue and action for
change (Chafe, 1980). Instead, the bias was toward preserving "things
as they are" and respecting structures, policies, and programs in place
to preserve the community as it was. Within this culture, the desire to
get past the events of November 3 may have served to circumvent the
deep analysis eventually conducted by the Truth and Reconciliation
Commission (Final Report, 2006, 326).

Recognizing that multiple factors had an impact on the community's understanding of November 3, the media still occupied a central
role in communicating the information people read or saw, and also
what they did not see or have access to in their daily lives. In this case,
as in most news events, the number of facts can often exceed the
amount of information a reporter can include in a story. Thus *how* the
news was reported was crucial. Regarding November 3 most media
stories were based on interviews with lawyers, government officials,
and police representatives. To a far lesser degree, stories featured comments and interviews from the CWP, the Klan, and the Nazis and very
rarely from the residents of Morningside Homes.

What emerged from an analysis of the mainstream daily newspaper
articles covering the events of November 3, 1979, was a rhetoric of blame
that cast the responsibility of what happened that day on individual
actors, not systemic failures (Final Report, 2006, 327). Further, the CWP
protestors were essentially caricatured in news accounts, particularly in
the six months following the event. Quotes attributable to CWP members were most often used to reinforce the portrayal of them as "dogged
conspiracy theorists" (Final Report, 2006, 328). At the same time, the
police were regularly praised in editorials and news accounts. The focus
by the media on the Klan's and the Nazis' actions as well as the CWP
images served to deflect attention away from other actors in the drama,
including police informants (Final Report, 2006, 328).

The neglect of the bigger stories in which November 3 played itself
out was glaring. Stories on police informant and undercover operations, labor and worker rights, First Amendment rights, racial tensions,
and social unrest were barely cited in newspaper reports and all but
disappeared as the reporting continued to narrow in on event details
and trial-specific particulars.

In contrast to the coverage in the mainstream dailies, the weekly

African American newspaper coverage described the events through an analysis of parallel developments of racist violence around the country (Final Report, 2006, 328). There is no doubt that the coverage in the weekly African American newspaper generally assumed that the KKK and Nazis were responsible for the killings on November 3. Therefore, the articles most often probed the role of the police and questioned the relationships of the FBI and other law enforcement agencies to Greensboro, even before knowledge of informants was made public.

To sum up the effect of the media coverage, the commissioners' Final Report said it was evident that the daily newspapers routinely invoked language that viewed two "extremist" groups equally at fault for what happened on November 3, 1979. In the daily newspapers, the police and local government officials were not considered blameworthy. For the primarily white readers of the daily newspapers, the respected news sources for the community "framed" or emphasized the news in such a way that the protestors and white supremacists were responsible for the violence inflicted that day (Final Report, 2006, 329).

African American newspaper readers saw the event in another light in large part because of dissimilar media coverage. Blacks read stories suggesting the history of Klan violence was continuing in 1979, perhaps as a result of the complicit or silent actions of police and government agents.

From the two very different presentations in the media, community members who were divided along racial lines learned to understand and remember November 3, 1979, differently. The truth commissioners pointed out that the media fulfilled its minimum obligations to report (some of) the facts, but failed to engage the deeper concerns that affected Greensboro at the time, concluding:

> The media had the floor to question the assumptions of race and class privilege that informed the prevailing cultural and ideological practices. To the degree that the media failed to delve into these issues, there was a missed opportunity to discuss, inform the community, and engage the questions that lead people to talk and learn from a momentous event. (Final Report, 2006, 335)

Winston Cavin, a reporter on the scene in 1979 and still working in a newsroom in 2006, explained to the TRC at the second public hearing,

"I think the coverage has changed over the years ... Over time, people look at events in a different light. Reporters who initially looked for someone to blame have taken a longer view" (Final Report, 2006, 336).

Significance of November 3, 1979, in the Twenty-first Century

As they pondered the impact of November 3, the truth commissioners confirmed that the most dramatic impact was of course the killing of five anti-Klan protestors and the injuring of ten others on November 3 (Final Report, 2006, 340). In addition, they believed November 3 affected Greensboro in multiple other ways that persisted into the twenty-first century. The individual trauma was pervasive, including a paralyzing fear in the black community. Feelings of isolation, survivor guilt, interrupted careers, depression, existential suspicion, and a general sense of helplessness followed. There was also economic and social retaliation against CWP members and their associates. Many experienced job losses, distortion of reputations, strained personal relationships, and threats of personal violence. The surveillance of CWP members and other activists led to a deep loss of privacy and civil rights, as well as a lack of receptivity to their calls for social justice.

The community impact following November 3 was also felt deeply. A general distrust in the police, justice system, and media followed. For some, November 3 made crystal clear that the police did not and do not protect poor or black people, and that the police abused their powers. Further, people viewed the justice system as a sham, and that the media reflected the views of the power elite rather than providing an objective accounting of news. In addition, following November 3, there was an increased awareness of smoldering race, class, and power tensions in Greensboro. Attempts to create change then and later were far from welcomed, and instead attacked with a fierce force by those in power. Citizens interpreted the effects on labor and political organizing as a mini "red scare" that had a profound and long-lasting effect to stop further protests. The distrust of outsiders and denial of responsibility for community problems by City of Greensboro leaders was cemented. In other words, any trouble on the home front was for city leaders only possible when outsiders or people "not like us" imported discord into an otherwise calm, happy city. The truth commissioners noted a tacit approval of violence against political dissenters was used to protect the status quo. To rationalize these practices, the city leaders and police had to dehumanize people, run covert operations, and put into motion an all-out mobilization to protect their positions.

Despite the significant negative repercussions following November 3, there were some positive outcomes. The truth commissioners remarked that a strengthened resolve by some citizens for political activism emerged as well as a district system for diverse political representation in city elections, and the establishment of the Greensboro Justice Fund with awards of more than $500,000 to groups in the South working for peace and justice (Final Report, 2006, 365–366).

Final Report Recommendations

The Greensboro Truth and Reconciliation Commission concluded that while the litigation surrounding November 3, 1979, was completed in 1985 when the third civil trial awarded $351,500 to the protestors, the pain and moral issues were not as neatly resolved. The three trials accomplished what was possible within a severely limited realm of justice:

> The "retributive justice" model of the U.S. legal system confines judicial inquiries to the proof of a defendant's guilt (criminal cases) or liability (civil cases), under a narrowly defined set of laws and rules of procedure . . . The courtroom is the realm of technical knowledge and expertise, with little leeway for richness of context or consequences that surround wrongs. (Final Report, 2006, 378–379)

By looking at events such as November 3 more comprehensively, the truth commissioners argued that their process offered a different and important gaze at what happened and why with a more promising goal of reconciling the community.

> The promise of "transformative justice" is in drawing the community to the table to discuss what wrongs were done and to whom and by whom. Transformative justice also facilitates exchange of diverse perspectives on why these wrongs occurred and what should be done. In this way, transformative justice

[used interchangeably with the term restorative justice] works in concert with retributive justice, not as a repeat or replacement of it. (Final Report, 2006, 379)

The Final Report recognized that the consequences of November 3, 1979, were both immediate and enduring. The deaths and injuries were most visible, but also deeply felt were the fear and isolation among city residents that permeated virtually every aspect of social life. The lasting impact showed itself in a splintered populace, divided by race, education, economic hardship, and class tensions.

In the spirit of offering hope that reconciliation was still possible in a city racked by division, the Truth Commission recommended a host of suggestions for the citizens of Greensboro, the local government, and community organizations. They offered new ideas and resurrected old ones that had yet to be implemented.

The TRC urged that the city undertake *meaningful gestures of acknowledgment* such as issuing a City of Greensboro proclamation recognizing the significance of November 3, 1979, as a notable event in its civil rights history; offering individual apologies, publicly and/or privately, to those who were harmed; issuing a police public apology for failing to protect the public; making monetary contributions in the victims' names; creating exhibits about November 3, 1979, for inclusion in the Greensboro Historical Museum and International Civil Rights Museum; hosting public forums for the community to discuss the TRC Final Report; sponsoring a healing workshop or retreat hosted by the religious leaders of Greensboro; and, erecting a public monument on the site of the shootings to honor those killed and injured.

The TRC also recommended *reforming institutional practices in local government* by paying all city and county employees a living wage and requiring contractors and subcontractors to pay workers a living wage; providing antiracism training to all city and county employees, as well as Greensboro-based businesses; preparing annual reports on the state of race relations and racial disparities in the City of Greensboro; and continuing and expanding programs to build trust and cultural understanding among citizens in the community. The seven truth commissioners recommended as well the creation of a Citizens' Police Review Board and increased funding to the Departments of Social Services and Public Health who serve low-income residents.

With regard to *education,* the truth commissioners recommended creating a curriculum based on the events of November 3, 1979, for use in public elementary and secondary schools.[6] They also suggested establishing a community justice center in Greensboro to encourage the teaching and application of restorative justice approaches to community problem solving.

Other recommendations included enabling legislation to expand the pool of potential jurors to be more representative of the community; organizing a citywide citizen group to comment on news process, content, quality, and ethics; affirming and enhancing leadership skills among grassroots leaders; and providing open citizen forums for discussion of community issues or crises.

The TRC reasoned that *criminal justice and civil remedies* were needed. For instance, they urged local officials to complete investigations into current allegations of corruption in the Greensboro Police Department, including surveillance of citizens, with reports publicly released and a town hall meeting held for citizen comment and questions. They further recommended that appropriate criminal prosecutions and/or civil action be pursued to reassure citizens and repair the damage to the police department's credibility.

Most important to the TRC was the recommendation to *encourage citizen engagement* via study and dialogue groups for individuals to examine the ideologies and beliefs present in the community and to explore workable solutions to existing problems, and participation of residents in antiracism and diversity education programs to explore historical perspectives on power, privilege, oppression, and economic and social justice as well as the individual's role in society today.

The truth commissioners were excited, but humble in forecasting what the Final Report could accomplish. Its greatest contribution to the community was to be a catalyst for important conversations and public dialogue that could call attention to the systemic inequalities experienced by at least some community members.

CHAPTER 7

The Public's Response

The wisdom of this process lies in the recognition that it is not possible to build a healthy community at peace with itself unless past wrongs are acknowledged and brought out into the open so that the truth of what happened can be determined and social trust renewed through a process of forgiveness and reconciliation. A community in which there is no trust is ultimately not viable and gradually begins to tear itself apart.

—TIMOTHY MURITHI

THOUGH NO ONE expected Greensboro to be suddenly "reconciled" when the Final Report was released, the report was viewed as an essential stepping-stone toward community-wide awareness, understanding, and critical discernment of the past and the present. In this way, the Final Report was never intended to be a static document. Rather, it was conceived to be an ongoing community resource for reconciliation as its readers acknowledged the many hidden stories, facts, and consequences pointing to how our histories are ethically, politically, and culturally bound. The community did engage the TRC process and Final Report using varied and creative means. A dialogic space was carved out for a few large events scattered among many small group gatherings before the release of the Final Report and for several years afterward.

Duncan Bell (2008) writes on the politics of memory suggesting that myths often arise from simplified narratives told over time. These simple narratives offer fixed and coherent meanings but fail to account for the diversity of experience in the community. He argues that the solution is not to simply forward a counternarrative, but rather to recognize that most events of the past are the subject of conflicting interpretations. Thus, "In order to facilitate a pluralistic radical democracy, it is essential to acknowledge multiple and often conflicting pasts, and the intrinsically power-infused and tension-ridden nature of communal mythological construction" (Bell, 2008, 149). In this way, the interests of the community, as distinguished by various populations, special interests, and distinct neighborhoods, for instance, are given the opportunity to make legitimate claims about the past and its impact on the present. Over time, the TRC supporters reasoned, the truth of the past would be revealed like the peeling back of an onion, one layer at a time, as people continued to come forward to share insights, feelings, and stories.

The people who attended events to discuss the truth and reconciliation process were predisposed to seeing interconnections in the community, particularly with regard to how one event might influence others and how various aspects of city life affect one another. As well, the participants seemed to embrace the idea that while they may not have personally caused past misdeeds, they could see the value in a collective critique of the past of their city operations. For these community members, it made sense to consider their individual roles and the collective community's responsibility in responding to the information collected by the TRC and offered in the Final Report. Brian Weiner's work on national apologies in the United States offers a similar justification. He says, "The past does intrude into the present and future, individuals are rooted in the collective, and present-day citizens may share in the responsibility, although not the guilt, for deeds done long ago" (2005, 188).

A Rhetorical Toolkit for Social Change

On the discourse road to truth and reconciliation in Greensboro, a variety of methods were used to generate conversation. These methods formed the rhetorical toolkit for the TRC supporters with features common to the tenets of direct democracy and illustrative of the approach used by contemporary activists (Del Gandio, 2008). That is, the TRC process promoted diversity in thought, perspective, speech, and action. Putting diversity into practice meant that people of traditionally underprivileged or marginalized backgrounds were specifically encouraged to speak and contribute ideas at meetings and events that could reinvigorate deliberations with detail-rich, authentic experiences. When it was successful, discussions turned potential confrontations into a rhythm of responses that deepened the community relationships even if differences of opinion remained (Lingis, 1994). The most assured way of integrating new, personal insights into the TRC process was by sharing stories. To augment the storytelling process, a variety of conversation formats were also implemented and special events were planned.

LOCAL TASK FORCE

Building a core group of supporters was a vital first step in the TRC work, thus key constituent groups were invited into the dialogic fold, including faith-based leaders; college and university professors; labor organizers; neighborhood groups; college students and high school youth; political party representatives; and, nonprofit group leaders (Jovanovic et al., 2007). Committees planned meetings with custom-tailored agendas to appeal to the specific interests of these various groups. E-mail and word-of-mouth invitations were supplemented by list-serve announcements on Greensboro's Peace and Justice Network. Additionally, members of the Local Task Force were tapped for their personal contacts. After initial meetings with the specialty groups, new supporters were identified and invited to the Local Task Force working meetings while at the same time encouraged to continue subgroup meetings that commonly would remain intact for a period of three to five months.

The stable Local Task Force was the "home" site for volunteer supporters to speak and share ideas. The Local Task Force created a space—a dialogue safe house in effect—in which people were welcomed to participate as much or as little as they desired. To do their work, the TRC supporters extended open arms to as many people as they could reach.

Co-chair and former Greensboro mayor Carolyn Allen, a measured, confident, and generally quiet elder of the community, insisted that government and citizens working together provided Greensboro's best hope for a secure future in remarks shared at the TRC-hosted Community Dialogue on November 5, 2005:

> The City of Greensboro must continue to strive to hold onto [the fact] that we need *everybody*, not just "leaders." One of the values of the truth and reconciliation process has been that people *are*

coming forward and we *are* learning where the aches and pains are thanks to the dedication of the commissioners, the staff, our volunteers, and the Local Task Force. We haven't grown enough yet, but we can!

SPIRITED TALKS: WELCOMING AND CHALLENGING

Jacques Derrida comments on the necessity of the "welcome" that Levinas wrote so much about as a condition for ethical living and the possibility of ushering justice into the world (Levinas, 1969). "Discourse, justice, ethical uprightness have to do first of all with *welcoming*. The welcome is always a welcome reserved for the face" (Derrida, 1999, 35). What Derrida and Levinas wrote about, the Local Task Force put into action in their encounters with community members. The TRC supporters recognized that before a discussion of justice could ensue, there had to be desire and reason to invest time in relationships that transcended even the activity at hand.

The welcome was made concrete by the Local Task Force members in six distinct ways: (1) Meetings began with very short introductory comments followed by self introductions around the room with an invitation to also talk about what brought the person to the process; (2) References were regularly made to the spiritual dimension of truth and reconciliation, highlighting the need for all involved to be generous in thought, deed, and spirit; (3) New people were especially thanked for joining the conversation with personal contact by others before, during, and after the meetings; (4) Comments from "new" attendees were encouraged even when their comments covered ground previously addressed. The more seasoned participants expertly weaved the newcomers' ideas into the conversation seamlessly; (5) Seasoned supporters searched for ways to connect new people to the process by tapping into personal interests, job affiliation, and previous civic engagement activities; (6) Phone and e-mail contacts collected at each meeting ensured that new people were added to established lists for sharing information and announcements.

The main values communicated in the welcome and introduced in dialogue were collaboration, patience, persistence, and creativity. Conveying these values created the opportunity for supporters to introduce new activities and projects of their own design that could appeal to diverse audiences.

Though most of the activities were organized and implemented without much difficulty, interpersonal tensions did sometimes arise. Individual initiative had to operate alongside collective decision making for instance, and the community's youthful energy was encouraged even as it relied upon elder wisdom for guidance.

The twenty-fifth anniversary of November 3 in 2004 threatened to harm many of the relationships that had developed among the TRC supporters. In an effort to draw more African American supporters to the TRC process, an idea surfaced to hold a parade and march that would in essence complete the one never finished in 1979. Mostly white supporters were fearful that the march would not communicate a desire for reconciliation, and instead would be construed by the community as an unwanted rebellious action just as the truth commissioners were beginning their work to build the important relationships they needed in the community.

To address the divergent views on the twenty-fifth anniversary march, additional meetings were held for black and white supporters to discuss their perspectives at length. Through a time-intensive process that asked disagreeing people to continue to talk, the decision was finally made with near universal support to host the march. As it turned out, the march was successful in attracting a good number of African American community members, along with a more politically active crowd including civil rights leaders, NAACP representatives, progressive-minded youth, and labor organizers, many of whom had not previously been exposed to what happened on November 3.

Another event provoked hurt feelings among TRC supporters in April 2005. An esteemed community member affiliated with the Quakers offered to organize a community gathering of faith, prayer, and reconciliation at a local Baptist church to attract more white supporters to the truth and reconciliation process. Several others attending the Local Task Force meetings—blacks and whites—volunteered with the multicultural, intergenerational team that planned the event. The subgroup secured the keynote speaker, Dr. Peter Storey, for the program that also featured presentations by city officials, truth commissioners, singers, dancers, and musicians for an event that netted an attendance of more than two hundred people. The event was celebrated afterward, but also reviewed and critiqued by the Local Task Force for the way it both followed and violated democratic principles of inclusion and collective decision making. On the positive side, the processes of planning, implementation, and reflection were ongoing by all involved. On the negative side, there were several instances where decisions were made without adequate input. A particularly difficult situation arose when an older white male instructed a younger black male to manage the food serving function at the event. The racial implications of that directive, for blacks to serve whites, prompted hurt feelings and anger.

Philosopher Bettina Bergo's commentary on reflexive and critical interaction is what Levinas considered essential for justice: "Prophetism inaugurates a discourse of reflection and interrupts that discourse. This dual activity of informing and interrupting is difficult to grasp within the framework of political life," yet is so necessary to enact everyday democracy (1999, 254). The challenges of advancing toward a goal while taking time to review progress are compounded in part by our society's insatiable thirst to always move ahead without adequately assessing the path of pain or discomfort that is sometimes left behind. In fact, it is the lack of deliberate ruminations that contributed to the inability to have honest discussions about the events of November 3, 1979. Indeed, the progress narrative to "move on" is deeply entrenched in our ways of being, our organizational structures, and even our communicative behaviors. In response, the Local Task Force not once, but many times, took time out to discuss the difficult issues, like the ones just mentioned, that arose during the TRC work.

STORYTELLING AS DIALOGIC COURAGE

Storytelling or the sharing of narratives was a key communication strategy used to "fill in the gaps" of previous court records and media reports surrounding November 3. Greensboro's Truth and Reconciliation Commission encouraged public hearing presenters to prepare their remarks in advance, though it was not required. The much-anticipated stories of the Communist Workers Party members and survivors recounting the blame they shouldered for the community disruption was heart wrenching. The Klan testimony, too, was riveting, as it conveyed the hardships of growing up poor in the South.

The Morningside Homes residents, all but ignored in previous investigations, were well represented during the TRC public hearings. These residents told stories of how they found themselves in the midst of ideological sparring. From the establishment, they heard of misguided assumptions and practices. From the communists, they were bombarded with revolutionary rhetoric. From the Klan, they were exposed to perpetual racist violence. The residents affirmed that police action then was reserved to help white people, not blacks. It was no surprise then that in the aftermath of November 3, there was no counseling provided to Morningside Homes residents and no meetings with the police designed to help them recover from the trauma. Instead, there were lock-downs, curfews, and armed patrols of the area. The way the residents saw it, they were victims on November 3 and victims again in the aftermath. The expressions by the former Morningside Homes residents during the TRC process offered powerful evidence of the inequities that reigned in Greensboro in 1979. Blacks and whites worked in the textile mills under horrific conditions, but blacks had the worst of the worst jobs. The residents' connections between 1979 and the *current* inequitable conditions in the schools, on the streets, and in virtually every sector of life, were palpable.

Tammy Tutt, an African American woman who was living in Morningside Homes in 1979, was dressed in formal black attire and hat, of the kind she might have worn to a funeral, when she spoke at the TRC's public hearing with brute honesty:

> In 1979, racist people were able to come into a predominantly black community and launch an attack on people who were demonstrating in a peaceful way. And the community itself did not say a word. I can still see that happen today. I see crack houses, violent gun carriers, stores that sell drug paraphernalia, cigarettes sold to children, small grocery stores who sell forty ounces and no grocery or very little grocery, and red lining . . . These are small and present attacks that are going on in communities today. And still the police are not doing anything. The city officials are still sitting by. And the community is not saying a word. (Tutt, 2005)

Tutt's story showed that the victims of November 3 were not only the surviving protestors.

Winston Cavin, a twenty-six-year-old reporter for the *Greensboro Daily News* on November 3, was assigned a story he would never forget. He had spoken often in the intervening years about the tragedy, including at a media forum at the University of North Carolina at Greensboro in April 2004.[1] However, he told the truth commissioners he had never revealed the more personal loss he withstood until his testimony to them. Something about the format and approach taken by the TRC allowed the more private details of his experience to be finally shared.

> I heard screams everywhere. Gunfire. Screams. Gunfire. Screams. Engines gunning as the shooters fled, that eerie silence. I could smell gunpowder in the air and heard the groaning of people who were dying. I was in shock but did what many people do after surviving or witnessing a tragedy: I went on automatic pilot. I ran across the street to the courtyard, scribbling notes like mad as I tried to comprehend what was happening. People were screaming, crying. There were bloody victims lying on the ground. A woman was cradling her husband's head in her arms, and there were the sounds of people gurgling their last breaths, unable to speak . . . I've suffered survivor guilt along with other psychological affects including anger and profound sadness . . . Over the years I've realized that assigning blame is too simple to be true. I hoped to find some reconciliation within myself as part of this process. (Cavin, 2005)

As he concluded his story, Cavin wiped away the tears he had held back from the public for more than twenty years.

For widowed Marty Nathan, speaking at the TRC hearings was a pivotal moment among many she had had since November 3 in paying tribute to the life of her husband of only a year at the time, Michael Nathan. At the TRC hearings, she took her seat on stage, visibly shaking but comforted by the gentle touches of her longtime husband, Elliot Fratkin. She could not help but cry as she recounted the story of the changes to her life following November 3, including having to care for her grieving mother-in-law. Nathan said she also had to bear the responsibility of tending to a six-month-old baby daughter who grew up without knowing her biological father. In addition to her own grief, and caretaking responsibilities, Nathan explained that she was called upon by friends and community members to be strong as they mourned the death of an affable, compassionate doctor who tended to the ills of poor children in his community:

> The papers and the courts were filled with stories describing how foreign and threatening we the victims were. I knew that my friends and I were neither foreign nor threatening, just jobless, impoverished, frightened and grieving. I went to bed every night unable to sleep, fearing that my small family's house would be firebombed or the windows would be shot into. We had chosen this house with these huge picture windows because we loved light; boy did I regret that. I lived off of Mike's social security ... try to put yourselves, just for a moment, in our position, and imagine not only that your loved ones and friends are brutally and very publicly murdered, but society openly and legally condones it. Our expectations of decency and justice had been raised, and our resulting sense of alienation and hopelessness was deep. (Nathan, 2005)

Nathan turned her story of grief into a lifelong mission to expose the truth. She explained to the truth commissioners, "You can't replace those brilliant young lost lives, but you can tell the world the truth, and tell our society how to prevent this from ever happening again." Nathan was hopeful that the TRC's Final Report would influence police policies and the citizen monitoring of police activities to protect not attack expressions of dissent and social justice as noble actions befitting a real democracy.

As audience members openly wept upon hearing stories like Tutt's, Cavin's, and Nathan's, they learned very personal details of the lives ravaged by November 3. The stories, rich with factual detail and charged emotions, had the effect of transforming a distant event into a moment of dialogic sharing.

CONVERSATION SPACES

The TRC supporters recognized that what was crucial for affecting a cultural change in the community was creating varied conversational spaces for spontaneous, informal talks, as well as structured discussions, lectures with questions and answers, and even cyber talks.[2] Informal discussions did not take place in designated conference rooms or auditoriums, but in the streets, in local coffee shops, and at neighborhood gatherings. As a result, the supporters discussed at a 2006 Local Task Force meeting how they could initiate talk in barbershops, hair salons, and other places of public gathering that would be important to members of the community who might not attend more formal events.

In fact, one of these conversations was captured on film for the movie, *Greensboro: Closer to the Truth* (Zucker, 2008), when young and older men in a shoe-shining store recalled a city leader years back who frequented the shop. When they later saw a Klan march go by, the city leader's face was covered by a robe, but his recognizable shiny shoes were visible. The men in the shop agreed it was time that the city faced its past and forge reconciliation.

In addition to the spontaneous talks, efforts were made to encourage groups to study the report. The TRC supporters believed that the discussions could be robust in reading groups, religious institutions, college and university communities, high school clubs and classes, neighborhood groups, and civic organizations.

Public, academic-based lectures were also organized. An educator list-serve was developed to facilitate the sharing of teaching and learning ideas.

Most of the work of the TRC supporters was accomplished in face-to-face encounters but computer technology was also used vigorously. Young people established a Facebook presence for the TRC and other social networking sites were used to facilitate questions, conversations, and recommendations.

The blogging community was active as well, with threads maintained by the TRC staff on their Web site. Over time, some city officials used their own blogs to comment on the TRC process and the daily newspaper's numerous blogs featured commentary by a range of community members.

COMMUNITY INFORMATION SESSIONS

In May and June 2006, immediately following the release of the Final Report, eight "Community Information Sessions" were hosted on Tuesday and Thursday evenings for residents to ask questions, air concerns, and consider others' views of the TRC process and its products. Each session was facilitated by at least two volunteers with the Local Task Force. The sessions were conceived as two-hour open house formats, where people could flow in and out as their schedules permitted. Instead, the attendees in every session arrived at the beginning time and stayed late to talk about the Final Report. The sessions—averaging nine people—drew a total of seventy-three participants to discuss among other topics, next steps in the truth and reconciliation process, the quality and content of blogs and media reports, a frank consideration of what truth means, and an exploration of what apologies could accomplish. The overarching theme that emerged from the discussions was that the Final Report, concerned as it was for social justice, was a valuable tool and bridge to the city leaders' focus on economic development.

INTERNATIONAL TRUTH AND RECONCILIATION CONFERENCE

Two months after the release of the report, in July 2006, an International Truth and Reconciliation conference was hosted in Greensboro, North Carolina, bringing together forty people from U.S. cities and countries from five continents. With help from the International Center for Transitional Justice, consultants to Greensboro's TRC process, representatives from South Africa, Peru, Northern Ireland, and Sri Lanka met with attendees from Rosewood, Florida; Abbeville, South Carolina; the state of Mississippi; Moore's Ford, Georgia; Tewa Puebla, New Mexico; and New Orleans, Louisiana, among other locales, to compare processes and notes on reconciliation efforts underway in their cities and countries. The conference attendees detailed some of their struggles with advancing justice based on the truth telling of their specific historical episodes.

As part of that three-day conference, a Saturday morning session was opened up to the Greensboro public entitled, "The Local Search for the Truth." Black and white members of the community filled more than sixty-five chairs to hear from the conference participants on the importance of recognizing how different kinds of violence are related, the prominence of grassroots organizing, and the importance of reclaiming the dimensions of democracy that encourage citizen action for justice. Among the many lessons gleaned that day was one voiced by a young African American college student in Greensboro who said, "We have to put the information in the [Final] Report into our hearts and do the work of reconciliation." That is, he was not looking or waiting for signs of formal reconciliation, but instead asking others to embrace the everyday opportunities that present themselves to forge new relationships grounded in respect and honesty.

A YEAR-LONG SERIES OF COMMUNITY FORUMS

As had been planned from the beginning, the year following the release of the report was devoted to planning and hosting five community-wide forums, each focused on a section of the Final Report for citizen comment and reaction. The first of these forums commenced in December 2006 and the final one was held November 3, 2007. More than one hundred people attended each event. The first discussion covered "What Brought Us to November 3rd" by focusing conversation on the introduction and methodology used in the Final Report. The second forum examined the sequence of events surrounding November 3, while the third forum examined what happened after November 3. The fourth community-wide forum focused on the overall conclusion and recommendations in the report in preparation for the fifth and final community meeting, which mobilized concerned citizens into working groups to implement selected recommendations from the TRC report.

COLLEGE CLASSROOM INSTRUCTION

The work of the community was helped by the efforts of faculty and students throughout the area. It was in classes that the most systematic study of the Final Report occurred with the reading linked to classroom instruction and assignments.[3] Some instructors used collaboratively developed study guides[4] to facilitate conversation among readers, while others linked the report to additional course readings on democracy, forgiveness, and social protest.

A workshop was developed for college faculty to provide a range of examples of how other professors had integrated the work of the TRC into their classrooms. The TRC staff promoted the workshop through a 2005 letter of invitation, recognizing the many opportunities the research provided to educators:

> The multifaceted work offers real-world opportunities to increase understanding about such issues as violence, justice, police-community relations, politics, hate groups, labor, race and class. Educators at colleges, universities and law schools around the country have taken advantage of the opportunity and the Commission has benefited from the service-learning work of numerous students.

Thus, the reach to young adults with this newly documented information was potentially quite large. For many of those students who graduated from the public K–12 schools in the area, the history of November 3 as revealed through the TRC process was brand new. That is, there is not one reference in North Carolina history curriculum about November 3, 1979, an event that left five people dead in the streets, involved more than five years of judicial activity, occupied headlines in stories spanning three decades, and injured an entire city's social infrastructure. When some students did learn of the events and the TRC process in college classrooms, they joined the effort to infuse their own youthful, creative sparks into the public conversations and learn from a generation of activists who had witnessed an era gone by.

Adam Eaglin, in 2007 a senior at Duke University, expressed his dismay at having to go to college to learn the history of his native Greensboro. In a newspaper article written for Greensboro's *News & Record,* he said:

> As someone who grew up in Guilford County, it's upsetting to realize that I gained only a shallow understanding of the sometimes-violent events that shaped my hometown ... If we, as a city and county, expect to raise children with a genuine engagement with the community, they need to know their history—the good and the bad ... By excluding the topic from our schools, we also institutionalize ignorance about the entrenched racism and harmful sentiments that Nov. 3 revealed. (June 13, 2007, A-11)

The college student urged the county's school board to integrate specific teaching and activities about November 3 into the curricula, against the protestations of the board's staff that it lacked resources to make local events part of classroom instruction.

Students did not stop with just asking for change, they took action. One college group that studied the report in a communication class at UNCG developed a five-day and alternative three-day curriculum on November 3 for eighth graders. Their curriculum guide included an overview of the tragedy and a fifteen-word vocabulary list including words such as reconciliation, racism, civil rights, and labor unions. The students developed a simple event timeline, discussion questions, mock quizzes, and activity guidelines for oral history presentations. The college students also created a crossword puzzle and bingo game to go along with field trip suggestions.

Another college group prepared materials useful for discussing November 3 and the Final Report in other college classes. They developed discussion questions and a series of journal entry prompts to encourage students to write about their views of media representations and activists in the community. They identified guest speakers and assignments for newspaper analyses, oral history collection, and remembrance ceremonies.

Other college students developed conversation circle guides with information packets highlighting the essential information from the Final Report for participants and a theatrical reading of the perspectives of those involved in November 3 to reinforce the TRC's position that understanding comes in hearing the stories of everyone involved. Students researched and then prepared scripts they read from to play the part of someone in the CWP, the Klan and Nazis, Morningside Homes, the Greensboro Police Department, the FBI, elected officials, and the media to detail each of their views surrounding the events of November 3.

Other suggestions and projects surfaced from college students including dramatic readings, dance performances, trial reenactments, audio walking tours, and painting exhibits. Perhaps the most talked-about college production was a spoken word written and performed by UNCG students under the direction of Alicia Sowisdral that drew tears from the audience members, including some of the truth commissioners. The stand-up, fiery oration critiqued textile mill life where workers faced difficult conditions and low wages that perpetuated a slave mentality so prominent in the South. Pointing out how young black men continue to be targeted by law enforcement and denied educational advancement, the hip-hop style poetry described how those conditions set the stage for November 3, the violence that followed, and the concealment of vital information that would have exposed a lasting system of injustice. The spoken word concluded with a call to "let this tragedy birth a new life, one of fairness and equality instead of suffering and strife" in the hopes of building a more just future.[5]

In the fall semester of 2006 following the release of the Final Report, more than three hundred college students at the University of North Carolina at Greensboro and Guilford Technical Community College were assigned to read what the Truth and Reconciliation Commission wrote about their community. Since then, courses at those same institutions as well as North Carolina A & T University, Guilford College, Bennett College, Greensboro College, and Elon University have used all or parts of the Final Report for courses in departments of philosophy, conflict resolution, community and justice studies, religious studies, sociology, political science, communication studies, and history.

ARTISTIC EXPRESSIONS

Responses to the TRC emerged in various forms of artistic expressions. Paintings, theatrical productions, original music, concerts, and poetry were among the many creative efforts launched to inspire discussion about November 3.

One of the most poignant visual art displays that emerged was a series of paintings by Guilford College student Aliene de Souza Howell. Her richly colored and textured renderings, some standing over six feet tall and exhibited at The Green Bean coffeehouse in downtown Greensboro, both reflected and evoked the emotions associated with November 3.[6] Aliene recounted:

> The more I found out about the Greensboro Massacre, the more I just sat, stunned, in disbelief. I needed to be involved with this, to do something towards change. I began volunteering at the Truth and Reconciliation Project, which was really inspiring because I was working around the survivors . . . I began painting

like I never painted before . . . I felt like a part of the story.
(Howell, 2005)

Aliene combined her volunteer experience with the TRC process with research and interviews to prepare herself to paint.

Scott Pryor, a Guilford College alum and former staff member with the Beloved Community Center working to launch the TRC, was among the singers, songwriters, and poets who performed at a 2005 concert. Tickets cost $25 for "Three Chords and the Truth: An Evening of Grassroots Music to Benefit the Greensboro Truth and Reconciliation Commission." Pryor's songs, delving into what he imagined were the views of the Klan, Nazis, police, and protestors, were intended to bring the community together through song.

Jean Rodenbough, a retired Presbyterian minister and writer, was a supporter of the truth and reconciliation effort, who came to the process later than most when she moved to Greensboro in 2005. But as she learned of the TRC, she listened carefully and crafted poetry in response. "Morning" is one of her works that linked the past to the present as a reminder that hope persists even in tragedy:

> Morning foretells death at noon.
> At Morningside, life is still—transfixed,
> afternoon arrives uninvited
> to the blood-stained street.
> Shouts linger, sorrow and hatred mingle.
> Mourning follows.
>
> How long does it take to forget?
> To erase spilled blood steeped into indelible memories?
> Weeping will linger. We remember.
>
> November is a cruel month
> when passions clash and justice
> goes on trial. All the struggles
> seem wasted. Even night
> cannot assuage the day.
>
> We mourn them, Jim and César, Mike,
> Sandi, Bill, for lives lost but not goals

which lead us by their purpose
through new times and new wrongs.

Years later: hope tiptoes in cautiously,
then boldly, as a community looks back
and defines the truth in order to reconcile.
Morning must come through the sunlight
of new things dreamed of, not yet
the joy of promise and fulfillment,
only a song heard in the distance.
Take heart, take courage, take hope.
Morning will come, will come indeed.

The TRC supporters were hopeful that the meaning of the report would be illustrated in ways "beyond words" or in ways more creative than typical prose allows.

STUDENT CONFERENCE BLENDS YOUTH ENERGY WITH ELDER WISDOM

In 2007 another community event was organized to encourage sustained dialogue and designed to attract young adults into the circle of support for truth and reconciliation efforts. College students from three area schools joined together to host a conference. The elder advisory team included Joyce Johnson, one of the organizers of November 3, and two professors. Knowing that older, more experienced hands could tip the scales of meaningful participation away from the students, the older adults were constantly monitoring their own actions. The point was to encourage youth involvement not direct it. By the time the conference was held, the students had learned how to solicit papers through national list-serves, organize workshops, and schedule creative performances from community members and academics around the country in con-current sessions. Among the highlights of the day were cash prize awards to the top presentations, attendance by city dignitaries, and the creation of a collective art project named the Peace Pole. Participant evaluations showed 75 percent of those in attendance planned to get involved in other community activities or work for social change in their home communities, demonstrating how a process like the TRC, one relevant to a wide range of community interests, can propel young people to counter the sometimes public apathy toward civic engagement.

Students learned the fundamentals of event planning and fundraising, grappled with the collaboration and communication obstacles that arose, shepherded eighty-five people through a full day of engagement with and discussion surrounding Greensboro's attempts for truth and reconciliation, and they discovered as well how others were applying concepts of truth and reconciliation to contemporary issues involving race, sexuality, immigration, and gang violence.

In planning the special events and convening community dialogues, the charge put before the organizers was to encourage as many people to speak as possible. This was seen as a much more important goal than the actual number of attendees.

REPORT RECEIVER DISCUSSIONS

More than sixty reading groups, political action organizations, church groups, and an array of other organizations agreed in advance to receive the TRC's Final Report and discuss it with their members. This outreach strategy by the TRC exemplified the varied and creative ways it was determined to engage the public. One such group, with seven readers, ranging in age from forty-five to seventy-five, met biweekly in the living room of a retired sociologist and therapist. The gatherings featured an around-the-room response style where each person shared his or her notes, feelings, and thoughts concerning the section of the report under discussion. One participant who had only lived in Greensboro four years said she could feel the fragmentation in the community and was compelled to participate in the reading group because she wanted to affect change. "I want to contribute to creating a different, positive force in the city. I was always pushing against something. Now I want to work on formations to provide positive examples of the changes we want to see." Since then, she has launched a monthly dialogue series in coffee and book shops throughout Greensboro to discuss critical community issues, nourish new ideas, and inspire possibilities for collective action.

DOCUMENTARY FILM SCREENING, *GREENSBORO: CLOSER TO THE TRUTH*

In April 2007, the documentary *Greensboro: Closer to the Truth* premiered at the city's downtown historic Carolina Theatre, an event heavily promoted by the supporters of the TRC. Tickets priced at $15 were purchased by more than two hundred in attendance that night to view the movie many had seen being filmed over the previous years. Since its release, the film has been shown repeatedly in college classrooms in Greensboro and at film festivals and community gatherings across the country to illustrate how one community revisited an unresolved chapter of its history. In 2009, *The Closer to the Truth Project* was launched featuring a facilitation and dialogue guide to be used with the film in communities wanting to deepen the work of social justice organizations, promote community healing, and foster greater civic participation among marginalized residents.

FAITH-BASED VIGILS

The roots of the TRC process were firmly planted in the houses of prayer all around Greensboro, and perhaps no more so than in the Beloved Community Center and Faith Community Church where November 3 organizer Reverend Nelson Johnson was the leader. Along with Quaker meeting sites, African American churches, Presbyterian ministries, Jewish temples, and other faith-based organizations, a number of spiritual gatherings were organized to study the Final Report. In some cases, overtures were made among white and black congregations to study the report together, modeling the need for understanding based on diverse views that the TRC Final Report recommended. Though these events were steeped in religion, they were publicized to the larger community with invitations issued to all, regardless of faith affiliation.

Collective Reflections

In 2008, more work continued with the support of the Beloved Community Center, one of the organizing entities of the Greensboro Truth and Community Reconciliation Project, and the leadership of the Local Task Force. In the fall of that year, a celebratory dinner with forty invited guests was held to reflect on the accomplishments of the truth process to date. Dr. Anthony Wade, the new executive director of the City of Greensboro's Human Relations Commission, attended with greetings from the mayor and other city officials. He said he was there to "pay homage to the work of the truth and reconciliation committee and the continuing efforts to bring healing to the community" (personal communication, October 17, 2008).

Foremost among those accomplishments was reclaiming the dignity and humanity of the survivors who had been blamed for so many years for the violence that ensued on November 3. Reverend Z Holler, Local Task Force co-chair, noted that the process challenged those long-held beliefs about the survivors. He said, "The beautiful thing I have observed and been a part of is a change in the attitude of the community toward the 1979 victims. They are now appreciated and respected." Survivor Signe Waller Foxworth concurred. She said, "When I testified, I appreciated being able to tell my story as I wanted. I was respected and listened to." Local Task Force co-chair Reverend Gregory Headen spoke of his feelings in ways that prompted nods of agreement around the room: "The entire truth and reconciliation project has been an inspiration for my life. There have been some hard places, but we prevailed. I had no idea that our work would have such influence all over the world."

Staff member Joe Frierson, a young African American male in his twenties, had recently returned to work with the GTCRP after taking a several-year hiatus to attend graduate school and work elsewhere. On that same night that Reverend Headen looked back with pride and forward with anticipation, Frierson recapped for all the process of the last many years:

> In 2002, the project began. We did it together, first drafting a declaration for truth and reconciliation and then preparing a mandate to guide the work of the TRC. We installed the first TRC of its kind in the United States. That would be the first of many hard roads to cross. Seven truth commissioners worked for two years with young people, elders, and all segments of the community. We are so proud of them ... When this all started, I had just graduated from North Carolina A & T State University and didn't

know the deep rooted causes, contexts, reasons, and doubts about November 3rd, 1979. But now, if you ask a graduating senior from A & T, UNCG, or Guilford College, they know about November 3rd. We're now sharing the truth with our youth community. (personal communication, October 17, 2008).

After Frierson, one participant after another rose to speak, and in doing so the enthusiasm in the room grew with remembrances, accomplishments, and challenges still to come.

Civil rights attorney for the widows and survivors, Lewis Pitts, said, "I have a feeling of hope that we can overcome the hostility that was in this community . . . My hope is that we can really begin to use words like labor, labor unions, and democracy to discuss our economy and our government" (personal communication, October 17, 2008).

Reverend Nelson Johnson concluded with praise that would be echoed by still others that night and again at future gatherings:

> I'm filled with the spirit of gratitude for how this journey has gone . . . If someone had told me a TRC in the United States would work, I'm not sure I would have believed it. But we had that. We worked to help gain the footing and dignity the process deserved, and to speak out. Greensboro is now poised to become a moral and justice capital. (personal communication, October 17, 2008).

From the issuance of the Declaration of Intent in January 2003 to the end of 2007 when the final "official" community dialogue was held, and into subsequent years, more than ten thousand people in Greensboro participated in some way with the truth-seeking process. Many attended strategy meetings over many years, some viewed the installation of the truth commissioners or witnessed the presentation of the Final Report, five thousand signed petitions asking the city council to support the work of the TRC, hundreds attended documentary film showings on November 3 and the truth process, and many more attended one or the series of public hearings and religious, educational, cultural, and other events supporting truth and reconciliation. For Signe Waller Foxworth, the involvement of so many people is proof positive that democracy depends upon and is inspired by diverse views and involvement of a community's members. Looking back on what transpired, she said to an audience at the University of

North Carolina at Greensboro on the occasion of the Center for Critical Inquiry's symposium on "Race, Personal History and Public History" in September 2008:

> It is one of the most democratic processes—perhaps the most democratic process—this city has ever seen . . . The Greensboro Truth and Reconciliation Commission completed its work in May 2006 with the publication of their mandated report, but the truth and reconciliation process continues . . . Racism and economic inequality plague us still, in many respects worse than a few decades ago. Capitalism, today globalized and dominated by a ruthless neo-liberal ideology, has enslaved, dispossessed, and starved most of the earth's people.

As promising as the TRC process was, Waller Foxworth added that perhaps she should have done even more. She said she and her companions "failed to be critical enough of the role of the modern nation-state in both capitalist and communist countries, both of which cry out for democratic reform." The Greensboro TRC process for her, as it was for the other survivors, the truth commissioners, and supporters in Greensboro and around the world, a step toward the democracy they envisioned where people speak out for truth and for the importance of forging reconciliation in communities divided.

Thirtieth Anniversary Celebration

The thirtieth anniversary and commemoration in November 2009 was the first large tribute after the release of the TRC Final Report. Four days and evenings of events were devoted to (1) Healing for personal and social transformation; (2) The advancement of workers, immigrants, and communities organizing for economic justice; and, (3) Truth and reconciliation today. The multiday program included workshops, guest speakers, art exhibits, original musical compositions, visitors from truth commissions organizing or operating elsewhere in the South, along with celebratory moments and awards.

Preparations for the thirtieth anniversary began six months earlier with approximately a dozen people meeting weekly and close to sixty people attending selected evening planning sessions. As was the case when the TRC project began, supporters and participants included students from North Carolina A & T, Guilford College, and UNCG, clergy and churchgoers, city government officials, representatives of the Local Task Force of the Greensboro Truth and Community Reconciliation Project, planning committee members, interested community members not affiliated with any particular organization, and people representing co-sponsoring organizations. For chief organizer Signe Waller Foxworth, the large crowds demonstrated a lively interest by the community to engage with the pressing social issues of the times. Survivors Marty Nathan, Sally and Paul Bermanzohn, Lucy Lewis, and others traveled some distance to be at the commemorative events, as they so often had previously done.

Revealing History

In February 2010, the International Civil Rights Museum opened, fifty years to the day after the 1960 Sit-In Movement was launched in Greensboro. Amid record low temperatures, hundreds turned out to witness the ribbon-cutting celebration, participate in a march from North Carolina A & T University to the museum's front doors, and to take the guided tour there, which moves people between two floors of exhibits as it tells the story of the Greensboro Four, and selected other civil rights actions in the United States and around the world. Interactive displays, "the hall of shame," original lunch counter stools, reenactment scenes leading up to the sit-ins, and a wall of remembrance are among the exhibits that museum-goers see in a forty-minute volunteer-guided group tour of the 30,000 square foot facility. Though the Greensboro sit-ins are the highlight of the museum, more time and space is devoted to other civil rights actions in America and around the world.

There is no mention, however, of the Greensboro Massacre in the struggle to achieve civil rights—not on the tour, in the museum, or on the museum's Web site. Deemed too controversial and violent for a museum touting the success of a nonviolent protest, November 3 was once again left out of Greensboro's "official" telling of its history.

This condition, say supporters of the TRC, upholds an image of Greensboro that is incomplete. Though Greensboro today takes great pride in the Sit-In Movement, it continues to deny struggles that were not so neatly packaged, like November 3.

Efforts like the Greensboro TRC provide a platform from which to talk openly and honestly about the community's vision, one cognizant of a past not always so glorious in hopes of crafting a future much brighter. The goal, TRC supporters say, is not to cast blame, but rather to influence city structures and community attitudes toward a peace and justice sensibility. The TRC was an exercise in democracy intended to showcase the voices of citizens' collective desire for justice. Even as problems in Greensboro remain, as they do in virtually every community across America, hope is grounded in what can emerge in vigorous dialogue inclusive of all people. With a more honest look at the past as well as the present, proponents argue that progressive changes can gain the necessary momentum to overcome obstacles and hurdles, prejudices and entrenched patterns, to communicate new, healthier values for a diverse society.

There was a fluidity to the movement of people involved in the TRC effort. That is, some stayed active and involved throughout, but far more chose to be involved for a limited time before moving onto other endeavors. For instance, for two to three years, one very active retired male attended three to four meetings per week. He developed partnerships with college youth, church leaders, and city officials. Eventually, though, he decreased his time at the TRC meetings and increased his involvement with the local affordable housing organization where he became chairman of the board. Still, this active community member returned to support major TRC events, as did most others who had been touched by the grassroots process. Another supporter, a retired physician, was likewise very involved in earlier planning meetings, but in time shifted his leadership abilities to another group that was advocating for the elimination of smoking in public buildings.

Just as people moved from the TRC to other projects for social justice, the TRC project also turned its focus toward other community concerns. Individuals and the larger organization located themselves in efforts to raise the minimum wage, to improve the achievement of African American males in school, and to support factory workers wishing to unionize at a nearby meat-packing company. And, when a racially motivated fight broke out at a local college, the participants of the TRC process immediately convened a series of community dialogues to discuss how to lend support to the school, the victims, and the larger community.

The many outreach efforts that one or more of the TRC supporters launched allowed for a "menu" of activities to effectively connect with one new audience after another. Not every supporter participated in every event, which reflected a process by which a larger concern for truth and reconciliation could make way for differing approaches to getting there. What did remain consistent was a commitment to educate and share the possibilities of truth and reconciliation in such a way that other people could speak freely about November 3.

CHAPTER 8

The Politics of an Apology

The past does intrude into the present and future, individuals are rooted in the collective, and present-day citizens may share in the responsibility, although not the guilt, for deeds done long ago.

—BRIAN A. WEINER

EVEN THOUGH 79 percent of the Greensboro citizens surveyed early in the process expressed support for a TRC to examine the events and consequences of November 3, most of the city's elected leaders held firmly to the belief that little good could come from a reexamination and discussion of that tragic event.[1] When the Final Report was issued, a community call was sounded for a public apology from the Greensboro city council. This chapter provides a glimpse into the politics of securing such a statement in the face of continuing opposition. The apology was finally made thirty years after November 3 and three years after the release of the TRC's Final Report.

A few city council members, city staff, and police officers read the Final Report, some read the abbreviated Executive Summary, but most did not read anything published by the TRC. With pressure from the community, Mayor Keith Holliday hosted a special session in July 2006 to discuss the Final Report. The council members convened in a conference room in city hall, sitting at a table that was surrounded by citizens barred from speaking, but there to witness the conversation. The mayor called on each council member present to contribute remarks in what he called a roundtable session; some did so by reading prepared remarks, others spoke extemporaneously, and two city council members did not utter a word. At the end of the seventy-five-minute session, Mayor Holliday suggested a statement of regret might be in order, but not an apology. He directed the Human Relations Commission to study the Final Report and make recommendations for action to the city council.

Nearly a year later, when no tangible work or response had come from the city, black councilwoman Goldie Wells asked that her fellow council members uphold their promise to publicly address the recommendations of the TRC Final Report. In addition to the directive Mayor Holliday had issued to the Human Relations Commission, Wells had introduced a resolution to rescind the opposition vote to the TRC process that was taken on April 19, 2005. That resolution was soundly rejected. It would later be revealed that Mayor Holliday, anticipating Wells's move, had talked privately with enough city council members to secure a majority vote that would for a second time oppose the TRC with an announcement that no follow-up action on the TRC's Final Report would be planned after all. Eighteen months after the original commitment to study the Final Report, Mayor Holliday was leaving public office and *no* action had been taken by any city entity in response to the TRC process.

Despite these setbacks, the TRC supporters' spirits were lifted by the fall 2007 local election that brought about a sea change—new city leaders were voted in and for the first time, an African American was elected mayor. Mayor Yvonne Johnson, one of the TRC's most visible supporters, became only the second woman to occupy that seat of honor.[2] Yvonne Johnson had been and remained a devout supporter of the TRC, seeing it as a viable avenue to needed reconciliation in the city.

After only a few months in her new position as mayor, Yvonne Johnson directed city staff and the Human Relations Commission to provide a response to the TRC process. From that, a fifteen-member committee was convened to read the TRC Final Report along with two other administrative reports written in 1980. The participation on that committee would eventually dwindle to a mere handful of people who drafted a position paper for city council consideration. That the committee was assigned to read more than the TRC Final Report was in all likelihood a political compromise to the officials who were still opposed to the work of the TRC. For unlike the comprehensive nature of the TRC Final Report, the two 1980-dated reports were incomplete—they lacked the crucial information of undercover operatives and prior knowledge by the Greensboro Police Department of the Klan and Nazi plans for November 3—those were facts that would not become public knowledge until the 1985 civil trial and in the TRC's Final Report.

The local election victory, coupled with the long-awaited action by the Human Relations Commission, demonstrated that the City of Greensboro was at last engaging with the TRC process. The change in the political landscape sparked by the supporters of the TRC showed how change was made possible by community members who lead and by leaders who (sometimes) follow.

In June 2009, three years after the release of the TRC Final Report, the Human Relations' task force presented its report to the city council for adoption. The council chamber was full with TRC supporters mainly, on the night of the presentation. Reverend Nelson Johnson was there, along with Z Holler, Joe Frierson, Signe Waller, Lewis Pitts, Kay Lovelace, Vance Arnold, and others who had devoted time to the work of the Local Task Force. There were also members present from the Human Relations Commission and the Commission on the Status of Women, both volunteer boards that extend the work of the city's Human Relations Department.

When the Human Relations Commission made its presentation, Dr. Abdel Nuriddin, vice chair, spoke of what he termed a "milestone event" for the city council to finally address the events of November 3. He believed that though a long list of city-sponsored programs convened through the years to dismantle racism, more effort was required by the City of Greensboro to ensure that fairness and justice became commonplace:

> If we want to be honest, there has to be changes of heart to create what we want. This [November 3, 1979] is just *not* going to go away. We can take a step here, moving in the right direction that will cause us to be a city where we are honest with one another so that we can be happy that we've made some progress.

Nuriddin completed his opening remarks by saying, "The responsibility is now in your hands. We've done what we can. Tonight, what you do will not totally satisfy everyone in the City of Greensboro, but it can be a step in the right direction."

The floor was turned over to Human Relations Commission chair

Maxine Bateman who presented the six official recommendations of her committee to the city council:

1. Issue the proposed statement of regret acknowledging the events and loss of lives that occurred in November 3, 1979 to address the critique that the City of Greensboro never acknowledged what happened in 1979.

2. Practice transparency regarding city government matters via public forums.

3. Utilize all media outlets for dissemination of city information to maximize community outreach efforts.

4. Reduce the perception of distrust by making all the documents related to November 3, 1979 available for wide public review.

5. Ensure that all city residents feel safe no matter where they live by providing equity in police services.

6. Take a conscious and deliberate position to prevent the exploitation of certain groups through information sharing and public deliberation.

The recommendations directly connected the consequences of November 3, 1979, to the lingering mistrust and unequal access to resources that continued in the City of Greensboro as documented by a State of Human Relations report on residents' experiences with prejudicial behavior and discrimination (City of Greensboro, 2008). The Human Relations Commission's report added, "There remains a distrust of City government and the police among Greensboro residents that must be addressed to improve race relations" (Greensboro Human Relations Commission, 2009, 2). Many audience members applauded the statement of regret but noted that it was far weaker than the hoped-for bold statement of apology.

Z Holler called for the city council to summon up the courage "to share our stories in all honesty . . . and acknowledge our own attitudes and actions in relation to the November 3 tragedy—with no excuses, no rationalizing or blaming others—just our part as flawed members of a flawed human race." In other words, Z Holler called on the leaders of Greensboro to build upon the positive truth-telling features that the TRC engaged in by responding in like fashion with open, honest, and frank talk. He concluded by saying, "It's time to look at it [November 3], and it's time to tell the world that we intend to be a city that respects all of its citizens."

Signe Waller Foxworth expressed appreciation for the work of the Human Relations Commission but was critical that its report failed to address the accountability of the police and the City of Greensboro in the events that unfolded on and after November 3. She said, "If there's no accountability for the past, there cannot be accountability for the present. Today, we're seeing police abuse against street organizations called gangs—they are unmercifully hounded by police."

An Episcopal priest concurred that the TRC's final report was "a gift." He said, "A [citizen] group did the hard work of two years that probably the city should have done to find out what happened. You're being given a gift and all you have to do is receive it." He added of the truth and reconciliation process, "It's not history, it's us."

Next, a robust middle-aged African American man and lifelong city resident rose to speak. He was visibly angry as he walked to the podium to declare:

> I have no choice but to speak of what is a gross waste of the city's time. This council tonight is wasting time on something that hap- pened in our history. The Klan-Nazi shooting was terrible, but I don't understand why this council has allowed itself to be brow beaten by a small group of citizens. I have a message from *normal* people like me. I'd like the City Council to say, we have a job to do and it's not attending to this history. The vast majority of the people in this city have no interest in the Klan, Nazis or Com- munists. Finally, there has been change and if you don't believe that, just take a look at the [African American, female] mayor.

Upon his departure from the podium, the tension communicated in the man's voice and through his body held the room silent. As he walked away, Nelson Johnson immediately approached him and shook hands briefly, even though the two held very different views. No other speakers from the floor at the meeting suggested that the TRC was a waste of time. On the contrary, a line of people spoke in favor of an apology by the city council.

Nelson Johnson read from his August 26, 2005, testimony to the Truth and Reconciliation Commission, recounting his apology to then mayor Jim Melvin. His testimony further reminded the city council that he regretted the use of a flyer that demeaned the Klan. In both these instances, where the humanity of others was forsaken, Johnson said he was wrong and declared, "I do apologize."

After motions, counter-motions, and procedural moves to table motions, an exasperated Councilman Mike Barber said, "We may as well get it over tonight." He was opposed to having any further public comments about the TRC at future council meetings. He was unconvinced that the impact of November 3 was relevant so many years later, and concerned about the possible liability the City of Greensboro might face by issuing a statement of regret. Barber, a lawyer himself, suggested that his fellow council members consider this: "The language I could accept regards this as a regrettable event, not that we regret."

Zach Matheny, the youngest member of the city council at age thirty-six, asserted a position that echoed one long promoted by former mayor Jim Melvin. "One thing I have noticed about the City of Greensboro is that we never celebrate our successes." Matheny's next comments caused audience members and fellow council members to recoil:

> No doubt it [November 3] was a tragedy. I'm sorry for the losses there. But when we look at it as a city, we have to celebrate what we have done . . . I'll tell you what my generation says. Look at our successes. Let us move on. Quit telling me to regret what I did not do. The City of Greensboro did not cause the events of November 3rd, 1979.

These words would be on the front page of Greensboro's *News & Record* the following day, causing more stir yet among bloggers, including Billy Jones, the Blogging Poet, who asserted Jim Melvin was still in control of Greensboro government and that some city council members, including young Zach Matheny, were his instruments of power (Jones, 2008).

Councilwoman Goldie Wells spoke next. "I went to the TRC Report [formal presentation] when it was handed out and I was *sure* the City Council would read it. I was shocked then as I am now that we will not deal with it. It will not go away until we deal with it."

It was Councilman Robbie Perkins's comments that stood out

most for his change of heart toward the truth and reconciliation process. Previously, he led the opposition vote to the TRC Final Report:

> I can remember sitting here, three to four years ago and making a motion to oppose the Truth and Reconciliation Commission at 1:00 or 2:00 in the morning. All of us were tired and frustrated. I've often thought about my motion in the context of the rest of my life. Two years ago, when we were all campaigning, I ran into two elderly gentlemen in East Greensboro who said, please do something and bring this to an end . . . What harm does it do to accept a statement of regret? I can't find anything to object to. The way to move on is to *do* something.

Following Perkins's comments, the city council took a ten-minute break during which time the city attorney quickly made substantive changes to the draft statement of regret.

At last and in response to significant writing changes, the city council in a split 5–4 decision voted to issue a statement of regret that first, rejected liability for any past tragedy, and second, acknowledged the work of city-sponsored efforts to lead the community toward social harmony. Of note is that in the originally proposed statement, one hammered out over nineteen months of work by the citizen committee, there were some important moves to recognize the work of the Truth and Reconciliation Commission as a component part of the many efforts in the city that had been organized to repair damaged relationships. Additionally, the original statement contained wording of a pledge by the City of Greensboro to do all it could to prevent any such tragedy in the future. Those points that implied the City of Greensboro could do better in the areas of human relations and civil rights caused some (white) members of the city council to take offense.

Consequently, a far weaker version of the original statement was prepared in minutes as a political compromise. The original statement is provided here, with the revised and accepted statement of regret written in *italics*. Each of the three sentences that comprise the revised statement of regret was written to "protect" the city from appearing responsible, in any way, for any past mistakes. As a result, though the statement of regret was a step forward, the TRC supporters said it lacked honest, authentic consideration of the city's full and complete role in a tragic event.

Sentence #1:

Proposed: The City Council of Greensboro, North Carolina is strongly committed to human rights and deeply regrets the events of November 3, 1979 that resulted in the loss of five lives and divided a community.

Revised: Without acknowledging or creating any city employee, or Public Official liability, the City Council of Greensboro, North Carolina is strongly committed to human rights and deeply regrets the events of November 3, 1979 that resulted in the loss of five lives and divided a community.

Sentence #2:

Proposed: We appreciate the work done by the Truth and Reconciliation Commission, the Citizens Review Committee and the Human Relations Commission, as well as the great effort of many individuals and organizations to promote healing among the residents of our community by replacing divisiveness with harmonious relationships.

Revised: We appreciate the work done by the Human Relations Commission, as well as the great effort of many individuals and organizations to promote healing among the residents of our community by replacing divisiveness with harmonious relationships.

Sentence #3:

Proposed: We the City Council of Greensboro, North Carolina value the rich diversity of our neighborhoods, celebrate both our similarities and differences as human beings, and pledge its support to the extent of its ability and authority to ensure that nothing like the events of November 3, 1979 ever occur again in our community.

Revised: We, the City Council of Greensboro, North Carolina value the rich diversity of our neighborhoods, celebrate both our similarities and differences as human beings, and pledge our support to help the community heal.

The local newspaper commended the city council's vote. The paper's editorial staff recognized the statement of regret as "hardly a mandate" but instead a small measure toward understanding the past to "better cope with future challenges" (Truth and Regrets, 2009, A-12).

Responses to the regret-accepting vote by the city council appeared in the Letters to the Editor section of the daily paper in the following days with predictably mixed sentiments. The first letter expressed dismay at the four council members who voted against the statement of regret, saying, "I regret the council's vote because it should have been a unanimous 'yes' to issue a statement of regret." Other letter writers seized on the moment to chastise their city council that would "regret" anything for which it had no involvement. Expressions of regret or apologies, it was clear, were not considered just words for they "cut to the core of our political identity" (Barkan and Karn, 2006, 22). But what some community members and city leaders failed to see was that the power of communicating regrets and apologies creates a "bridging discourse" as a catalyst for more apologies that in turn signal a more compassionate community. That is, "The discourse of apology allows its participants to transform their ethical striving into substantive political action and makes the world—however scarred and bruised—a bit more like the one we want to live in" (Barkan and Karn, 2006, 24).

Joe Frierson, the youthful project director for the Greensboro Truth and Community Reconciliation Project, recognized the city council's apology as a guarded affirmation of the ongoing process for reconciliation. "There's a part of our community that feels there is a process capable of getting to the truth. There is a base of citizens interested in that process. Collecting stories worked and the groundwork for that came from folks working in grassroots organizations" (personal communication, July 14, 2009).

TRC supporter, historian, and civil rights activist Lewis Brandon III agreed and added that Greensboro's experience at uncovering the truth may not have been of great interest to local government leaders, but it was inspiring to other cities around the country and throughout the world:

> There have been other communities, too, looking at Greensboro. Mississippi has instituted its own process. We've been to Georgia, Alabama, Virginia, and Canada. And when we were in South Africa, Alex Boraine said he wanted to offer Greensboro's process as an example to other locales because of the grassroots foundation of our effort. (personal communication, July 14, 2009)

Brandon remarked that citizens could not be frozen in their efforts to advance democratic decision making by those who do not want to participate.

The effort to secure the city council's involvement, even at the very end of the project, was not easy as the stories in this chapter illustrate. However, as Nelson Johnson and others would repeat regularly during the TRC process, social change work is never without difficulty.

CHAPTER 9

Measures of Success

Communication is a struggle against interference and confusion.

—ALPHONSO LINGIS

THE TENETS OF participatory democracy were evident throughout the TRC process, but not without challenges. With the benefit of time to reflect back, this chapter answers the question so many ask, namely, did the TRC in Greensboro work?

Unlike its better-known counterpart in South Africa, Greensboro's TRC was not formed as a response to a history of human rights abuses. It instead examined how one event reflected the history of blacks in America, the labor movement in this country, the role of local and federal law enforcement to maintain peace, and alternative political conceptions of the good life. Though Greensboro's TRC looked at the violence of a single day, in so doing the TRC revealed that any one moment in history is in fact a reflection of the pattern established in years of cultural behaviors that are in turn codified in practices and norms, and then revealed in laws and institutions and the acceptance and support of those laws and institutions.

Together the grassroots group that initiated the work, and the independent commission tasked to investigate, analyze, and write a Final Report, asserted that the city of 250,000 could indeed do the hard work of facing up to a scarred history by holding onto hope for a revitalized community. In other words, the process was a realization of the potential of U.S. democracy where people are in the seat of power to not only elect their representatives, but also call for change when it is needed, and contribute time and energy to the communal life they want. The Greensboro Truth and Reconciliation commissioners' gaze on the past was a catalyst for a renewed commitment to carry forth the mandate for justice. In an imperfect union such as ours, the truth commissioners said, that means constantly seeking to improve the institutions, the policies, and the ways in which we interact with one another to ensure that equality and justice are actually, not just rhetorically, within the grasp of all.

So, in the years after the release of the report, and decades after the incident that sparked its need, people ask, what did Greensboro's Truth and Reconciliation Commission achieve? How is Greensboro different, they ask? Implicit in that question is, of course, how is Greensboro better, as a result of the time, money, and effort that went into investigating November 3, 1979, holding public hearings, collecting interviews from hundreds of people, hosting forums that provided guidance to the commission's task, and organizing reading groups and follow-up conversations that considered the details of the report.

Has there been change? Did Greensboro find the truth? Did community members and city officials reconcile in ways that made the effort worthwhile? Did the process provide a sufficient model for other cities to use in confronting past injustices? Was the silence of the past broken by the dialogue of the present? The answers to these many questions are best considered in three parts.

Yes, Greensboro and its residents are different and better as a result of the TRC. Since the report was released, Greensboro elected its first African American mayor. Yvonne Johnson's victory came one year before the election of Barack Obama as the first African American president of the United States. Together, Mayor Johnson and President Obama represented a significant change in citizen views of U.S. politics. For the majority of the electorate in Greensboro, North Carolina, who voted in the city election and for the majority of citizens in the United States who cast their votes in that federal election, there was a swell of support to shepherd into office two people who had generally sat at the margins of mainstream society by virtue of their race, and in the local example, by her gender as well. There are other changes in Greensboro.

Since 2006, Greensboro sprouted new, energetic movements for social change. The Greensboro HIVE (History, Information, Vision, and Exchange) established that year and open until 2010 was a collective operated in the Glenwood area, a historically crime-ridden section of the city. The HIVE's operating committee and volunteers established social justice-oriented programs, hosted dinners for the homeless, and initiated dialogue-generating events to strengthen the bonds of community as the mostly young people involved explored the possibilities for progressive change. The Raise the Minimum Wage Campaign, also initiated in 2006, was a citizens' initiative to increase Greensboro's minimum wage to $9.82 per hour, the rough equivalent of what the minimum wage in 1968 would yield in purchasing power forty years later. A Brown-Black Alliance formed in 2008 brought together clergy members in the African American Pulpit Forum of Greensboro, community supporters, and leaders and individuals associated with the Almighty Latin King and Queen Nation, the Almighty Black Peace Stone Nation, the Crips, the Five Percenters, the Piru Bloods, and the Nation of Islam. Seeking to transform the reputation of these "gangs," the alliance cleaned up the graffiti in the community, educated youth and adults on the history and original intent of the groups now labeled as gangs, and created opportunities to build unity among African Americans and Hispanics. In 2009, the Greensboro Currency Project was launched to develop an alternative paper currency to boost the local economy and free residents from a deep dependency on commercial banks. By distinguishing between real wealth—people's generosity, talents, skills, and abilities—from phantom wealth—paper assets—the project aimed to pursue alternative energy investments and provide loans with very favorable terms for people who most needed it to secure basic human needs. In 2011, individuals and groups were continuing to organize people's movements to address issues around which local government officials were dormant or uncooperative. These initiatives included efforts to stop the reopening of the White Street Landfill in a low-income, minority residential area and the planning of a participatory budgeting process for citizens to affect city government fiscal decisions. In addition, a vocal collective of several hundred formed an Occupy Greensboro coalition in support of the Occupy Wall Street movement. In Greensboro, the group set out to change home foreclosure laws and processes, in addition to waging protests against the banking industry and hosting teach-ins on financial topics and social movement history.

Greensboro's long tradition of activism preceded the activities of the Truth and Reconciliation Commission, but a renewed spirit and collective enthusiasm swept through the city when the TRC's Final Report was released. For instance, the Peace and Justice Network of the Triad formed in 1999 increased its visibility and outreach activities by hosting events, sponsoring its first fundraising concert, and organizing a year-long workshop series to build a stronger alliance among progressive activists to resist imperialistic approaches to growth. They avowed organic, holistic-based principles for communal living.

The question of whether the TRC "worked" can also be answered by saying that Greensboro was better in some ways but not all as a result of the TRC. Though the citizens of Greensboro experienced changes of the kind just noted, there were many who still clung to the ways of old. In 2007, the sitting police chief resigned under pressure from the city manager after news reports uncovered that there existed a "black book" of African American police officers that was used for line-up questioning of crime victims. The special investigations unit that assembled the black book also placed a tracking device on one of its own high-profile black officers in attempts to tie him to organized crime. All of this activity was carried out under the chief's watch, but when questioned by the city manager, the chief claimed he was unaware of this covert, often-illegal activity. We are better off, some reason, because the police chief resigned after being locked out of his office by the city manager. We are no better off, others suggest, because the follow-up investigation once again failed to arise from a citizen-commissioned Police Review Board. Instead, the investigation was conducted by internal resources and then eventually by external consultants who themselves were ex-officers. The lack of citizen involvement in police oversight, despite task force panels recommending such action over a period of decades in Greensboro, demonstrated the city's lack of faith in one of the basic principles of democracy, namely that people should set the agenda and be responsible for their own governance, including how law enforcement is carried out. Police Citizen Review Boards are common in cities across America, but not in Greensboro where repeated proposals to establish such an entity have been blocked by the local government.[1]

The third part to the question of the TRC's effectiveness must admit as well, that change was not entirely complete. For instance, a

City of Greensboro Human Relations Commissioner who indicated she had read the TRC Final Report remained unconvinced that the police shouldered any responsibility for the events that transpired that day, despite the detailed evidence presented in the report. Instead, she clung to the long-held story, as did then Mayor Keith Holliday, that the police were absent from the scene of the violence simply because they got their communication channel wires crossed. In spite of the intensive work of the TRC, many people refused to change their minds, holding on instead to the dominant understanding, or narrative, played and replayed by public officials and reported in local newspapers following the incident in 1979. The Final Report's painstaking detail showed the facts of radio communication, the litany of internal memos, and the chain of interactions in place to expose that in fact commanding police officials were fully aware of the possibility for violence, where it would come from, and how it might happen that day. The lesson to be drawn here is that the facts are necessary, yet insufficient to welcome a change of heart, a change in point of view, and a change in understanding. We like to pride ourselves on the assumption that if people just knew the facts, they would respond accordingly. But experience has shown us otherwise.

In the case of November 3 and the work of the TRC, revealing the truth of what happened that day and the consequences that followed was a critical first step for the community to consider more than what they had been led to believe up to that point. "Yet, the community was not involved to the extent it could have been in Greensboro and this challenge might prove useful lessons for other communities," explained TRC executive director Jill Williams (2007). For instance, the business interests in the city did not participate, despite multiple overtures to do so. An editorial in the area's *Business Journal* described the situation as a missed opportunity for building good will:

> Business leaders in Greensboro are always looking for opportunities to attract national attention to the city and have it seen as a progressive Southern community. Ironically, the business establishment is distancing itself from the landmark social initiative that, thus far, appears to be achieving those goals. (Catanoso, 2004)

In summary, the people in Greensboro learned that the real work of community change—addressing injustices, forgiving ourselves where we have been wrong, welcoming new ideas, collaborating with others, adjusting our understanding, and reconciling competing views—comes not only from reading a report, but also from ongoing conversations, critical questioning, reflection, cooperative action, and more inclusive decision making in the community that the report hoped to inspire.

Until the TRC released its report in 2006, the locus of blame fell to what the city leaders considered extremist groups—the KKK/Nazis on the one side, and the labor union organizers who were members of the Communist Workers Party on the other. The absence of the police that fateful day was treated simply as a miscommunication, effectively releasing the city from any responsibility. The TRC Final Report concluded otherwise, affirming in some respects that the lingering mistrust of law enforcement in this southern city was not unfounded.

Whereas the truth commissioners were charged with finding the truth of what happened on November 3, it was up to the community to achieve reconciliation. But *achieving* reconciliation is really a misnomer, for community reconciliation is an ongoing process without an ending even possible. In Greensboro, community members sought out and created the dialogic space for discussions, educational activities, trainings, and other interactive moments to enthuse an impulse for reconciliation rather than retribution.

The survivors and their supporters found within the structure of the TRC an opportunity outside the persecutory powers of the legal system for what they considered a better method of engaging the community to ask questions that could lead to substantive social change and lasting community justice. To assuage fears that the TRC was simply the means by which future court action would follow, the widows of November 3 wrote to the city attorney that they unequivocally waived any and all rights to future criminal or civil action.[2]

The experiences of the people in Greensboro who supported the truth and community reconciliation enterprise reveal a lot about the courage, skills, commitment, and challenges that accompany such a process. Putting the work of the TRC into perspective, the executive director Jill Williams pointed to the usefulness of difficult conversations:

> If the Greensboro experience inspires any hope for other communities, it comes from the power of those who are traditionally

silenced sharing their stories of violence and fear within a democratic process they organized themselves, and against the dis-
approval of the local government and other powerful community
members . . . the truth and reconciliation process in Greensboro
opened up a space in which even the most privileged in town
were engaged—willingly or not—in a dialogue about race and
class disparities. (Williams, 2007)

The supporters of the TRC were from the beginning, and for five years
of concentrated effort, prepared to address concerns and opposition
voiced by others in order to advance substantive change.

Despite what they could not know initially, all of the truth commissioners and most of the truth and reconciliation supporters
remained committed to advocacy for social change throughout the
many-year process. The composition of the Local Task Force was initially a membership-like body but then transformed into a more fluid
association of citizen activists. Its activities were shaped around the
strengths of those available for meetings and assignments and tapped
into the energies of those willing to invest their time for however long
they could. This approach comports well with what economist Richard
Florida recognized in the needs of highly creative people. He says they
"do not desire the strong ties and long-term commitments . . . rather
they prefer a more flexible, quasi-anonymous community—where
they can quickly plug in, pursue opportunities and build a wide range
of relationships" (Florida, 2002, 220). The approach, likewise, was
effective in addressing the common challenges that social change
agents face: creating de-centered movements with many different
issues advanced simultaneously; developing new forms of leadership
that move authority out of the hands of one into the hearts of many
who want more nonhierarchical modes of activism; learning to communicate across contexts; building multicultural alliances with people
locally and from around the world; and dealing with the media landscape that is so often unfriendly to social change initiatives (Del
Gandio, 2008). The Local Task Force meetings provided that place
where people of all ages could quickly get connected, as they so desired.
It was a place to get educated, see others taking action, get help in dealing with obstacles they encountered, and make inroads into a project
deemed important not only for Greensboro, but also for other locales.

Not unexpectedly for such a long project, some people's activity would wane through the years. Sadly, some of the supporters passed away during the process, others had to tend to personal crises of their own including divorce, parent care taking, and serious health maladies. Some students and older adults moved away from the area, and some people's fire for the project simply smoldered after their initial excitement.

For many though, their involvement with the TRC deepened their commitment to social justice more broadly. This was especially the case for the youth contingent. Some young people turned their focus from the TRC to law school entry and graduate school study related to matters of reconciliation, peace, and counseling. One student became a television news reporter, citing her experience with the TRC as the ground upon which she was able to discuss relevant news issues in the interview that landed her the job. Other students later participated in the U.S. Social Forum and attended and even organized other protest actions addressing police harassment, gay rights, and antiwar mobilization. Other youth traveled to distant countries to serve in various nonprofit organizations dedicated to peace and justice. Their appreciation expressed to the older adults involved in the TRC project was captured most poignantly by a student attending North Carolina A & T State University who, on the occasion of a Local Task Force meeting in November 2007, said:

> I want to say thank you. It means a lot to me to see adults sitting around talking about truth and reconciliation. I see adults working and eating, but not usually sitting around talking about important concepts that I am just learning about.

From the very beginning, a high premium was placed on the promise of the TRC process to inspire such intergenerational learning, action, sharing, and celebration.

For Local Task Force co-chair Z Holler, the reason why the TRC process attracted young and old alike was because what was at stake was the quality of life in the community. He cited recent instances of rancorous debate that eclipsed attempts at genuine dialogue, where fights on high school campuses escalated to deadly actions, where the steady loss of jobs and economic opportunities were manifest, and where looming immigrant hostility was building. These local, national, and world events were leading people to feelings of deep alienation, explained Holler. The TRC, he said, provided an antidote to the pervasive cultural condition bankrupting the opportunities for enriching multicultural experiences. In detailing his vision of why the truth and reconciliation process was a viable means by which to address our troubles, Holler wrote:

> There is an urgent need for those who love this community and this nation to find ways to engage emerging community issues with honesty and hope. We need to listen and learn from one another and from our past. We need to dream new dreams together, and be about the work of building a vibrant, confident community full of promise for our own youth and attractive to all who have contact with it. This is the goal of our Truth and Community Reconciliation Project, which currently seeks healing through a shared understanding of November 3, 1979. (Holler, 2003)

The community understanding deemed necessary for a cooperative future, was pursued through varied discourse forms to tap into the interests, energies, and care of Greensboro's residents.

Strategies to Ensure Many Voices Were Featured in Community Conversations

The Truth Commission's process followed on the heels of what was initiated by the grassroots Greensboro Truth and Community Reconciliation Project to include as many voices as possible in the truth-seeking process and attending reconciliation activities. In their Final Report, the truth commissioners said:

> We have demonstrated this power [of moral suasion] in bringing to the table, against many dismissive predictions to the contrary, not only former communists, but former Klansmen and Nazis, residents of the Morningside neighborhood, police officers, judges, trial attorneys, city officials, journalists and citizens from all parts of the city. In the words of one attorney, we have demonstrated that this process can "begin to melt the ice" within which many in this community have been frozen and unable to reach each other. (Final Report, 2006, 15)

TRC staff and volunteers walked from door-to-door in public housing communities to collect statements from residents living in the area in 1979, and sent out trained statement takers to anyone interested in providing comment on the activities or aftermath of November 3. Informational events were held at the city's public libraries, universities, and churches while other outreach efforts focused on individual meetings with constituent groups such as former workers in the mills. The three public hearings involving six full days brought not only hundreds of people each day to hear fifty-four speakers, but also attracted sixty journalists to cover the proceedings.

NEWSPAPER COVERAGE BOTH HELPS AND HURTS THE EFFORT

The daily newspaper, Greensboro's *News & Record,* was considered both the villain and partner in the truth and reconciliation process, according to community members. Most of what was deemed helpful information and coverage by the TRC supporters appeared on the editorial pages. They considered the news reporting less detailed, sometimes inaccurate, and in some cases, absent altogether. Community activist and TRC supporter Ed Whitfield commented on what he saw as uneven and erroneous reporting in the fall of 2005 upon the completion of the TRC public hearings:

> The *News & Record* recently ran a front-page article declaring that there was little substance to the commission's work and claiming that its analysis of the testimony revealed that there was nothing new or noteworthy—"no tearful apologies" and "no startling revelations" . . . The article itself goes on to make several errors of fact, major omissions and misleading judgments that have been pointed out in detail on local internet blogs. John Robinson, the news editor . . . defended the front-page article saying its errors were minor ones. In particular he admitted that he wished that the article had included Nelson Johnson's apology to Mayor Jim Melvin but said that its omission did not alter the point of the article that there had been no apologies. (Whitfield, 2005)

Whitfield called newspaper editor Robinson's defense of factual errors a disservice to the community and a continuation of the manipulation of facts that had been the pattern in newspaper reporting since 1979.

The area's weekly newspapers were considered the community's best source of TRC information, not the daily newspaper, according to TRC supporters. Regular, in-depth articles in the free alternative tabloid, *Yes Weekly!* became the most authoritative voice on the TRC happenings. Senior reporter Jordan Green spent more investigative and writing hours reporting on Greensboro's truth and reconciliation process than any other journalist. Another weekly paper, the *Carolina Peacemaker,* part of the Black Press USA Network, remained a faithful outlet as well for TRC news throughout its process.

One of the TRC's Final Report recommendations was to "host a citywide citizen group that would comment on news process, content, quality and ethics" (Final Report, 2006, 388). This suggestion was taken up immediately by *News & Record* editor John Robinson, who responded, "Count us in" (2006, B-2). He assured readers that the newspaper staff would "do a bit of fact-finding to discover the most effective model" for such a citizen group. That model, it would turn out, was not as envisioned by the TRC and instead an Internet-based readers' panel. Fashioned more as a public opinion survey to help advertisers, the newspaper skirted the opportunity for meaningful citizen involvement in its editorial processes.

The letters to the editor in all the newspapers suggest that the community remained split in its feelings about whether talk was a viable means to reconciliation or whether reconciliation was even necessary in the community. Some argued that the Truth Commission's Final Report highlighted some of Greensboro's long-held ills about which continuing conversation was necessary. Others suggested that the Truth Commission and its supporters exaggerated the extent of the problems in Greensboro and that whatever challenges confronted the community should have been taken up with current issues, not past events. The split of support in the letters to the editor mirrored what executive director Jill Williams and the truth commissioners discovered in their walks and talks in selected neighborhoods:

> There were white and black people both in favor of and opposed to reexamining the events of November 3, 1979, but the reasons for the support and opposition were generally quite different . . . white people tended to understand the 1979 events as being acts of outsiders and having nothing to do with Greensboro. If they opposed the process, it was often because they saw no

connection between 1979 and today and felt that the process
unfairly presented the city in a negative light to the outside world.
(Williams, 2007)

Williams said the TRC's door-to-door campaign in poor and working-
class communities also revealed some African Americans were
opposed to the TRC process but for them, she said:

> The opposition seemed to grow largely out of a sense of hope-
> lessness that anything would really change, the need to focus lim-
> ited resources on more immediate concerns, and even a fear that
> participating could result in retaliation from the police, the Klan,
> employers, or the Housing Authority. (Williams, 2007)

As for supporters, Williams heard more often from whites that they
saw the TRC process as one that could hopefully encourage reconciliation, whereas from African Americans, there was much more concern for truth telling.

WORKING AGAINST FORCES TO EXCLUDE

The move to include many voices was strong, but the force by some
to stay distanced from the TRC process was also robust. For instance,
Jim Melvin, the mayor of Greensboro in 1979 who remained an active
and vital leader in the community, never engaged with the formal truth
and reconciliation process. He did not provide a statement to the Truth
Commission, nor did he participate in any of its events. However,
Melvin did grant interviews to the media and appeared in Adam
Zucker's (2008) documentary about the process. He also spoke to participants at a chamber of commerce-sponsored program, Leadership
Greensboro. Two former mayors were scheduled to speak—Jim
Melvin, who was opposed to the TRC, and Carolyn Allen, who was
among those who initiated the TRC process. Melvin spoke first and
then left before engaging in deeper discussion, but at least he did talk
about November 3, said Allen. She continued, "He didn't say much
beyond what he had already said, but at least both of our voices were
heard at the same time" (personal communication, July 23, 2010).

Opposition came as well from current elected leaders. Mayor Keith
Holliday repeatedly forecasted that the TRC would amount to little

more than "a witch hunt," a conjecture that did not materialize. For city councilwoman Florence Gatten, the TRC was a misguided effort that effectively dismissed all the good work others had done in the intervening years since the tragedy. Gatten pledged early on to spend thirty minutes a day to defeat the launch of the TRC. Despite her efforts, the citizen initiative carried on its mission.

The TRC, using multiple discourse forms, provided improved models of conversation surrounding difficult issues. The results were impressive in prompting others to take collective action, less remarkable in terms of tangible local government changes, and not fully successful in bringing together people with different positions on the need for a TRC.

The lessons gleaned from this effort point to the need for the kind of community conversations that are largely removed from public discourse activity, yet imperative for implementing authentic democratic action. One of the TRC's greatest impacts, then, was in modeling and teaching citizens that their words and actions matter deeply in the self-governing processes necessary for life, liberty, and the pursuit of happiness.

CHAPTER 10

Greensboro's Legacy Is Hidden No More

Reconciliation cannot be thought of as a narrow prescription but rather a broad and vast one that creates a new culture of respect for differences and human rights.

—ANDREW RIGBY

THIS FINAL CHAPTER considers the lessons learned from Greensboro's TRC to understand how a specific community comes to know, appreciate, and talk across differences to reach for truth and initiate reconciliation. The lessons are gleaned from the activities of commissioners and citizens who honored the community's history, present condition, and future possibilities rooted in cultural practices, spiritual touchstones, political structures, and social practices.

In the United States, there are tremendous forces that resist movements for change, even ones that have modest aims of more fair treatment for all. Rhetorical scholars of social change movements remind us that those who possess the power to determine a community's fate assume the worst from others who challenge them. As a result, any questioning is seen as an attack on the establishment that must be defeated (Bowers et al., 2010). Nevertheless, a cursory look at our history reveals that the eight-hour workday and mandated breaks would not have come about without a collective movement to stop the common practices of overtime hours without pay. The fight was a long and protracted one where company executives and government officials waged campaigns to discredit and disrupt actions by those seeking change. Occupational health and safety codes were not granted without sustained pressure and struggle from union organizers and human rights advocates.

The health of a community depends upon its social change

advocates to drive the conversations that are not always wanted, but are so desperately needed to balance the scales of justice. The work then of social change agents is not always comfortable. Being mindful of the importance of relationships is too often pitted against the need for expressing critiques of existing customs. In the face of that, many of us hear the common refrain that sends a warning flag into the air— if you want to keep your friends, do not talk about politics, religion, or money. As it would turn out, the Greensboro TRC addressed in great detail all three of those difficult subject areas. As a result, many people working with the TRC who without previous experience in social change efforts were at times thrown into unfamiliar waters.

A student learning about the TRC and reading the Final Report in her university class was at a neighborhood café one evening, discussing November 3 with her dining partner. Others evidently overheard her conversation in the restaurant because as two men passed her table to pay their bill, they paused and warned, "Do you think you or anyone can change history? Those commies got what they deserved." When the young woman left later, she found her car in the parking lot with the tires slashed. Other isolated incidents of negative reaction from total strangers on the subject of November 3 and the Greensboro TRC became opportunities for discussion in college classes and at the Local Task Force meetings.

Nelson Johnson, a social change professional, was less fazed by the pejorative comments. They were ones he had heard repeatedly since 1979. He was instead preoccupied by the question, how do you hold institutions accountable for their actions? He had learned from experience that rarely are critiques seriously considered. Instead they are dismissed, he said, for not adhering to the cultural, political, and economic practices of the time. November 3 was one of those events that did not fit with the dominant community narrative of a progressive city protecting the interests of its citizens. In fact, Project Censorship included Greensboro's story of the cascading injustices related to November 3 as the second most censored story in 1981 (see www.projectcensored.org). Johnson believed the TRC could provide the foundation for the community to challenge what until then they had not questioned sufficiently in law enforcement practices, protest action, cooperative economic structures, education reform, and free speech.

The timeliness of the TRC project in Greensboro and around the world should not be understated. As civic engagement continues to spiral downward and citizen action suffocates under the threats to rule of law, the TRC provides the reasons and model for how to engage with one another surrounding the significant issues of our time.

The lessons Greensboro's citizens learned through this process of pursuing truth and reconciliation are many. The participants who had long histories in activism provided valuable support to social change newcomers. At the same time, the relative newcomers among the students, faith leaders, retirees, and others provided priceless support to the more seasoned change agents. Together, they demonstrated how strong, diverse alliances can be forged. Perhaps above all else they worked in tandem to acknowledge the many aspects of community life that fashion our conception of what is ultimately right, good, and truthful, and in doing so inspired hope for a community more benevolent and just (Hyde, 2006). The collective action for truth and reconciliation in Greensboro highlights the following ten lessons.

1. *Southern civility needs to regain its posture as an asset in building strong relationships with respectful discourse. To do so, it must overcome its past, documented proclivity to suppress dissent and thwart democratic practice.*

Civility can embrace the important features of hospitality, appreciation, and responsibility that serve to open up spaces for conversation. However, in the South, civility has too often used courtesy and good manners to side step meaningful talk that hinders dissent (Chafe, 1980). The result in those cases has been a reduction of spaces where conflict could be expressed in ways to prompt social change. The TRC was important, as was the Final Report, but what was most important to advancing strong democratic action were the instances where conversation spaces were opened up to the difficult conversations that had previously been avoided.

The story for November 3 has many similarities to the initial thrust and stalemate experienced by the sit-in leaders in 1960. However, whereas the sit-in protestors could point to a visible contradiction in human and civil rights policy that required change, the Greensboro Massacre of 1979 targeted something more insidious—government misconduct and labor management practices that reflected segregationist attitudes.

People remained civil after November 3, but as a result of not talking honestly about the events and its consequences, Greensboro's community members experienced feelings of "existential mistrust" (Arnett and Arneson, 1999). They harbored feelings of suspicion in the motives of city leaders on the one hand, and activists on the other hand. That mistrust manifested itself in two ways. First, people simply gave up on their right to self-governance as a democratic principle. Second, acts of dissent came to be deemed "crazy" or violent, but certainly not civil.

To overcome the resistance to civic engagement that inherently includes conflict, the TRC process identified and enacted a very important lesson to resurrect the best that southern civility offers. That is, the commissioners, staff, and TRC supporters invited people into difficult deliberative processes not once or even twice, but many times over. They did so by being attentive to and reflective about the possible impediments to meaningful dialogue. They learned that invitations of this sort cannot be perfunctory, but instead must be genuinely respectful of people's views whatever they may be. The goal was to enact civility, even as others reacted with less grace, as a valuable end in itself and as a means to more conversations.

2. *Injustices built into and "normalized" in the fabric of systemic practices warrant questioning and change.*

In Greensboro, the task was arduous—to confront the injustices that gave rise to the violence of November 3. Injustice from one vantage point, however, is defined differently from other perspectives. For some, this very fact of life is reason to find fault with everyone and every institution when wrongdoing occurs. That was what author Elizabeth Wheaton concluded in her 1986 book, *Codename Greenkil,* after following and reporting on the Greensboro Massacre. But the TRC process proceeded differently, probing for the underlying systemic practices that influenced the subsequent decisions and behaviors by law enforcement as well as activists.

Though people generally would rather believe the police are above reproach and that government officials do not cover up information, the TRC process showed citizens that at least with regard to November 3, concealed information and lack of protection were the byproducts of long-standing practices. Nelson Johnson said the situation continued, even throughout the TRC process itself. He detailed a troubling situation in an "Update on Recent Developments Involving the Task Force" for the Truth and Reconciliation Commission:

> Shortly after our Task Force meeting last Tuesday, April 18, 2006, Police Chief Bellamy visited me at the church. He shared that I along with twenty-six other people had been electronically eavesdropped upon by the police. He told me that twenty-five of the twenty-seven were African Americans. At least one meeting of the Task Force and perhaps more held at the church had also been spied upon. He stated that a woman wearing an electronic listening device attended the Task Force meeting . . . He also told me that the privacy of [TRC executive director] Jill Williams had been similarly invaded. He said he did not know why the previous police leadership had authorized the surveillance activity.

A few days later, Johnson met and learned from the city manager that indeed the criminal activity within the ranks of the police was broad. Johnson showed that the "normalized" practices of police misconduct that had been reigning in Greensboro since before 1979 continued and thus required collective citizen action in a call for change.

Lucy Lewis, another survivor, continued her work as well to advance economic and racial justice, in part because those concerns had not been made visible enough, she said, in the taken-for-granted features of our capitalist economy that encourage wealth for some at the expense of pain and suffering of others. For Lewis, truth telling about these conditions that were punctuated by November 3, was vital and had to precede the road to reconciliation. When the truth is aired, and healing begins, she said changes must be introduced and reparations made in the form best suited to the situation.

Commissioner Cynthia Brown, looking back on her involvement and the TRC process itself, expressed mixed feelings of satisfaction and frustration. Though establishing the truth of what happened in 1979 was the preeminent accomplishment for which she was satisfied, Brown told an audience of community members and students in 2011 that she remained disappointed that Greensboro's TRC did not have the ability to subpoena and prosecute perpetrators of the violence that day. For her, those restrictions on the TRC's activities limited the possibilities for justice in the community.

3. *When managing image and liability take priority over taking eth-ical action, the deep consideration of the human condition is lost.*

Just as social change agents need to maintain a focus on the root issues of their concerns, so too should communities when confronted with crises. If the City of Greensboro had first attended to the needs of its community members on November 3, then it may have been more willing and better able to assess the response and responsibility of its police force to achieve the goals of public safety. As it was, though, the City of Greensboro responded to the tragedy with a defensive posture rather than an honest reflection of what transpired. In doing so, the door was effectively shut on any meaningful engagement with the commu-nity's members and a review of how the events of November 3 unfolded.

The approach advocated by TRC supporters was that caring for peo-ple as individuals needs to be the priority in private and public actions. This is a position advocated as well by philosopher Emmanuel Levinas, who conceives of ethical engagement as the moral foundation of justice. That is, absent the care for the other, the possibility of justice is bank-rupted. For Levinas then, ethics is a people-centered approach to meting out justice. This approach places the demand upon elected officials to shed the instinctive defense of the status quo to preserve appearances, in favor of an admittedly more time-consuming approach of engaging contested positions to ensure the public trust. The TRC respected this value—that every person has a story worth hearing—in conducting its research and analysis.

Candy Clapp spoke to the Truth and Reconciliation Commission about how she felt abandoned by the city's leaders after November 3:

> After the smoke cleared it was a silence . . . We knew people were dead. . . . I still have fear of crowds because of what happened that day. We didn't have a clue what we would see the next day. It was like the children didn't matter to the City of Greensboro. They knew we were there, but they didn't seem to care. Nobody came back from the City to question us about what we were feeling . . . Nobody but the church could tell us anything to make it better, and preachers could only tell us to hold onto our faith, God would make it better. God would handle it. (Final Report, 2006, 229)

Clapp suggested, and the TRC agreed, that Greensboro's elected offi-cials and staff should have met with and counseled the victims of the tragedy that took place in their city limits. That, they argued, would have been the ethical and just course of action.

4. *Overcoming opposition to honest, authentic dialogue is daunting, but possible, and necessary for social change.*

In the absence of sustained talk about uncomfortable issues, those working within the structures of power will assume all is well, and that all are happy. This is a lesson we have learned from U.S. history. "Former slaves often did not tell the worst of it to young people, who never felt the lash, which means that an end to the lore began soon after freedom" (Ball, 1998, 81).

TRC supporters admitted that community members needed to share responsibility for not previously confronting difficult matters. Many people preferred to speak of the community's successes and achievements, rather than unveiling any shortcomings. Being optimistic, with a focus on the future, enamored by progress, and always hopeful are not bad qualities, but can mask society's dysfunctions.

Sadly, those who speak honestly about problems are not always admired. Instead they are often cast as nay-sayers (or worse) that undermine a common faith. Yet, undermining our faith, when it is faith unfounded, is precisely the first step toward improving the condition of our world. Professor, author, and activist Robert Jensen spoke to Greensboro's progressive contingent about this, and in a book written to dismantle white privilege he wrote:

> History matters. It matters whether we tell the truth about what happened centuries ago, and it matters whether we tell the truth about more recent history. It matters because if we can't, we will never be able to face the present, guaranteeing that our future will be doomed. (Jensen, 2005, 44)

Jensen says a society with deep inequality at so many levels is unsustainable. The prophetic words ring true in Greensboro as it struggles to uplift a downward spiral of community confidence.

One strategy to help people address difficult concerns was to allow time to rest between sessions of talk. In doing so, the TRC supporters held onto a commitment to continue talking and learning to see what could come from the later, collective discussions. This approach not only recognized that people have lives apart and distinct from political conversations, but also supported space for public discourse to occur absent the pressure of weekly events and time-limited sessions.

Further, the TRC provided invaluable documents to help people prepare for the needed conversations. This was especially true for survivor Alex Goldstein, who in 1979 was just a child to Signe Waller. He said, "I've gained more insight and can communicate better with other people about that situation [November 3]. Also, I can now refer people to Adam's documentary and the full report and executive summary" (personal communication, March 30, 2010).

Communication ethics scholar Clifford Christians says, "Communities are knit together linguistically; because the lingual is not neutral, but value laden, our social bonds are moral claims" (2007, 440). Our social bonds in effect depend upon talking, and talking about difficult or agonizing experiences as well as more joyful ones to reveal the depth of our emotions and social critique. In doing so, views and values are vetted to develop a "critical moral consciousness" necessary for community making (Christians, 2007, 443).

The extent of the obligation of an individual to his or her community remains a site of discursive struggle. But the issue is not just one of abstract importance; it has meaningful and practical implications for the quality of our community relationships. A strong community is one that involves all of its constituent groups in making decisions and promoting positive change. More difficult to ascertain is how and under what conditions community groups should work to advance social change that may lift up some members of the community but cause other sectors to change their ways or sacrifice their traditions. Attending to the core principles of democracy—equality, justice, individual rights, the common good, deliberative practices, and diversity—helped Greensboro's TRC prioritize those judgments.

Ethical commitments, civic responsibility, community identity, and leadership practices are vital processes for productive dialogue that can lead to a community's quest for improvement. The process is ongoing, and as such, requires a sustained commitment by citizens, as was the case for the work surrounding truth and reconciliation in Greensboro.

5. *Seeking and granting forgiveness are moral endeavors that we perform to recognize past harms, seek absolution, and assign responsibility.*

Forgiveness has most often been regarded as a moral act engaged by moral actors, one-on-one. More recently, scholars and activists have asked what ought to be the role of forgiveness at the level of societal wrongdoings. In Greensboro, there was no consensus reached on this subject. Still, the definition of and possibility for engaging in acts of community forgiveness were assumed to be essential conditions to affirming the truth and working toward reconciliation.

To better assert what Greensboro's experience teaches us, it is useful to consider an extended definition of forgiveness that reminds us of the impact of power differentials within relationships. Philosopher Kate Norlock (2009) writes that considerations of forgiveness need to attend to matters of gender, for instance, and Greensboro's experience would add race, and class, to examine who forgives, why, and how. It is around these questions that forgiveness discourse and negotiation takes place, not just between victim and offender, but also among a variety of relationships in which we are all situated. In doing so, forgiveness Norlock says and Greensboro demonstrated, is both an attitude and a communicative act.

> Forgiveness is held to be a moral, and therefore at least partially deliberative, action or set of actions, which functions as a remedy in responding to blame or condemnation, releasing offenders from the fullness of their blameworthiness, in relational contexts which therefore require considerations of power between relata. (Norlock, 2009, 2)

The Greensboro truth commissioners encouraged community members to apologize and forgive one another as remedies and alternatives to other speech acts of blame and retribution. A forgiveness mode, they argued, attended to the personal features of people who were harmed. At the same time, being willing to forgive required that we ask what responsibility we bore—personally and at the community level—for how people were disparaged for expressing dissent. The TRC process provided an opportunity as well for enacting forgiveness anew as a show of respect. Forgiveness, the truth commissioners affirmed, is a relational endeavor.

But even the subject of forgiveness caused defenses to flair. "I didn't do anything" and "You can't blame me for what others did" were common enough exhortations. Edward Ball, a descendant of a slave owner and author of *Slaves in the Family* (1998), says, "We're not responsible for what our ancestors did or did not do . . . but we're accountable for it" (416). The distinction Ball makes for us is that rather than taking blame for doing wrong, we need to look at the enduring consequences of past actions that we have allowed to continue. In the case of slavery, blacks continue to experience disadvantages in nearly every social indicator. Thus, Ball says, we ought to do something to remedy that situation.

That is, "Our task is to live on the edge of the guilt, to use it to challenge ourselves and each other to do better" (Jensen, 2005, 51). Applying this admonition to Greensboro, the TRC supporters hoped that the city's elected leaders would take heed of the protracted community outcry for a Citizens' Review Board to review charges of police misconduct.

6. Reconciliation is best viewed as a process to be enacted over and over again rather than as an end state.

Reconciliation, the truth commissioners reminded us, was not a one-time event, but instead an ever-unfolding process of communication that allows us to live less encumbered by past hurts and with greater compassion. The lesson learned was that reconciliation is something we can choose to enact every day in our interactions with others. That we are different and hold differing beliefs than others is to be expected. But our differences can be the source of inspiration rather than a marker of division. For example, during the TRC process, supporters and critics in Greensboro encountered opposition sometimes and downright hostility at other times. Reconciliation is made possible in the moment by even one person running interference to ensure that the lines of communication are kept open and flowing.

Without a doubt, it is more difficult to engage with others who hold different values and different conceptions of community well-being, or even different routes to a similar goal. However, repeated engagement, inevitable conflict, and necessary reconciliation is vital to any living environment and contingent upon adapting, flexing, considering options, compromising, and trying new approaches that allow a better solution for the environment to emerge.

To reconcile the past, for the hope of a better future, Greensboro

TRC supporters knew they had to carefully attend to the needs of others. Time was the requisite feature of that possibility.

7. Efforts for restorative justice are tasks for community members to organize and lead, and for politicians to support.

Howard Zehr says, "Restorative justice should be built from the bottom up, by communities in dialogue assessing their needs and resources and applying the principles to their own situations" (2002, 10). Before Greensboro used this route, restorative justice emerged as an alternative frame for adjudicating harms experienced by the Mennonites applying faith and peace principles to what they saw as a harsh world in the 1970s. Even earlier, Native Americans in North America and New Zealand set the precedents for what would later be called restorative justice.

Restorative justice, then, is steeped in the values of democracy and the rule of the people to determine their fate. Communities need rich informal community structures, social networks, and infrastructure to complement formal, institutional systems and practices to advance its values. Restorative justice, as a democratic practice, casts a wide net for grassroots community leaders to take full advantage of the power of the people to speak alongside elected officials. In doing so, a diverse leadership base is established with strong opportunities for the expression of varied, even dissenting views that bode well for a deliberative community (Gastil, 2008). Greensboro learned this lesson, and in advancing truth and reconciliation built that necessary broad base of support.

The challenge in the United States and in Greensboro is to influence the activities of the legal community that is oriented toward punitive measures by capitalizing on fear and control. Legal training is not sufficiently provided for restorative practices or victim advocacy, says Zehr (personal communication, April 23, 2010). The quest for restorative justice, however, contributed to a new dialogue in Greensboro, one where relationships were regarded as essential to community well-being. Further, the restorative justice frame suggested that the health of the larger community warrants care to maintain and strengthen its resolve. In this way, the restorative justice movement's greatest contribution to Greensboro was in generating talk within the community of its values and the episodes in history that challenged those values.

8. *Public education needs to provide a thorough understanding of local issues, as well as national and international issues, and political decision making in order for students to understand and engage with the democratic practices of self-government.*

The TRC supporters in Greensboro saw the enduring impact of connecting young people to the community. The youth participated by listening to testimonies, asking questions at Local Task Force meetings, and offering critique in classrooms and in public. The local community was clearly the hub of what made possible that deep engagement. The TRC process provided ripe facts, figures, and stories about an episode in history for cultivating the democratic arts of investigation, conversation, reflection, and action in relation to the themes of freedom, equality, dissent, and communal responsibility. The youth found themselves in step with cultural critic and educator bell hooks, who asserts, "Whenever we love justice and stand on the side of justice, we refuse simplistic binaries" in favor of deep, critical questioning and thinking (2003, 10).

Thus, November 3 and the truth and reconciliation process provided educators the opportunity to examine how a community's culture influences its decisions, policies, and daily practices. In doing so, students were pressed to consider the various meanings and ideologies implicated in political action. Students were encouraged to enact democracy as a process of deliberation among free and equal citizens to consider community options compatible with a pluralist democracy. In the case of November 3, such discussions recognized the various parties to the conflict not as enemies, but rather as adversaries whose passions were worthy of consideration in light of democratic principles (Mouffe, 2000). To be clear, while the Klan and Nazi passions of hatred and bigotry must be rejected, their experiences as members of the exploited working class are worthy of sensitive discussions.

Thus, education steeped in the local political landscape effectively linked learning to democratic foundations and provided knowledge about how to intervene in civic life. Equipping young people with those basic building blocks of civic education was deemed a vital mission for many of the TRC supporters echoing the call by critical education philosophers:

> knowledge, power, values, and institutions must be made available to critical scrutiny, be understood as a product of human

labor (as opposed to God-given), and evaluated in terms of how they might open up or close down democratic practices and experiences. (Giroux and Giroux, 2006, 211)

To accomplish this kind of critical engagement, some of Greensboro's teachers related the classroom instruction to TRC themes and encouraged robust debate surrounding the merits and shortcomings of the citizen-initiated process within specified philosophical and political theories:

> On first or second or even third try, most students will fail to adequately engage *both* the theory and the world in their oral or written responses. Without adequate practice and feedback, students have a tendency and good reason to fall back on the default position, that of simply asserting an opinion devoid of grounding or supportive evidence. (Bloch-Schulman and Jovanovic, 2010)

In fact, community discourse likewise exhibits a pattern of views or opinions devoid of reason, reflection, or evidence. The TRC project thus paved the way for educators to teach students *how* to be active, participating citizens.

The benefits derived from teaching about November 3 and the TRC process were many. Foremost among them was that specific, relevant instruction instilled a citizen ethic strong enough to propel a number of students into the public sphere to take action. Struggling for a better world required that students as citizens scrutinized how private actions comported with public issues while being able to see as well how undemocratic forces denied economic, social, and political justice (Giroux, 2007).

9. *There is cause to celebrate the advances and stories of citizens who make strides in achieving social change.*

In 1979, the participants in the November 3 protest march were seasoned community organizers and activists. They had reached across race and social class to mobilize diverse people in search of better educational opportunities, economic benefits, and political goods. During the TRC process, thousands of supporters learned to build sustained collaborations. Reverend Cardes Brown articulated as much at the first community-wide town meeting hosted to discuss the Final Report in December 2006:

> This has been a most encouraging movement. So often when we
> speak, there are no ears to listen. That day of shame has held the
> city hostage ever since. That day seemed uneventful to the com-
> munity and now all these years later, there's still an effort to sup-
> press and keep it from going forward. But we are here!

His acknowledgment was an appreciated and necessary form of celebration to keep people encouraged about their activities in what was
an admittedly long-term process.

Councilwoman Dianne Bellamy-Small, too, put her faith in the
TRC process to uphold the power of ordinary citizens to organize and
act. She reprimanded her fellow council members for standing in the
way of that possibility:

> There is no reason the citizens cannot be more engaged in the
> destiny of our community. But all people must feel empowered
> to engage the process for freedom and that we do not have
> broadly enough yet . . . There is a belief in this city that if we
> ignore or hide the truth from the public that a different reality
> will be realized. There is a behavior in this city that if anyone tries
> too hard to stand for truth, equity or justice, they will be discred-
> ited or neutralized. There is an attitude in this city that some who
> play along to get along will be safe from the practices of prejudice
> and racism. But there must be a thought-out call to action to stop
> these beliefs, behaviors and attitudes from continuing in the 21st
> century and in the future of Greensboro . . . Truth, reconciliation,
> and healing are all a part of the growth of a just community,
> strength of a state, and the liberty of a nation.

In addition to the instances of talk that celebrated the many small steps
forward on the road to social change, the TRC supporters found time
and space to write letters of support to the newspaper, host public
events to recognize progress, and to engage in other small and large
practices of celebration simultaneous with the hard, serious work
required.

For survivor Signe Waller Foxworth, the tremendous effort was
worth every minute and every dollar invested:

> The truth and reconciliation process is a glorious chapter we can
> add to the city's history. And maybe it will not be fully appreci-
> ated for quite awhile. It had massive participation from a lot of

people, was so innovative, and inspired so many. It gave courage
to the people. (personal communication, May 19, 2010)

10. *Democracy is people inspired, people initiated, and people sustained.*

Democracy in America depends upon the full participation of its
citizens and the understanding of history as it impacts people today.
Taken together, these practices can ignite the collective will of the people to lead and enact programs and policies to accommodate the needs
of the populace. It is that trust in the promise of democracy, and the
will to have people's voices heard, that fueled the efforts in Greensboro,
North Carolina, to initiate the first truth and reconciliation commission in the United States.

It is the people who must reclaim the roots, values, and hopes for
democracy against the threats of special-interest politics and large corporate interests. In Greensboro, the people followed a quest for truth
and reconciliation inspired by a passion for authentic equality, opportunity, dignity, and fairness that could fill in the landscape of the
community.

Greensboro resisted, embraced, fought, and welcomed all at the
same time the work of the TRC. That is, the community was not uni-
fied in its adoption of a process for restorative justice, one that would
eventually point the finger of accountability inward to its own city and
police force for not preventing the violence that occurred on the streets
of an African American neighborhood. That lack of a common story
might be considered cause for concern, but it could also be regarded
as the most important reason for continued dialogue. Our social bonds
are worth fighting for against the tyranny of those who ask us to forget
a painful past or deny the depth of our emotions and social critique.

The heart of our human existence is steeped in the democratic
arts of community making, where we live in the presence of others
who can make us better, and to whom we can contribute our individual gifts. Greensboro's truth and reconciliation process expressed the
possibility for developing a more just, caring, and inclusive community. It was a historic process that was driven by determined people
who asserted their voices for a strong democracy they believed had
always been theirs for the making.

Mandate for the Greensboro Truth and Reconciliation Commission

There comes a time in the life of every community when it must look humbly and seriously into its past in order to provide the best possible foundation for moving into a future based on healing and hope. Many residents of Greensboro believe that for this city, the time is now.

In light of the shooting death of 5 people and the wounding of 10 others in Greensboro, North Carolina on November 3, 1979, and

In light of the subsequent acquittal of defendants in both state and federal criminal trials, despite the fact that the shootings were video-taped and widely viewed, and

In light of the further investigations, passage of time and other factors which allowed a jury in a later civil trial to find certain parties liable for damages in the death of one of the victims, and

In light of the confusion, pain, and fear experienced by residents of the city and the damage to the fabric of relationships in the community caused by these incidents and their aftermath,

The Greensboro Truth and Community Reconciliation Project, including the signers of its Declaration, calls for the examination of the context, causes, sequence and consequence of the events of November 3, 1979.

We affirm that the intention of this examination shall be:

a) Healing and reconciliation of the community through discovering and disseminating the truth of what happened and its consequences in the lives of individuals and institutions, both locally and beyond Greensboro.

b) Clarifying the confusion and reconciling the fragmentation that has been caused by these events and their aftermath, in part by educating the public through its findings.

c) Acknowledging and recognizing people's feelings, including feelings of loss, guilt, shame, anger and fear.

d) Helping facilitate changes in social consciousness and in the institutions that were consciously or unconsciously complicit in these events, thus aiding in the prevention of similar events in the future.

This examination is not for the purpose of exacting revenge or recrimination. Indeed, the Commission will have no such power. Rather, the Commission will attempt to learn how persons and groups came to be directly or indirectly involved in these events; it will assess the impact of these events on the life and development of this community. It will seek all possibilities for healing transformation.

In addition to exploring questions of institutional and individual responsibility for what happened, as a necessary part of the truth-seeking process we urge the Commission to look deeply into the root causes and historical context of the events of November 3, 1979.

Members of this community, young and old, still find the events of November 3, 1979 nearly incomprehensible. We owe it to ourselves and to future generations to explain what happened and why. Many citizens and institutions of this city have acknowledged the wisdom of, and necessity for, such a process.

It is in this spirit that we affirm the South African Truth and Reconciliation Commission's motto: "Without Truth, no Healing; without Forgiveness, no Future."

Therefore, toward these ends,

1. The Greensboro Truth and Community Reconciliation Project (referred to here as "the Project") hereby establishes a Greensboro Truth and Reconciliation Commission (GTRC), charged with the examination of the context, causes, sequence and consequence of the events of November 3, 1979.

2. The GTRC will consist of seven (7) Commissioners who shall be persons of recognized integrity and principle, with a demonstrated commitment to the values of truth, reconciliation, equity and justice. The majority of the commissioners will be current residents of the

Greensboro area; at least two commissioners will be from outside the Greensboro area. All will be selected in accordance with "The Selection Process for the Greensboro Truth and Reconciliation Commission" document, which is attached. The Commission will designate its chair(s).

Commissioners will serve on an honorary basis and in their personal capacity, but may be reimbursed for expenses incurred in the discharge of their responsibilities.

3. The Commissioners will carry out their mandate by reviewing documents, inviting people to come forward with information, consulting with experts and by any other means, public or private, they consider appropriate.

4. The Commission may decide to carry out some activities in private in order to protect, to the extent possible, the security and privacy of individuals and the integrity of its ongoing truth-seeking, but in general the Commission's activities will be carried out in a manner that is as public and transparent as possible.

5. The Commission will issue a report to the residents of Greensboro, to the City, to the Project, and to other public bodies, encompassing the items outlined in paragraph 1 and in keeping with the intentions and spirit of the mandate. The Commission will ensure that its findings are fair, based on the information compiled and reviewed, and adequately documented in its report. The Commission may take steps to protect the identity of individual sources, if requested. The Commission will also make specific, constructive recommendations to the City, to the residents of Greensboro, and to other entities as it deems appropriate, particularly to further the intentions set forth in the mandate.

6. The Commission will have no authority either to pursue criminal or civil claims or to grant immunity from such claims. Its focus is reconciliation through seeking, understanding and reporting the truth.

7. The Commission will convene a first meeting, as determined by the Commissioners, no later than 60 days from the date on which the Selection Panel confirms and announces the selection and acceptance of its members. From its first meeting, the Commission will have a period of 15 months to fulfill the terms of its mandate. This period

includes initial planning and set-up, the determination of its internal procedures and selection and appointment of its key staff. The Commission may call upon the Project staff and other resources for administrative support during its initial planning and set-up phase. If absolutely necessary, the period of the Commission's mandate may be extended for up to 6 more months, with the permission of the Project.

8. The Commission will carry out its mandate while operating independently from any external influence, including the Project. It may reach cooperative agreements with organizations, institutions and individuals in order to strengthen its capacity and resources, in so far as such agreements do not compromise the Commission's independence. The Commission will have full authority to make decisions on its spending, within the limits of available funds, and may elect to have a fiscal sponsor through another institution so long as that relationship is consistent with the spirit of the mandate and the Commission's substantive independence.

9. At the completion of its work, all documents of the Commission, its notes, findings, exhibits and other collected materials, shall be permanently archived in Greensboro in an institution whose purpose and tradition is in keeping with the objectives and spirit of the Commission mandate. The identity of this institution and the structure of the archive will be determined by agreement between the Commission and the Project. If deemed appropriate, multiple institutions and locations may be used for archival purposes. Such an archive shall, to the extent feasible and respectful of any recommendations by the Commission with regard to the continued confidentiality of records, be accessible to the public.

The passage of time alone cannot bring closure, nor resolve feelings of guilt and lingering trauma, for those impacted by the events of November 3, 1979. Nor can there be any genuine healing for the city of Greensboro unless the truth surrounding these events is honestly confronted, the suffering fully acknowledged, accountability established, and forgiveness and reconciliation facilitated.

Guiding Principles of the Greensboro Truth and Reconciliation Commission

We, the members of the Greensboro Truth and Reconciliation Commission, are committed to carrying out our work in accordance with the ideals and objectives set forth in our Mandate. In this spirit, we have also adopted the following guiding principles:

PRINCIPLE ONE: Because we recognize that injustice anywhere affects us everywhere, we will seek the truth in all its layers and will seek to provide creative ways for all members of our community to explore their experiences and feelings, engage in fruitful dialogue, and work together in our search for both truth and reconciliation.

PRINCIPLE TWO: Because we enthusiastically embrace the twin principles of honesty and openness, we will work hard to assure that every part of our examination is open, fair and impartial.

PRINCIPLE THREE: Because we are a totally independent entity, not accountable to or dependent on any particular group or segment of our community, we will earnestly seek to hear and will honestly value everyone's story. No evidence or testimony will be rejected. In every aspect of our work we will give respect to and provide opportunity for expressions of diverse viewpoints.

PRINCIPLE FOUR: We commit ourselves to the ideal of restorative justice, freed from the need to exact revenge or make recriminations. The work that we do, and the report that we ultimately will issue, will be inspired by the belief that divisions can be bridged, trust restored and hope rekindled.

November 2004

What Is Reconciliation?

The following document was generated by the Greensboro Truth and Reconciliation Commissioners in response to numerous questions from community members about why, who, how, and what the TRC is reconciling.

We all want to live in a loving, just and sustainable community. We want to live where the rights, dignity and sacredness of all people are valued. When any person has been harmed by the actions of another, we all need to work together in order to find a way to help that person heal. This is especially important when someone harms a group of people. It becomes even more important when that harm has been both intentional and long lasting.

Reconciliation means to bring together those parts that were torn apart and make them whole again. Reconciliation means to repair the brokenness in our community.

Reconciliation does not happen all at once. It takes time. There has to be a process, with many individual steps. The first step is to find out what is the truth. What actually happened? How did those events in the past cause harm to people in our community? In what way were they harmed? This is not an easy task. Each person involved will have his or her own story about what actually happened. Each person may feel strongly that they are telling the truth, even when one person's version differs from another person's version. However, when all of the various versions of the truth are told clearly, and harmonized, we can finally understand the whole truth.

Communities are made up not only by people, but also by institutions. When people within a community are hurt by violence or oppression, institutions often are involved. This means that institutions must be part of the truth telling and part of the reconciliation that follows.

Once we tell and understand the whole truth, we then can take the next steps toward reconciliation. We can describe clearly the harm that was done, to individuals and to groups. We can explain how the actions of the past caused harm. We also can show how that harm continues to cause problems in the community. We can understand how the ongoing harm leads to mistrust, fear, and division. This is what we mean when we speak of a broken community.

Knowing the whole truth helps individuals, groups, and institutions who caused the harm to face what they have done. Sometimes, until the whole truth has been uncovered, those who did the harm are unable to see how their actions hurt other people. They are not able to see that their actions also hurt the community.

Several things must happen for reconciliation to be fully achieved:

Those who have hurt others need to understand just how their actions caused harm. Sometimes the harm is physical. Other times it is emotional, cultural, or spiritual. Often, the harm has economic consequences.

Once those who hurt others understand the harm they have done, they should be supported in their efforts to apologize, and in so far as possible, to undo the harm.

The community that works for reconciliation should create ways in which those who have done harm and those who were harmed can talk honestly to one another. This will make it easier for there to be healing between them.

Sometimes, we will discover that certain social conditions or public policies allowed people to harm others. In some cases, community institutions may even have encouraged the harm. When this is the case, we should take steps to change these social conditions or public policies so they may never contribute to harming others again.

As more and more people learn the whole truth, they should be encouraged to see how they may have participated, unknowingly, in the problem. It may be that they stood by and did nothing to stop the harm. Perhaps they shared attitudes that indirectly suggested it was OK to act in harmful ways. When people know these things, they are less likely to support hurtful behavior in the future.

Once the people of a community have gone through a process of discovering the whole truth about a hurtful event in their past, they will be more aware of the signs that problems exist. In the future, they will be more able to prevent people from doing harmful things.

We believe that we must work together in order to make our society more just. We think that justice is the way a society expresses love toward the people who are part of that society. In an ideal society, each person will act in a just and loving way toward all the other people in that society. When harm is done, we all work together to undo the damage. That is reconciliation. It also is real justice.

Unresolved past hurtful events divide a community. We can help the people in such a community reunite in common purpose by seeking truth and working for reconciliation. A reconciled community will be a strong community, where people work together for the common good.

Final Report General Summary

The Greensboro Truth and Reconciliation Commission (GTRC) took a two-year look at Nov. 3, 1979. On that day in Greensboro, N.C., in the absence of police, white supremacists clashed with and ultimately opened fire on communist demonstrators—a handful of whom also had guns—holding a "Death to the Klan" rally in a black public housing neighborhood. Five demonstrators were killed and at least 10 injured. TV news crews recorded the violence. The killers claimed self-defense and all were acquitted.

The GTRC was initiated by survivors and victims of the tragedy and others seeking a greater understanding of what happened and why. We were democratically selected and independent. We worked in impartial service to all of Greensboro, with an ultimate goal of authentic community healing from this trauma, based on truth.

Key Findings:

KLAN AND NAZIS

- On the morning of Nov. 3, 1979, Klan and Nazi members headed for the parade starting point intending to break the law, carrying an arsenal of weapons and heavy firearms. They planned at the least to assault demonstrators by throwing eggs, and to provoke a violent confrontation.

- The heaviest burden of responsibility is on Klansmen and Nazis who—after an initial stick fight with demonstrators—returned to their cars, retrieved weapons and fired at mostly unarmed demonstrators, when the caravan's path of exit was cleared and they could have fled.

COMMUNIST WORKERS PARTY (CWP)

- We find that CWP members did not seek or deserve to be killed. They do, however, bear some responsibility, although lesser, for underestimating the danger of taunting the Klan with provocative language and for beating on caravan cars with sticks. A few members also fired guns after the Klan and Nazis began firing.

- The demonstrators' protest issues were grounded in the economic and social concerns of the community—in which the Greensboro members had worked for many years—but their communist ideology and tactics were not widely embraced.

- The WVO/CWP's top-down leadership style was neither empowering nor democratic, and it marginalized the concerns of even its own members. Demonstrators had a responsibility to consult rather than inform Morningside Homes residents about the rally planned there. Many felt angry and traumatized afterward.

GREENSBORO POLICE DEPARTMENT (GPD)

- We believe that loss of life could have been avoided had police been visibly present. The police had a paid informant in the Klan who played a leading role in bringing about the confrontation and provided advance information about the Klan and Nazis plans, including the likelihood that they would be armed. Yet police made the deliberate choice to be absent, which they explained as a low-profile plan to avoid a clash between marchers and police.

- Police did not warn march organizers of the Klan and Nazis plans, nor of the fact that they had given a Klansman a copy of the parade route and starting point.

- Minutes before the shooting occurred, officers were explicitly called away from the area around the parade starting point.

- A police intelligence officer followed and photographed the caravan as it approached the parade and kept other officers updated. Yet officers did not move in to intervene or visibly accompany the caravan. Key commanders claim they were not monitoring hand radios and so did not stay abreast of the caravan's approach. All but one of the caravan vehicles were allowed to flee the scene of the shooting.

- The Commission feels these decisions recklessly endangered the welfare of all involved, including Morningside Homes residents. Nearly all Commissioners believe police absence was the result of some intentionality on the part of some officers involved in planning and intelligence-gathering for the march.

CITY AND COMMUNITY RESPONSE

- City officials endeavored to protect the city's image by attempting to distance Greensboro from the underlying issues that contributed to the event, using tactics including CWP scapegoating.
- The City's elected officials and managers responded to the tragedy by clamping down on citizen protest in the interest of "security," through tactics such as curfews, National Guard presence, surveillance and public service announcements discouraging attendance at subsequent protests.
- The GPD intentionally downplayed its own role in the violence by failing to disclose it had advance intelligence about the likelihood of violence and falsely claiming the CWP had deceived police about the parade starting point.

INJUSTICE IN THE JUSTICE SYSTEM

- The verdicts in the three trials conflicted with what seems to be a common sense assessment of wrongdoing based on the videotape, resulting in a greater distrust of the justice system.
- A flawed system of jury selection created all-white juries unrepresentative of the community, contributing to the acquittals.
- We disagree with jurors' acceptance that the first two shots fired by the Klan were "calming" shots, and with the juries' assessment that the defendants acted in self-defense.
- The civil trial jury that found Greensboro police and the white supremacist shooters jointly liable for one of the five deaths was a modest dose of justice, but it still left four other deaths unexplained.

RACISM IN GREENSBORO

We found that the events of Nov. 3, 1979, are woven through with issues of race and class. Our report discusses underlying issues including racial and economic justice, white supremacy, and the failure of the police and justice system to provide equal protection to all residents.

Consequences and Recommendations

As an exercise in transformative justice, we find that deep brokenness existed prior to Nov. 3, 1979, and led to the violence. The harm from this event extended beyond those who were killed, wounded or psychologically traumatized to include all residents of Greensboro, which lost ground on human relations progress made after school desegregation. Our recommendations seek to address these harms through public acknowledgement, institutional reforms, and citizen engagement and transformation.

- We recommend that the City, the police department and individuals responsible in any way for the tragedy or the harms suffered in the aftermath publicly and privately acknowledge and apologize for their roles, and take specific steps toward reconciliation such as commemorations and community forums. The apologies and self-reflection already offered through this process give us hope that this is possible.

- We recommend that the City and Guilford County confront local disparities by committing to a living wage for all workers, providing anti-racism training, establishing short-term and permanent citizen review committees to ensure police accountability, and creating a community justice center.

- We recommend that the current investigations into alleged GPD corruption be thoroughly and expeditiously completed, that the reports of these investigations be publicly released, and that a town hall meeting be held to solicit citizen questions and feedback. If appropriate, criminal prosecutions or civil action should be pursued to help heal the department's credibility.

- We encourage all citizens to take an active role in understanding racism, poverty, oppression and privilege around them and the ways in which their own actions play a role in perpetuating disparities.

The executive summary and full report can be accessed at www. greensborotrc.org.

Discussing the Greensboro Truth and Reconciliation Commission's Executive Summary in a College Classroom

TIME REQUIRED: 1½ to 2 hours

PURPOSE: To discuss the executive summary of the GTRC report and place in context with specific disciplinary interest/theories.

COMMUNICATION GUIDELINES: We'd like to target participation by everyone. To do that, we need to listen and we need to express our views. Hopefully we will consider the different views to see what we can learn from one another. We need to understand the facts. By the end, we should have more questions that arise from our engagement with the material and our collective dialogue about it.

I. VIEWING OF SOME FILM OR EVENT FOOTAGE:
   Up to 30 minutes.

II. DISCUSSION

In small groups or one larger body, depending on size:

1. What is the method by which the TRC did its work?

2. What do you see as the main purpose of the report in terms of generating future activities/discussion in the city? In other words, why spend all this time to create a report?

3. Who did the TRC find responsible for the events of November 3, 1979? In what ways?

4. How did the findings in the report differ from what was discovered in the legal process spanning three court trials and seven years?

5. What key issues emerge from the report that are especially interesting to your field of study?

6. What consequences of November 3 do you see in the community today? Provide specific examples.

7. What recommendations are ones with which you as an individual could have an impact?

III. CLOSING

Wrap up the discussion OR use this initial discussion as a gateway to encouraging the reading of the full report (or parts of it). Some questions to consider:

1. What have we learned today, or what do you know now, after reading the report and discussing it that you didn't know previously?

2. What do you still have questions about?

3. What intrigues you most? What will you want to read more about in the full report?

Lyrical Reflections of November 3rd, 1979

Life at the mill ain't been no thrill
America's part of the KKK and they're ready to kill
we're overworked and underpaid.
Lord knows there are some changes to be made
The bastards upstairs won't give us a break
They don't realize our lives are at stake
This isn't just about race it's more about class
even these white workers are being treated like trash
We try to speak out and are seen as a threat
but if they think I'm gonna shut up
that's something they can forget
they don't want us meeting or putting up signs
but for them to rally against us is just fine
I don't even know when things all fell apart
at what point did the inequality start
I'll tell you what, if we're going to be saved
lord knows there are some changes to be made

In 1863
Good ol' Abe declared to give us free
Which puts the years from now
To one hundred and forty-three
Since slavery ended, so it's said . . .
So why is it that now
I can't get ahead?

Don't get it twisted
It wasn't no moral change of heart
This was a time of war
And a political decision to mend
The schism
And to get applause from those abroad
The federacy
wanted slavery
and Reconstruction
Still enslaving the
Freedmen wanting
To be men
Wanting to vote and treated
As equal, then
Now
We back there again
Treated as a second class
Citizens
It's '79 tryna stay alive
Wit these wages
We sleeping in cages
Give me my damn money
You see we hungry!
LOOK at these racial disparities
Education, wages, housing, health care, insanity
Twice as many of us living below poverty
Why can't we be what we wanna be?
When all we want to be is free . . .

free to be a young black man
who can take a stand
without you assuming there's a gun in my hand

they tell me speech is free?
well not for me
my words are interpreted by what you see
a criminal
a liar
a troublemaker
a threat
and I ant even said nothing yet
but im the one you love to hate
not an equal citizen but an enemy of the state
so I flip a table or throw a chair
what I gotta do for you to see me here
embody the stereotype of anger and rage
just to play a part on America's stage
where the stories that are told
depend on the power you hold
Change is gonna come
I'm gonna show you I am someone
Tired of being overlooked
It's time we write our own history book
not just about black and white
this is a story of civil rights
the truth is we deserve to be heard
even if you can't understand a single word

you think I don't see how you're looking at me
thinking cause I'm white I ain't got no right
to speak to another
about these stupid assumptions we assign by color
I don't need you to like me
I don't need you to care
but I need for myself to make you aware

even if it's just for this moment right now
your gonna listen while I lay it down
Death to Klan is the headline that ran
in every paper around town
going around saying the CWP
would burn the Klan to the ground
like the fiery crosses left on many a lawn
warning those who didn't belong
but theirs was a metaphor an institutional claim
not a reality where thousands were hanged
the Klan and the Nazis perpetuate hate
that's a matter of fact not up for debate
their words are vicious their actions the same
torture and killing is how they play the game
meritocracy is a myth if you want to buy in
to this commodity culture we're living in
nobody starts with the same fair chances
life is all about circumstances
most of which are controlled by another
especially if you a person of color

but there were a few
who knew what they had to do
lead, organize and educate the masses
time to transcend all social classes
so they took the road to China Grove
with no thought of the consequences our future would hold
pointing the finger at working conditions
forcing people to see the problems in the system
In the fight for equality
Five were gunned down
You didn't want to remember

So you rearranged the ground
And you say they weren't victims
for choosing to be there
But I doubt they chose
which bullet to wear
Sandi, Cesar, Mike, Bill and Jim
they all believed this was a fight we could win
But the truth was concealed about the events of that day
A group of men and women acting in ignorant ways
And still many deny the reason why
I guess it's easier to swallow a lie
The killers were tried but slapped on the hand
where was the justice promised from our great land?
Instead the story was twisted and called a shootout
That day the light in Greensboro's hall of justice went out.

There is hope if you can see
America's just a baby democracy
there's still much to be learned in the land of the free
and to be brave we must not fear reality
So what now?
Past the point of assigning blame
no longer will we carry this shame
we want recognition and justice at last
the only way to evolve is to learn from the past
we can't turn back time we cannot undo
but we must continue to seek what is true
we are asking the city to say it out loud
we're sorry for the innocent blood on the ground
we're sorry the police didn't serve and protect
we're sorry the police weren't present that day
to protect the people and keep the Klan away

and now let this tragedy birth a new life
one of fairness and equality instead of suffering and strife
let all city workers be paid a living wage
and encourage those filled with hatred to overcome their rage
let's instill in the youth the integrity to do for yourself
without exploiting somebody else
so future generations can lay a new foundation
and continue to build a more just nation.

NOTES

Introduction

Epigraph. *The Researcher as Detective,* plenary address to the Southern States Communication Association, 2007.

1. Greensboro, North Carolina, fared poorly in these features of community life in comparison with other cities across the country according to the Harvard-based Saguaro Seminar's Social Capital Benchmark Studies released in 2001 and 2007 and available at www.cfgg.org.

2. I rely here on Paolo Freire's definition of radical as someone who is "critical, loving, humble and communicative" (1973, 10) in working to resolve or lessen social injustices.

Chapter 1: The Greensboro Massacre, November 3, 1979

1. The Communist Workers Party was the new name of Jerry Tung's U.S. Maoist organization, based in New York with branches around the country, started in 1973 first as the Asian Study Group, then the Workers' Viewpoint Organization and finally the CWP. By 1985, the CWP dissolved and was replaced by the short-lived New Democratic Movement.

2. Eddie Dawson was a paid informant for the FBI from 1969 to 1976. In 1979, the Greensboro Police Department hired Dawson to provide inside information on the Klan, despite his documented history of criminal activity and race-based violence.

3. Bernard Butkovich's identity and role were revealed for the first time in a July 1980 *Greensboro Record* newspaper article that reported he was at the meeting where the United Racist Front formed on September 22, 1979, and where the decision was made to attack the WVO/CWP on November 3 (Woodall, 1980, A1–2).

4. Z Holler's first encounter with Nelson Johnson and the other survivors was in 1979, but it continued through the years. In 1991, he co-founded with Johnson and Barbara Dua, the nonprofit Beloved Community Center. Later, Holler was named a co-chair of the Local Task Force of the Greensboro Community Truth and Reconciliation Project with former mayor Carolyn Allen and the Reverend Gregory Headon.

5. The National Anti-Klan Network was later renamed the Center for Democratic Renewal. Klan Watch became Hatewatch and is maintained by the Southern Poverty Law Center (www.splcenter.org), which in 2010 reported on the activities of 1,002 hate groups in the United States.

6. Some of these reports are archived and available at the Civil Rights Greensboro Digital Collection, http://library.uncg.edu/dp/crg/.

Chapter 2: Grave Consequences

Epigraph. Johnson, Survivor, Public Hearing Testimony, September 30, 2005.

1. Sandi Smith's parents made arrangements for her body to be buried elsewhere, in a family cemetery.

2. See http://www.leadershipforchange.org/awardees/awardee.php3?ID=314.

3. Details about the South African "Living Learning Experience" included photographs and a compilation of recommendations by James Lamar Gibson in the November 2007 "Newsview" originally posted to, but no longer available, at www.belovedcommunitycenter.org.

4. See Civic Ventures' program at http://www.encore.org/prize/winners-fellows.

Chapter 3: An Unfolding History of Social Unrest

Epigraph. Rorty, *Achieving Our Country*, 1997, 106.

1. Chinese Americans and African Americans originally founded the Workers' Viewpoint Organization in New York, according to November 3 survivor Jean Chapman. In North Carolina, WVO members lived primarily in Greensboro's Piedmont Triad and in Durham and saw their goal of equality as dependent upon defeating capitalism, which for them was tainted by slavery and exploitation of black people and others without adequate power or representation (Final Report, 2006, 79–82). Just prior to November 3, 1979, the WVO in Greensboro transitioned to the Communist Workers Party for the latter's clout as a political party, according to survivor Signe Waller (see page 32 in Waller's 2002 book, *Love and Revolution: A Political Memoir* and page 81 of the Truth Commission's Final Report).

2. More than one hundred court challenges have been filed since the film's release to prevent its showing (Final Report, 2006, 103).

3. It was at this point in time, according to documents used in the federal civil trial, that the WVO became a target of FBI investigation.

4. In the Final Report of the United States Senate Select Committee to Study Governmental Operations with Respect to Intelligence Activities entitled, "Intelligence Activities and the Rights of Americans" (1976), the committee's investigation confirmed "substantial wrongdoing" with regard to domestic intelligence gathering (v). They further reported, "We have seen segments of our Government, in their attitudes and action, adopt tactics unworthy of a democracy, and occasionally reminiscent of the tactics of totalitarian regimes" (3). In summarizing the main problems of intelligence, the committee noted, "Unsavory and vicious tactics have been employed—including anonymous attempts to break up marriages, disrupt meetings, ostracize persons from their professions, and provoke target groups into rivalries that might result in deaths" (5).

Chapter 4: Truth and Reconciliation Commissions Seek Healing, Not Vengeance

Epigraph. Gutmann and Thompson, *The Moral Foundations of Truth Commissions*, 2000, 42.

1. For more information on many of the world's TRCs, see the U.S. Institute of

Peace that maintains a Truth Commission Digital Collection at www.usip.org/library/truth.html.

2. For an excellent review of the many stories that circulated around this incident, read *Fire in a Canebreak* (2003) by Laura Wexler.

3. On the occasion of the fifth anniversary of Greensboro's TRC Final Report release, representatives from these cities convened in Greensboro to share stories of their efforts to launch truth commissions.

4. See http://www.atrr.org/documents/narratives.pdf.

5. See the writings of Hannah Arendt, Emmanuel Levinas, Martha Minnow, and Martin Buber.

6. Simon Wiesenthal's classic book, *The Sunflower* (1998), illuminates his questions and struggle to forgive a dying Nazi, as well as reflections from other world experts on the dilemma.

7. In 2002, the Friends of the Greensboro Public Library initiated the One City One Book project to encourage reading and discussion throughout the city. Despite the survey results, Greensboro Public Library assistant director Steve Sumerford reported that the first book selection was one about racial injustice (personal communication, April 14, 2003). Book club readers, high school and college students, and attendees at public lectures and theatrical performances discussed Ernest Gaines's novel, *A Lesson before Dying* about a wrongfully accused, convicted, and executed black man in the 1940s South.

8. See Bureau of Labor Statistics at http://www.bls.gov/eag/eag.nc_greensboro_msa.htm.

9. See American Community Survey Briefs, Poverty: 2009 and 2010 at www.census.gov/prod/2011pubs/acsbr10-01.pdf.

10. The USA PATRIOT Act is an acronym for Uniting and Strengthening America by Providing Appropriate Tools Required to Intercept and Obstruct Terrorism Act of 2001.

11. Specifically Moses Cone Healthcare Systems, R. F. MicroSystems, HondaJet, and Federal Express are among Greensboro's larger corporate employers.

Chapter 5: Greensboro's Truth and Reconciliation Commission: Principles and Processes

Epigraph. Tutu, *No Future without Forgiveness,* 1999, 30.

1. Though suspicions softened, they did not fade away completely. A number of sitting city council members speaking on their own and on behalf of some of their constituents remained unconvinced that any good could come from the process and refused to read the Final Report. Still, other city council members and community members expressed appreciation and even changed views as the work progressed and was completed.

2. With funding from the College of Arts and Sciences, the TRC was the subject of a two-year-long UNCG Ashby Dialogue series on the hidden legacy of November 3, 1979.

3. These "Guiding Principles" are included in the Appendix.

4. In 2009, nearly 47 percent of Buies Creek's residents lived in poverty according to www.citydata.com/city/Buies-Creek-North-Carolina.html.

Chapter 6: The Commission's Final Report: Recovering the Truth

Epigraph. Final Report, 2006, 23.

1. The Greensboro's Truth and Reconciliation Commission's Final Report, Executive Summary, Public Hearing Testimonies, and other documents are accessible on-line at www.greensborotrc.org.

2. See Mandate for the Greensboro Truth and Reconciliation Commission prepared and approved by the Greensboro Truth and Community Reconciliation Project that appears in Appendix A and in the original Final Report (2006) on pp. 457–459.

3. For a more thorough discussion of restorative justice, see this book, chapter 4.

4. In a Social Capital study released in 2006, mistrust of local government leaders and police officials was significantly higher in Greensboro than in most other parts of the country. In fact, Greensboro's level of generalized mistrust—trust of people beyond your immediate social circle—was the highest of any of the twenty communities surveyed in 2006, and by sizable margins (Easterling and Foy, 2007).

5. In concert with my position as a communication activist and a supporter of the Greensboro Truth and Reconciliation process, I agreed to conduct and be compensated for the media research requested by the Greensboro Truth and Reconciliation Commission's staff research director, Emily Harwell. The results of that research appear in the TRC's Final Report in chapter 11 and the Appendix.

6. A curricular activity based on the eight media frames of November 3, 1979, detailed in the Final Report, was developed and is available from "Teaching Tolerance," a project of the Southern Poverty Law Center. It can be downloaded from http://www.tolerance.org/activity/what-truth for use with students to "understand that different perspectives of the same event can sometimes be true and that different perspectives of the same event are sometimes not equally accurate."

Chapter 7: The Public's Response

Epigraph. Murithi, *Practical Peacemaking*, 2006, 31.

1. Cavin participated in one of thirteen panels organized from 2003 to 2005 as part of a two-year-long Ashby Dialogue series at UNCG devoted to interdisciplinary study and inquiry into "Greensboro's Hidden Legacy: The Impact of November 3, 1979 on the City Today." The Ashby Dialogue, funded by UNCG's College of Arts and Sciences, honors the late Dr. Warren Ashby, a UNCG faculty member from 1949 to 1985 who believed that the university was the home for "freedom in the search and service of truth."

2. Of note is that even before the TRC was operational, conversations were initiated to prepare the community for the truth and reconciliation effort. Then UNCG graduate student Carol Steger prepared a sixteen-page booklet entitled *A Call for Dialogue* (2004) and with a team of community supporters, organized workshops for more than two hundred people. The booklets, facilitator training, workshop manuals, and participant packets were paid for by individual donations and a grant from the Community Foundation of Greater Greensboro. The booklet is available free at www.uncg.edu/cst.

3. In 2002 at a coffee shop meeting, Mayor Keith Holliday said he remained firmly opposed to the TRC yet supported educational inquiry into November 3. Ironically, it was the TRC that enabled the educational experiences Holliday suggested by providing a research-based, well-detailed volume to read, study, and question.

4. See Appendix for a sample study guide.

5. See Appendix for the full text written by Alicia Sowisdral with Jeanna Covington, Michael C. Craig, Shanell Smaw, Savon Williams and others.

6. Some of Howell's paintings and more of her thoughts are at http://inthefray. org/content/view/989/177/.

Chapter 8: The Politics of an Apology

Epigraph. Weiner, *Sins of the Parents,* 2005, 188.

1. In August 2003, UNCG students collected benchmark data about citizen knowledge of November 3 and the Greensboro Truth and Community Reconciliation Project. Three hundred surveys were administered to 67 percent white, 30 percent African American, and 3 percent other racially identified citizens. Of those, 56 percent said they were unaware of the 1979 incident (Jovanovic, 2003).

2. Greensboro's first female mayor was Local Task Force co-chair Carolyn Allen, who served for three terms, 1993–1999.

Chapter 9: Measures of Success

Epigraph. Lingis, *The Community of Those Who Have Nothing in Common,* 1994, 70.

1. Citizen review of police conduct began in the 1950s and 1960s in response to the civil rights movement. By 1998, 80 percent of the largest cities in the United States had some form of citizen review according to a report issued by the National Institute of Justice at www.nij.gov/pubs-sum/184430.htm.

2. A letter signed by the widows of November 3, 1979, was written and sent to Greensboro's city attorney when rumors circulated to discredit the work of the TRC as a "front" for the survivors to use in extracting or extorting money from the city's coffers.

Chapter 10: Greensboro's Legacy Is Hidden No More

Epigraph. Rigby, *Justice and Reconciliation,* 2001, 183.

REFERENCES

American Community Survey. 2006. United States Census Bureau. Available at http://factfinder.census.gov.

Amjad-Ali, Charles. 2008. Comparing the TRCs around the world: Ethical, moral and theological assessment. Paper presented at Healing through Faith: A Conference for Faith Leaders of the Liberian Diaspora. Minneapolis, MN. Retrieved February 18, 2009, from http://liberiatrc.mnadvocates.org/Healing_Through_Faith_Conference.html.

Amstutz, Mark R. 2005. *The healing of nations: The promise and limits of political forgiveness.* Lanham, MD: Rowman & Littlefield.

Anderson, Rob, Leslie A. Baxter, and Kenneth N. Cissna. 2004. *Dialogue: Theorizing difference in communication studies.* Thousand Oaks, CA: Sage.

Arnett, Ronald C. 1986. *Communication and community: Implications of Martin Buber's dialogue.* Carbondale: Southern Illinois University Press.

Arnett, Ronald C., and Pat Arneson. 1999. *Dialogic civility in a cynical age: Community, hope, and interpersonal relationships.* New York: SUNY Press.

Ball, Edward. 1998. *Slaves in the family.* New York: Ballantine Books.

Barber, Benjamin. 1994. *Aristocracy for everyone: The politics of education and the future of America.* New York: Oxford University Press.

Barkan, Elazar, and Alexander Karn. 2006. Group apology as an ethical imperative. In E. Barkan and A. Karn (eds.), *Taking wrongs seriously: Apologies and reconciliation,* 3–30. Stanford, CA: Stanford University.

Barry, Dan. 2003. A word choice and challenge long forgotten. *New York Times,* October 25, A14.

Bauman, Zygmunt. 2005. *Liquid life.* Cambridge, UK: Polity.

Bell, Duncan. 2008. Agonistic democracy and the politics of memory. *Constellations* 15 (1): 148–166. doi:10.1111/j.1467–8675.2008.00478.x.

Belvin, Brent H. 2004. Malcolm X Liberation University: An experiment in independent black education. A thesis submitted to North Carolina State University in partial fulfillment for the Degree of Master of Arts in History. Raleigh, NC. Retrieved April 23, 2009, from http://www.lib.ncsu.edu/theses/available/etd-07082004012843/unrestricted/etd.pdf.

Bergo, Bettina. 1999. *Levinas between ethics and politics: For the beauty that adorns the earth.* Dordrecht, The Netherlands: Kluwer Academic Publishers.

Bermanzohn, Paul. 2005, July 15. Public hearing testimony. *Greensboro Truth and Reconciliation Commission.* Available at www.greensborotrc.org/hear_statements.php.

Bermanzohn, Sally A. 2003. *Through survivors' eyes: From the sixties to the Greensboro Massacre.* Nashville, TN: Vanderbilt University.

Bloch-Schulman, Stephen, and Spoma Jovanovic. 2010. Who's afraid of politics? On the need to teach political engagement. *Journal of Higher Education Outreach and Engagement* 14 (1): 83–100.

Bohm, David. 1996. *On dialogue.* New York: Routledge.

Bowers, John W., Donovan J. Ochs, Richard J. Jensen, and David P. Schulz. 2010. *The rhetoric of agitation and control.* 3rd ed. Long Grove, IL: Waveland.

Braithwaite, John. 2002. *Restorative justice and responsive regulation.* New York: Oxford University Press.

Buber, Martin. 1955. *Between man and* man. Trans. R. G. Smith. Boston: Beacon.

Catanoso, Justin. 2004, June 28. Triad talk. *Business Journal* 6 (43). Available at www.triad.bixjournals/com/triad/stories/2004/06/28/tidbits1.html.

Cauce, César. 2005, October 1. Public hearing testimony. *Greensboro Truth and Reconciliation Commission.* Available at www.greensborotrc.org/hear_statements.php.

Cavin, Winston. 2005, September 26. Public hearing testimony. *Greensboro Truth and Reconciliation Commission.* Available at www.greensborotrc.org/hear_statements.php.

Chafe, William H. 1980. *Civilities and civil rights.* New York: Oxford University Press.

Chafe, William H., Raymond Gavins, and Robert Korstad. 2001. *Remembering Jim Crow: African Americans tell about life in the segregated south.* New York: New Press.

Chapman, Yonni. 2005, July 15. Public hearing testimony. *Greensboro Truth and Reconciliation Commission.* Available at www.greensborotrc.org/hear_statements.php.

Christians, Clifford G. 2007. Cultural continuity as an ethical imperative. *Qualitative Inquiry* 13 (3): 437–444. doi:10.1177/1077800406297664.

City of Greensboro Department of Human Relations. 2008, December. *A Strategic Study of the State of Human Relations in Greensboro: Uncovering Institutional Discrimination to Promote Equal Opportunity.* Greensboro, NC: Ruth DeHoog, Terrolyn Carter, Robert Davis, Eric Jones, Spoma Jovanovic, Arthur Murphy, Stephen Sills. Available at http://www.greensboronc.gov/departments/Relations/study.htm.

Civic Ventures. 2011. Purpose prize, all winners and fellows. For 2008, Rev. Nelson J. Johnson and Joyce Johnson, see www.encore.org/rev-nelson-johnson-and.

Civil Rights Greensboro. 2011. Digital collection. Available at http://library.uncg.edu/dp/crg/.

Coman, Jim. 2005, August 4. Summary interview with the *Greensboro Truth and Reconciliation Commission.* Available at www.greensborotrc.org.

Compa, Lance. 2000. Unfair advantage: Workers' freedom of association in the United States under international human rights standards. *Human Rights Watch.* New York. Available at www.hrw.org.

Cose, Ellis. 2003, June 2. How to mend a massacre. *Newsweek* 141 (22), 63.

Cose, Ellis. 2004. *Bone to pick: Of forgiveness, reconciliation, reparation, and revenge.* New York: Atria Books.

Covington, Jeanna. 2007, December 21. Beloved Center members journey to South Africa. Greensboro, NC: *Carolina Peacemaker.*

Darsey, James. 1997. *The prophetic tradition and radical rhetoric in America.* New York: New York University Press.

Debbage, Keith G. 2008, December 17. 2009 State of the city report: Greensboro, North Carolina. Prepared with Suzanne Gallaway for The Greensboro Partnership. Available at http://greensborochamber.org/PDF/stateofcity2009.pdf.

Debbage, Keith G., Ruth DeHoog, and Jim Johnson. 2008, September. Long-term socio-demographic challenges facing the greater Greensboro area: New opportunities. A report to the Bryan Foundation Board of Directors.

Del Gandio, Jason. 2008. *Rhetoric for radicals: A handbook for 21st century activists.* Gabriola Island, British Columbia, Canada: New Society Publishers.

Derrida, Jacques. 1999. *Adieu to Emmanuel Levinas.* Trans. P. Brault and M. Naas. Stanford, CA: Stanford University.

Doxtader, Eric. 2001. Making rhetorical history in a time of transition: The occasion, constitution, and representation of South African reconciliation. *Rhetoric & Public Affairs* 4 (2): 223–260.

Doxtader, Eric. 2003. Reconciliation: A rhetorical concept/ion. *Quarterly Journal of Speech* 89 (4): 267–292, doi:10.1080/0033563032000160954.

Duncan, Alison. 2005, October 1. Public hearing testimony. *Greensboro Truth and Reconciliation Commission.* Available at www.greensborotrc.org/hear_statements.php.

Eaglin, Adam. 2007, June 13. Teach local students about Nov. 3, 1979. *Greensboro's News & Record,* A-11.

Earnhardt Pirkle. 2009, September 22. United Methodist Publishing House's *Living the good life together: "Challenges to forgiveness,"* part 2. Available at www.ep-video.com.

Easterling, Doug, and Capri G. Foy. 2007. 2006 social capital community benchmark report. Greensboro, NC: Community Foundation of Greater Greensboro.

Fernandez, Jennifer. 2010, March 22. 1064 homeless people counted on annual survey. Retrieved from www.news-record.com.

Florida, Richard. 2002. *The rise of the creative class.* New York: Basic Books.

Freire, Paulo. 1973. *Education for a critical consciousness.* New York: Seabury Press.

Gabel, Peter, and Paul Harris. 1983. Building power and breaking images. *New York University Review of Law and Social Change* 11: 369–411.

Gaines, Ernest J. 1993. *A lesson before dying.* New York: Vintage Books.

Gastil, John. 2008. *Political communication and deliberation.* Thousand Oaks, CA: Sage.

Geertz, Clifford J. 1973. *The interpretation of cultures: Selected essays.* New York: Basic.

Gilligan, C. 1982. *In a different voice.* Cambridge, MA: Harvard University Press.

Gilmore, Glenda E. 2008. *Defying Dixie: The radical roots of civil rights, 1919–1950.* New York: W. W. Norton.

Giroux, Henry. 2007, February 17. Higher education in a time of crisis: Rethinking the politics and possibilities of critical pedagogy, an interview with Chronis Polychroniou. Available at www.cosmopolisonline.it/20071201/giroux.php.

Giroux, Henry A., and Susan Searis Giroux. 2006. Corporate culture versus public education and democracy: A call for critical pedagogy. In Lee Artz, Steve Macek, and Dana L. Cloud (eds.), *Marxism and communication studies: The point is to change it,* 203–216. New York: Peter Lang.

Goodall, Harold Lloyd. 2007. The researcher as detective. Plenary address to the Southern States Communication Association.

Goodall, Harold Lloyd. 1999. Casing the academy for community. *Communication Theory* 9 (4): 465–494. doi:10.1111/j.14682885.1999.tb00208.x.

Green, Jordan. 2005, September 21. Jordan Green confesses: He's an ex-activist. *YES! Weekly,* 21, 24.

Greensboro Human Relations Commission. 2009, June 16. Truth and reconciliation review report to the City Council. Available at http://greensboro.granicus.com/ViewPublisher.php?view_id=2.

Greensboro Truth and Community Reconciliation Project. 2007, November 3. Towards an inclusive vision for Greensboro. Available at www.beloved communitycenter.org.

Greensboro Truth and Reconciliation Commission. 2005, September 20. Educators to brainstorm ideas for "teaching through the TRC" *press release.*

Greensboro Truth and Reconciliation Commission. 2006. *Final report.* Available at www.greensborotrc.org.

Griffith, D. W. (Director). 1915. *The birth of a nation* [Motion picture]. U.S.A. Available at www.imdb.com/title/tt0004972/.

Gutmann, Amy, and Dennis Thompson. 2000. The moral foundations of truth commissions. In Robert I. Rotberg and Dennis Thompson (eds.), *Truth v. justice: The morality of truth commissions,* 22–44. Princeton, NJ: Princeton University Press.

Hanh, T. N. 1988. *The heart of understanding.* Berkeley, CA: Parallax Press.

Hatch, John B. 2008. *Race and reconciliation: Redressing wounds of injustice.* Lanham, MD: Rowman & Littlefield.

Hayner, Priscilla B. 2001. *Unspeakable truths: Confronting state terror and atrocity.* New York: Routledge.

Holler, Z. 2003. *The Greensboro Truth and Community Reconciliation Project . . . The right thing for just such a time as this.* Pamphlet.

hooks, bell. 2003. *Teaching community: A pedagogy of hope.* New York: Routledge.

Howell, Aliene de Souza. 2005, February 6. Greensboro's vulgar heart: An artist explores a little known tragedy through painting. *In the Fray Magazine* at http://inthefray.org/content/view/989/177/.

Hyde, Michael J. 2006. *The life-giving gift of acknowledgment: A philosophical and rhetorical inquiry.* West Lafayette, IN: Purdue University Press.

Jensen, Robert. 2005. *The heart of whiteness: Confronting race, racism, and white privilege.* San Francisco: City Lights.

Johnson, Joyce. 2005, September 30. Public hearing testimony. *Greensboro Truth and Reconciliation Commission.* Available at www.greensborotrc.org/hear_statements.php.

Johnson, Nelson. 2005, August 26. Public hearing testimony. *Greensboro Truth and Reconciliation Commission.* Available at www.greensborotrc.org/hear_statements.php.

Jones, Billy. 2008, May 1. Proof that Jim Melvin controls the city council. Retrieved June 26, 2009, from http://bloggingpoet.squarespace.com/billy-jones-bio.

Jost, Muktha, Edward Whitfield, and Mark Jost. 2005. When the rules are fair, but the game isn't. *Multicultural Education* 13 (1): 14–21.

Jovanovic, Spoma. 2003. August 2003 survey results: Assessing the knowledge and understanding of November 3, 1979 and the Greensboro Truth and Community Reconciliation Project.

Jovanovic, Spoma, Carol E. Steger, Sarah Symonds, and Donata Nelson. 2007. Promoting deliberative democracy through dialogue: Communication contributions to a grassroots movement for truth, justice, and reconciliation. In L. R. Frey and K. M. Carragee (eds.), *Communication Activism,* 53–94. Cresskill, NJ: Hampton.

Kerber, Guillermo. 2003. Overcoming violence and pursuing justice: An introduction to restorative justice. *Ecumenical Review* 55 (2): 151–157. doi:10.1111/j.1758–6623.2003.tb00191.x.

Krog, Antjie. 2008. ". . . if it means he gets his humanity back . . ." The worldview underpinning the South African Truth and Reconciliation Commission. *Journal of Multicultural Discourses* 3 (3): 204–220. doi:10.1080/174471 40802406891.

Lakoff, George. 2002. *Moral politics: How liberals and conservatives think.* 2nd ed. Chicago: University of Chicago Press.

Lama, D. 1999. *Ethics for a new millennium.* New York: Penguin Putnam.

Leadership for a Changing World. 2011. A program of the Ford Foundation in partnership with the Institute for Sustainable Communities and the Robert F. Wagner School of Public Service, New York University. Washington, DC. Available at www.leadershipforchange.org.

Levinas, Emmanuel. 1969. *Totality and infinity.* Trans. Alphonso Lingis. Pittsburgh, PA: Duquesne University. (Original work published in 1961.)

Levinas, Emmanuel. 1998. *Totality and infinity: An essay on exteriority.* Trans. A. Lingis. Pittsburgh, PA: Duquesne University. (Original work published 1961.)

Levinas, Emmanuel. 2006. *Humanism of the other.* Trans. N. Poller. Chicago: University of Illinois Press. (Originally published in 1972.)

Lingis, Alphonso. 1994. *The community of those who have nothing in common.* Bloomington: Indiana University Press.

Lipari, Lisbeth. 2004. Listening to the other: Ethical implications of the Buber-Levinas encounter. *Communication Theory* 14 (2): 122–141. doi:10.1111/j.1468–2885.2004.tb00308.x.

Lipari, Lisbeth. 2009. Listening otherwise: The voice of ethics. *The International Journal of Listening* 23: 44–59. doi:10.1080/10904010802591888.

Magarrell, Lisa, and Scott Roehm. 2003, July. Truth commission concept and processes: A brief introduction and overview (working paper presented to the Greensboro Truth and Community Reconciliation Project's Local Task Force Workshop). New York: International Center for Transitional Justice.

Magarrell, Lisa, and Joya Wesley. 2008. *Learning from Greensboro: Truth and reconciliation in the United States.* Philadelphia: University of Pennsylvania Press.

Massango, M. J. S. 2006. African spirituality that shapes the concept of Ubuntu. *African Spirituality* 27 (3): 930–943.

Minow, Martha. 1998. *Between vengeance and forgiveness: Facing history after genocide and mass violence.* Boston, MA: Beacon.

More, Mabogo P. 2004. Philosophy in South Africa under and after apartheid. In Kwasi Wiredu (ed.), *A companion to African philosophy,* 149–160. Malden, MA: Blackwell.

Mouffe, Chantal. 2000. *The democratic paradox.* London: Verso.

Moyers, B. 2008. *Moyers on democracy.* New York: Anchor Books.

Murithi, Timothy. 2006. Practical peacemaking wisdom from Africa: Reflections on ubuntu. *The Journal of Pan African Studies 1* (4): 25–34.

Nabudere, Dani W. 2005, March 1. *Ubuntu philosophy, memory and reconciliation.* From the International Documentation Network on the Great African Lakes Region. Retrieved February 2, 2009 from www.grandsclacs.net/doc/3621.pdf.

Nathan, Martha. 2005, October 1. Public hearing testimony. *Greensboro Truth and Reconciliation Commission.* Available at www.greensborotrc.org/hear_statements.php.

Noddings, Nell. 1984. *Caring: A feminine approach to ethics and moral education.* Berkeley and Los Angeles: University of California Press.

Noddings, Nell. 1995. Caring. In V. Held (ed.), *Justice and care,* 7–30. Boulder, CO: Westview Press.

Norlock, Kathryn. 2009. *Forgiveness from a feminist perspective.* Lanham, MD: Lexington Books.

Partners Ending Homelessness. 2010. Why is homelessness an important issue in Guilford County. Available at www.partnersendinghomlessness.org.

Patterson, Donald W. 2010, April 9. Guilford Mills' local legacy to end with layoff of 150. Retrieved from www.news-record.com.

Pearce, W. Barnett, and Stephen W. Littlejohn. 1997. *Moral conflict: When social worlds collide.* Thousand Oaks, CA: Sage.

Peters, John D. 1999. *Speaking into the air: A history of the idea of communication.* Chicago: University of Chicago Press.

Phelps, Teresa Godwin. 2004. *Shattered voices: Language, violence, and the work of truth commissions.* Philadelphia: University of Pennsylvania Press.

Pierce, Gorrell. 2005, July 16. Public hearing testimony. *Greensboro Truth and Reconciliation Commission.* Available at www.greensborotrc.org/hear_statements.php.

Poulos, Christopher N. 2009. *Accidental ethnography: An inquiry into family secrecy.* Walnut Creek, CA: Left Coast Press.

Ricks, Lenehn, Courtney Glass, Jeremy Skinner, and Sylvia Dove. 2007, Spring. *Southern truth and reconciliation: Narrative summaries and chart.* For Reparations, Reconciliation, and Restorative Justice taught by Professor Ifill. Baltimore: University of Maryland. Retrieved April 19, 2009, from http://www.atrr.org/documents/narratives.pdf.

Rigby, Andrew. 2001. *Justice and reconciliation: After the violence.* Boulder, CO: Lynne Reinner Publishers.

Robinson, John. 2006, June 4. Citizen group suggestion fits our philosophy. Greensboro's *News & Record,* B-2.

Rorty, Richard. 1997. *Achieving our country: Leftist thought in twentieth-century America.* Cambridge, MA: Harvard University Press.

Ross, Fiona C. 2003. *Bearing witness: Women and the truth and reconciliation commission in South Africa.* Sterling, VA: Pluto.

Ryder, John. 2008. Prospects for a thick democracy. *Americana-E-Journal of American Studies in Hungary* 4 (1). http://americanaejournal.hu/vol4no1.

Schlosser, Mike. 2005, August 4. Summary interview with the Greensboro TRC. Available at www.greensborotrc.org.

Sit In Movement, Inc. 2011. Civil rights movement: The Greensboro chronology. Available at www.sitinmovement.org/history/greensboro-chronology.asp.

Social Capital Benchmark Survey. 2000. Guilford County summary of findings, March 1, 2001. Available at www.cfgg.org/downloads/studies/Social_Capital_Benchmark_Study_Phase_1.doc.

Social Capital Benchmark Survey. 2006. Top line results from Phase Two, March 15, 2007. Available at www.cfgg.org/downloads/studies/Social_Capital_Benchmark_Study_Phase_1.doc.

Southern Poverty Law Center. 2010. A year in hate and extremism, 2010. *Intelligence Report* 141 (Spring). Available at www.splcenter.org.

Steadman, Tom. 2003, April 20. Commission faces criticism, questions. Greensboro's *News & Record,* A-1.

Steger, Carol E. 2004. *A call for dialogue: Greensboro, North Carolina's opportunity to move toward wholeness.* Available in electronic form at www.uncg.edu/cst.

Stewart, John. 1995. *Language as articulate contact: Toward a post-semiotic philosophy of communication.* New York: State University of New York Press.

Towns, Armond R. 2007. Rosez 4 a gun: Da demonz of a young black male. Lincoln, NE: iUniverse.

Truth and Regrets. 2009, June 18. *Greensboro News & Record* editorial, A12.

Tutt, Tammy. 2005, October 1. Public hearing testimony. *Greensboro Truth and Reconciliation Commission.* Available at http://www.greensborotrc.org/hear_statements.php.

Tutu, Desmond Mpilo. 1999. *No future without forgiveness.* New York: Doubleday.

The Ubuntu Experience. 2006, June 1. Interview with Nelson Mandela. Available at www.youtube.com/watch?v=ODQ4WiDsEBQ.

United States Census. 2010. Available at www.census.gov/2010census/.

United States Institute of Peace. 2011. Truth commission digital collection. Washington, DC. Available at www.usip.edu.

United States Senate Select Committee to Study Governmental Operations with Respect to Intelligence Activities. 1976, April 26. *Intelligence activities and the rights of Americans, Book II* (Report No. 94–755). U.S. Government Printing Office.

Verdoolaege, Annelies. 2008. *Reconciliation discourse: The case of the truth and reconciliation commission.* Amsterdam, The Netherlands: John Benjamins.

Waller, Signe. 2002. *Love and revolution: A political memoir: People's history of the Greensboro Massacre, its setting and aftermath.* Lanham, MD: Rowman & Littlefield.

Waller, Signe. 2005, February. *A city of two tales: The Greensboro massacre of November 3, 1979, in fact, context and meaning.* "A narrative report that reflects the collective knowledge and understanding of the survivors of the 1979 killings" prepared for the Greensboro Truth and Reconciliation Commission.

Weiner, Brian A. 2005. *Sins of the parents: The politics of national apologies in the United States.* Philadelphia: Temple University Press.

Wexler, Laura. 2003. *Fire in a canebreak: The last mass lynching in America.* New York: Scribner.

Wheaton, Elizabeth. 1987. *Codename GREENKIL: The 1979 Greensboro killings.* Lanham, MD: Rowman & Littlefield.

Whitfield, Ed. 2005, October 13. Is it worth the attention? *Carolina Peacemaker.* Available at www.carolinapeacemaker.com/News/search/ArchiveContent.asp?NewsID=62475&sID=.

Wiesenthal, Simon. 1998. *The sunflower: On the possibilities and limits of forgiveness.* New York: Schocken Books.

Williams, Jill. 2007, Spring. Truth and reconciliation comes to the south: Lessons from Greensboro. *Public Eye Magazine* (21), 2. Available at www.publiceye.org.

Wise, Leah. 2005, August 27, 2005. Public hearing testimony. *Greensboro Truth and Reconciliation Commission.* Available at www.greensborotrc.org/hear_statements.php.

Wolff, Miles. 1990. *Lunch at the 5 & 10.* Revised and expanded ed. Chicago: Ivan R. Dee.

Woodall, Martha. 1980, July 14. Nazis say federal agent infiltrated unit, knew of plans for Nov. 3 motorcade. *Greensboro Record,* A1.

Zehr, Howard. 2002. *The little book of restorative justice.* Intercourse, PA: Good Books.

Zinn, Howard. 1980. *A people's history of the United States: 1492 to present.* New York: Harper Collins.

Zucker, Adam. 2007. *Greensboro: Closer to the truth.* United States: Longnook Pictures.

INDEX

SPOMA JOVANOVIC worked alongside other community members in Greensboro, North Carolina, to document the grassroots effort to convene the first Truth and Reconciliation Commission in the United States. She is associate professor of communication studies at the University of North Carolina at Greensboro.